# UNITED STATES HISPANIC CATHOLICS TRENDS AND WORKS 1990–2000

# THE HISPANIC THEOLOGICAL INITIATIVE SERIES

## VOLUME I

The University of Scranton Press (www.scrantonpress.com) and the Hispanic Theological Initiative (HTI) have established a book series concerning the religious experience of U.S. Latinas and Latinos. it is interdisciplinary and ecumenical.

The goals of this series include: 1) encouraging scholarly reflection on the religious experience of U.S. Hispanics and disseminating that knowledge to the wider public; 2) providing Latino/a scholars with a venue for publishing their work with an emphasis on the career of HTI's scholarship awardees.

The first goal is achieved by both the reissue of classic texts in the field of U.S. Hispanic religious studies as well as the publication of similar titles that the Latino/a community itself suggests.

The second goal is accomplished through the annual HTI Dissertation Series Award. Latino/a junior scholars submit their dissertations for competition for the best doctoral dissertation dealing with U.S. Hispanics religious experience. Winners receive a $3,000 cash prize, and the opportunity to present their work during HTI's Annual Summer workshop at Princeton Theological Seminary. Winning entries are also published in the Hispanic Theological Initiative Series.

Questions concerning application for the award should be directed to:

Hispanic Theological Initiative
12 Library Place, Princeton, NJ 08640
http://www.htiprogram.org/
Tel: (609) 252-1721
Fax: (609) 252-1738
Toll Free: 1-800-575-5522
Email: HTI@ptsem.edu

Questions concerning the series publication should be directed to the series editor:

Kenneth G. Davis, OFM, Conv.
200 Hill Drive, St. Meinrad, IN 47577-1021
Tel: (812) 357-6542
Fax: (812) 357-6792

# UNITED STATES HISPANIC CATHOLICS TRENDS AND WORKS 1990–2000

by

Kenneth G. Davis
Eduardo C. Fernández
Verónica Méndez

**UNIVERSITY OF SCRANTON PRESS**
**Scranton and London**

Library of Congress: Cataloging-in-Publication Data

Unites States Hispanic Catholics : trends and works, 1990-2000 / [edited]
by Kenneth G. Davis, Eduardo C. Fernández, Veronica Méndez.
  p. cm.
  Includes bibliographical references and indexes.
  ISBN 1-58966-014-5 – ISBN 1-58966-002-1 (pbk.)
    1. Hispanic American Catholics–History–20th century. 2. Hispanic
  American Catholics–Bibliography. I. Davis, Kenneth G., 1957- II.
Fernández, Eduardo C.  III. Méndez, Veronica, 1942-

BX1407.H55 U55 2002
282'.73'08968–dc21                                    2002024343

Distribution:

University of Scranton Press
Chicago Distribution Center
11030 South Langley Avenue
Chicago, IL   60628

PRINTED IN THE UNITED STATES OF AMERICA

# CONTENTS

# PREFACE

The following pages contain a unique chronicle of trends among U.S. Hispanic Catholics during the 1990s. Father Kenneth G. Davis, O.F.M. Conv., conceived the idea of producing a yearly compilation of data on books, articles, and events relevant to the ever-growing and diverse presence of Hispanics in the United States. Davis obtained the loyal support of *Review for Religious*, which published the chronicle, titled "U.S. Hispanic Catholics: Trends and Recent Works," from 1990 to 1999. For ten years, the chronicle provided unquestionably the most thorough report of its kind for church leaders and for scholars of U.S. Hispanic religion, culture, and recent history. In 1995, Davis began to coedit the compilations with Father Eduardo Fernandez, S.J., and in 1998, Sister Verónica Méndez, R.C.D., joined the team as a third coeditor.

*Trends and Recent Works* is a veritable treasure chest that one would be hard pressed to find anywhere else. In it the reader will find regular reports on developments in the academic study of Latinos, especially in theology and religious studies. The wide gamut of Hispanic church-based organizations is diligently surveyed, as are personalities who made news, along with emergent Hispanic leaders. No part of the United States is neglected, and the editors do a good job of giving due attention to the wide diversity of Hispanic identities—Mexican, Puerto Rican, Cuban, South and Central American.

This is the best summary of trends and events in U.S. Hispanic Catholic history currently available. Father Davis brings a unique talent and plain old diligence to the task of chronicling this important decade, perhaps the most significant to date in the history of U.S. Hispanics; for this period gave rise to a new class of Hispanic intellectual—one that had never existed before. *Trends and Recent Works* witnesses to the "boom" in theological publications of and by U.S. Hispanics that started to take place in the 90s. No longer was Father Virgilio Elizondo out there on his own. Moreover, this chronicle makes it clear that Hispanic women have begun to take their place at every level of leadership in church and society, and in intellectual life. Now a seemingly endless group of women and men, Latinas and Latinos, has begun to regularly publish in the areas of theological method, popular religiosity, women's issues, pastoral care—to name just a few of the areas of interest. The decade chronicled here witnessed the emergence or coming of age of U.S. Hispanic organizations such as the National Catholic Council for Hispanic Ministry (NCCHM) with its national gatherings, the Academy of Catholic Hispanic Theologians of the United States (ACHTUS), and the Asociación Nacional de Sacerdotes Hispanos (ANSH). Other important national organizations like the Mexican American Cultural Center (MACC) in San Antonio and the Southeast Pastoral Institute (SEPI) renewed their commitments and launched new initiatives to become stronger than ever. These and many other developments among Hispanic organizations throughout the country are duly recorded for posterity here.

In these pages one will find detailed narratives on the more salient developments in church, society, and academia. The editors emphasize the extensive bibliography by or about U.S. Hispanics, both articles and books. Brief annotations alert the reader to the articles' or books' principle themes. More extensive book reviews highlight some of the more important publications of this decade. The reviews are generally quite well done, and reveal a critical eye that one would expect in a publication targeted to academics rather than to the more general readership of *Trends and Recent Works*. One will also find extensive reports on new programs and resources that respond to the religious, social, political, and economic life of Hispanics. In the reporting, consistent attention is paid to the growing world of Hispanic Protestantism. Consequently, these chronicles also witness to an emergent ecumenism, still not well known or even acknowledged among U.S. Hispanic Catholics and Protestants.

These year-by-year chronicles, together with the valuable Appendices, an updated Bibliography that includes Internet resources, and both name and subject Indices, constitute a rich source of information and insight into the ever-widening world of U.S. Hispanic influences on church and society. Father Davis and his associates have produced a unique resource that captures, better than anything currently available in print, the themes, struggles, hopes, and significant accomplishments of U.S. Hispanic Catholics. Scholars and the general reading public will find a great deal to analyze and interpret in these careful, wide-ranging reports.

Allan Figueroa Deck, S.J.
Loyola Marymount University
July 10, 2000

# ACKNOWLEDGMENTS

Each of us would like to thank our respective religious communities for all of their support throughout our careers as religious and as scholars. Specifically, each community made a financial contribution to this book without which it would not have been possible to publish it so soon.

We are all grateful as well to David Fleming, S.J., the editor of *Review for Religious*. Not only are all the ten chapters of this work based on articles that appeared in that journal, but Father Fleming in particular has been supportive since the beginning. Over ten years ago, an unknown, recent doctoral graduate approached him about publishing a yearly article concerning United States Hispanic Catholics. He accepted, and those articles make up the bulk of this book. Today that acceptance seems logical, but then it was remarkable. And we are profoundly grateful.

Allan Figueroa Deck, S.J., has been a friend and mentor to us all. We are honored that he agreed to write the preface to this work.

Daniel Grippo helped to edit this volume, and Richard W. Rousseau, S.J., of the University of Scranton Press has been supportive for years in publishing books about the religious experience of United States Hispanics. We thank both. We also thank research assistant Margaret Donlevy, clerical assistant Kim Byerly, and Timothy Matovina and *Living Light* for allowing us to use his review of Ken Davis *Primero Dios*.

Reading the index is a roll call of all the people who made the original ten articles possible. They are the people we wanted to celebrate. We thank them for their hard work on behalf of our people and for their contributions to this book.

Finally, we thank God and dedicate this work and our lives to the greater glory of Diosito.

# CONTRIBUTORS

Kenneth G. Davis, O.F.M.Conv., is assistant professor of pastoral studies at St. Meinrad School of Theology in St. Meinrad, Indiana.

Reverend Allan Figueroa Deck, S.J., is the executive director of the Loyola Institute for Spirituality and adjunct professor of theology at Loyola Marymount University.

Eduardo C. Fernández, S.J., recently published his first book, *La Cosecha: Harvesting Contemporary United States Hispanic Theology.* He is assistant professor of theology at the Jesuit School of Theology at Berkeley.

Verónica Méndez, R.C.D., is a member of the team of E.P.N.E. (Estudios Pastorales para la Nueva Evangelización) of the New York Province of Jesuits, and vocation director for her community. Sister has lectured and written articles on United States Latinas and Latinos.

# 1990 IN REVIEW

The year saw a plethora of interesting developments. Perhaps most noteworthy is the newly organized National Catholic Council for Hispanic Ministry (NCCHM), which met for the first time in Mundelein, Illinois, on June 17, 1990, to begin to coordinate national and regional organizations and movements of Hispanics. In 1990, NCCHM represented 18 such organizations, all committed to the following six objectives: (1) to provide a forum for reflection on the status of Hispanics in church and society at the local, regional, and national levels; (2) to network for mutual support and collaboration among religious, professional, and civic organizations serving Hispanics; (3) to advocate on behalf of United States Hispanics in the area of human rights, together with like-minded associations; (4) to promote the articulation of pastoral and social issues and concerns of special interest to Hispanics through forums, workshops, and publications; (5) to promote the fuller participation of Hispanics in church and society; (6) to facilitate communication among grass roots communities, the church, and civic and professional organizations.

Other important meetings included the annual convention of the Academy of Catholic Hispanic Theologians of the United States (ACHTUS), which met in Berkeley, California, and the founding convention of the National Association of Hispanic Priests (see *Mensaje*, Oct.–Nov., 1990). This group, (a merging of former organizations PADRES and ASH), hopes to coordinate the mutual support and ministry of Hispanic priests throughout the country. The first president, Eduardo Salazar, S.J., was also named by *Replica* magazine as one of the top 20 leading Hispanics.

During the summer the Conference (formerly Committee) of Religious in Hispanic Ministry hosted its annual seminar on vocation/formation and Hispanics in Sacramento, California. And in Mexico, César Chávez, founder of the United Farm Workers Union, was awarded the Order of the Aztec Eagle (Mexico's highest honor bestowed on foreigners) by President Carlos Salinas de Gortari (see *Noticias*, Nov. 1990).

We saw an increase in the opportunities for catechetical and ministerial formation. More and more dioceses nationwide now offer either yearly institutes or continuous programs for the certification of pastoral agents. For instance, in 1990, the Archdiocese of Los Angeles offered 30 different conferences in Spanish, with a total attendance of more than four thousand.

National seminars included two hosted by the Federation of Pastoral Institutes on behalf of the National Hispanic Secretariat. One dealt with base communities, and the other with the rising proselytism of some evangelical groups among Catholic Hispanics.

Emory University was the site of a successful conference, Somos Un Pueblo. And the Instituto de Liturgia Hispana held its biennial convention, whose 1990 theme was *popular religiosity*. Liturgists may also wish to consult the Institutos newsletter, *Amen*, as well as the trimestral, bilingual magazine of the Oregon Catholic Press called *Liturgia y Canción*. Liturgy Training Publications annual aid for lectors, *Manual para Proclamadores de la Palabra*, is certainly worthy of consideration.

The most important coming publications include the Notre Dame study of Hispanic Catholics headed by Jaime Vidal. Three fellowships to doctoral students of history have been offered, and a complete history of the Hispanic Catholic peoples of the United States will be written in conjunction with the Comisión de Estudios de Historia de la Iglesia en America Latina. Also, the United States Catholic Conference will be issuing a letter to commemorate the fifth anniversary of the Tercer Encuentro. Good news as well from Ayer Publishing Company, Inc., of Salem, New Hampshire: It has acquired copyrights to the Arno Press titles and has already reprinted Carlos Cortes classic *Church Views of the Mexican American*. And Saint Mary's Press is in the process of publishing several works on Hispanic youth ministry. As part of their consultation, they are publishing a new bilingual newsletter on youth ministry called *Construyendo Nuestra Esperanza*. For those involved in youth ministry, another resource is the series of thirteen cassettes produced by Ethnic Communications called *Grito Juventud*. Each is a mini-drama (in Spanish) based on topics ranging from valuing oneself to the importance of education.

Brief new works of interest include the new bilingual catechism by Sister María de la Cruz Aymes, S.H., and Francis Buckley, S.J., called *Familia de Dios* (a companion video is also available). Catechists ought also to be aware of the biannual, bilingual newsletter *Voz Catequetica*, published by the National Conference of Diocesan Directors of Catechesis for Hispanics. Education ministry among Hispanics continues to be one of our success stories.

Claretian Publications is offering two new bilingual newsletters: *Nuestra Parróquia* highlights successes in Hispanic ministry, and *El Momento Católico* touches upon a different topic of importance in each issue (see *Catholic Trends*, Oct. 27, 1990).

Quite a few articles, (few advancing new research), were published and will be included in the closing annotated bibliography. But note here that two Catholic journals dedicated entire issues to Hispanics. *New Catholic World* continues its proven commitment to Hispanic Catholics with its November/December issue, Hispanics in the American Church: The Opportunity and the Challenge. A fine editorial and important book review augment nine articles. The most innovative of these are Bishop Ramirezs answer to the widespread criticism that nothing is being done with the *National Pastoral Plan for Hispanic Ministry*, and the pair of articles on base communities and Hispanic vocations. The author of this last article, David Garcia, is at the office of vocations in San Antonio, Texas, and has collaborated on a booklet on Hispanic vocations.

The *U.S. Catholic Historian*, in its Winter/Spring issue Hispanic Catholics: Historical Explorations and Cultural Analysis, offers some detailed analyses of many aspects of the origin of the Hispanic Catholic Church. There are also works on twentieth century Arizona and Colorado and on contemporary Miami, as well as essays about unsung heroes and heroines. This is vital for all serious students.

The guest editor of that issue, Moises Sandoval, has also published a slim new work titled *On the Move: A History of the Hispanic Church in the United States* (Maryknoll, pp. 152, paper, $8.95). Because of its brevity, this book might have done better to try to cover only contemporary events (such as those which transpired after Sandovals 1983 history *Fronteras*). However, it is the mature fruit of a veteran of Hispanic Catholic activism and includes timely, trenchant criticism. Indeed, the contemporary scene receives most attention; unfortunately, little is mentioned about recent strides in catechesis and education among Catholic Hispanics.

Another important publication is Gerardo Marin and Raymond J. Gambas study, *Expectations and Experiences of Hispanic Catholics and Converts to Protestant Churches*. Much anecdotal conjecture had gone into explaining why thousands of Hispanics are abandoning the church; this monograph makes an attempt at thoughtful analysis. The authors report that over 18 percent of (nonacculturated) Hispanics leave the church, usually after arriving in the United States and usually in their youth. Hispanics are dissatisfied when the church is not involved in, or relevant to, their concrete situations. Reasons for this disaffection include a lack of leadership training or Bible study, parishes that are massive and cold rather than communal, and priests who do not understand the needs of Hispanics. By contrast, evangelical churches often offer small, all-Hispanic communities with native pastors who involve the people extensively in ministry (for example, evangelization). This analysis supports much previous reflection by Hispanic Catholic leaders; one can only hope it helps to motivate decision makers.

Perhaps the most important lengthy work to appear in 1990 is Mary Beth Rogers' *Cold Anger: A Story of Faith and Power Politics* (University of North Texas Press, pp. 222, paper, $14.95). It charts the rise of Ernesto Cortes and Community Organized for Public Service (COPS) of San Antonio. It is the remarkable chronicle of how poor and marginalized people are empowered by their faith, and organized by indigenous leadership, to lobby for basic rights and dignity. Many people credit this movement for the 1981 election of the first Hispanic mayor of San Antonio, Henry Cisneros.

While the work of Cortes has been recognized by such diverse institutions as Public Television, the MacArthur Foundation, and *Texas Business* magazine, he himself is convinced that the power of COPS is not a single individual but rather its famous iron rule: *Never, ever, do for people what they can do for themselves.* This rule, the peoples real circumstances (that is, no clean water, sewers, or paved streets), and a liberationist reading of Scriptures have led to the revolution of community organization. The will (*voluntad*) springs from the peoples faith; the skills (*capacidad*) from the teachings of the Industrial Areas Foundation. Together they fill what was once a political vacuum: Where before only organized money mattered, now the organized poor balance this. People are reminded that politicians are their employees and that it is necessary to watch over the employees because absolute power corrupts, and also because, on the part of the poor, absolute powerlessness also corrupts—corrupts ones dignity and citizenship. The poor begin to think of themselves as employers (*dueños*), with an influence over their own destiny. Whereas before institutional violence erupted in hot anger (violence), today it is successfully channeled into cold anger, faith in Jesus who was also persecuted, and confidence in the ability of the people to end persecution.

The key to the success of this community organization is its church base. While scrupulously ecumenical, in the context of Hispanic San Antonio, it is predominantly Catholic. Therefore, Cruz first learned and then taught the papal encyclicals and the United States bishops writings on social justice, as well as the works of theologians such as Hans Küng. The university for COPS is the living room, rectory, and community center of the barrio. In this university (and during so-called teachable moments such as role playing), people are disabused of the notion of acting on behalf of others: They must adhere to the iron rule of teaching people how to act for themselves. People learn that energy comes from cold anger and that this is what drives them to strive for true power, the power of building consent from the people who are served and forcing those who are elected to be accountable to this power. Learning to believe in the correct use of power, and finding the energy to demand it for oneself, constitutes the first (that is, internal) revolution, on which all others must be founded.

The book sketches Cortes own internal revolution, which followed that of many a Chicano. He skidded close to leaving the church, even flirted with the idea of being an evangelical minister. It was the I.A.F. that convinced him of the relevancy of his faith and the importance of his own work, which is a ministry. While he was never attracted to the seminary, he did help write the tough, disciplined, but simple rules of community organization (pp. 95–96).

Chapter Eleven begins the actual telling of the history of COPS. Chapter Twelve links the work of COPS with liberation theology (although Cortes himself expresses some nuanced differences). The book is nowhere romantic: It faces the tensions between evangelical and Catholic, the church of vision and that of operation, the difficulty of translating the success of San Antonio to other cities. Defeats, (for example, the 1988 bond issue), are dealt with as completely as successes. Racial and religious tensions, infighting, and setbacks are all part of the rough-and-tumble game of organizing power. The beauty of this book is its unbounded optimism concerning the connection between faith and politics. A Christian need not live in some pristine quarantine in order to be saved; a Christian may, indeed must, hunker down in the dirty bunkers of everyday life and fight for power for the poor. As has been said many times, evil triumphs only when enough good persons do nothing.

Rogers does a splendid job of making this connection between faith and power and presents Cortes in a believable fashion. She is at her best when she speaks of Texas politics as an insider, and when she reflects on her own Protestant faith. The book limps, however, in its simplistic view of contemporary Catholicism and especially in its analysis of base communities. Nevertheless, Rogers offers a compelling portrait of a

Catholic Hispanic who is inspired by his faith and dedicated to his people, an example and a lesson to the rest of the nation.

## Other Significant Writings

Amorós Alicea, José A. Fe, Desarrollo y Solidaridad: Reflexiones en Torno a la Encíclica *Sollicitudo Rei Socialis*. *Apuntes* 10 (3): 51–58. A positive review of the encyclical, based especially on the work of James W. Fowler.

Candelaria, Michael R. *Popular Religion and Liberation: The Dilemma of Liberation Theology* State University of New York Press, pp. 194, paper, $12.95. The relationship between popular religiosity and liberation theology is a burning one; this book uses specifically the theology of Scannone and Segundo to search for similar themes (for example, incarnation) between the two disciplines. Ample notes, bibliography, and index.

Carrasco, David. *Religions of Mesoamerica* Harper & Row, pp. 174, paper, $8.95. Strictly an introduction to the Olmec, Mayan, Aztec, and other indigenous religions of Mesoamerica before the Spanish conquest. Notes, glossary, and brief bibliography. Suitable as an undergraduate text.

Cervantes, Carmen María. Catholic Education for Ministry Among Hispanics. *The Living Light* 27 (Fall 1990): 46–50. A fine résumé of the history of Hispanic catechesis based on a chapter of her dissertation.

Davis, Kenneth G. A.A.: Making It User Friendly. *Apuntes* 10 (2): 36–43. The author concludes that Alcoholics Anonymous can be inculturated among the Mexican-descent community and suggests ways that the pastoral agent can aid this inculturation.

———. Father, Were Not in Kansas Anymore. *The Priest* 46, no. 7 (July 1990): 14–16. An anglophone priest explains why the whole United States Church is enriched by the presence of Hispanics.

Deck, Allan F., S.J. The Crisis of Hispanic Ministry: Multi-culturalism as Theology. *America* 163, no. 2 (July 14–21, 1990): 33–36. This controversial article marks a shift in emphasis for this prolific writer who argues that cheap ideology and easy ecumenism are substituting for the hard work of effective ministry.

———. The Hispanic Presence: A Moment of Grace. *The Critic* 45, no. 1 (Fall 1990): 48–59. A review of the riches of the Hispanic faith and culture. An excellent overview of the contemporary scene, highly recommended especially to novices in the field.

Duin, Julia. Hispanic Catholics. *New Covenant*, January 1990, pp. 9 –11. A popularly written but accurate account of the experience of Hispanic Catholics, their successes, and some of the reasons 60,000 are abandoning the church annually.

Lampe, Philip E. Is the Church Meeting the Needs of Hispanics? *Living Light* 27, no. 1 (Fall 1990): 51–55. Suggests that Hispanic laity is content with the ecclesial status quo. However, studies only churched, Catholic Hispanics from a particularly effective diocese, with no reference to their level of acculturation.

Miranda, J. Hispanic Churches in America. In Robert D. Linder et al, eds., *Dictionary of Christianity in America* (Intervarsity Fellowship of the USA). A balanced, current treatment.

Polischuk, P. Hispanic American Pastoral Care. In Rodney J. Hunter, ed., *Dictionary of Pastoral Care and Counseling* Nashville: Abingdon. A sensitive treatment with a correct emphasis on holistic care. A good bibliography of social science materials included.

Rodriguez-Holguin, Jeanette Y. Hispanics and the Sacred. *Chicago Studies* 29, no. 2 (August 1990): 137–154. A well organized if overly ambitious attempt to identify five concrete tasks in Hispanic pastoral care.

Smith, Darren L., ed. *Hispanic Americans Information Directory 1990 –1991* Detroit: Gale Research, Inc., 1990. Of more than forty five hundred entries, less than one percent are strictly Catholic, making for glaring oversights. For cultural, research, political, business, and communications purposes, however, it is unparalleled.

Ward, James Garcia. Project 13: Hispanic Vocations and Formation. *Apuntes* 10 (1): 15–16. This lamentably brief article sketches the history and accomplishments of a team of Hispanics who developed strategies for recruiting and sustaining Hispanic vocations to the priesthood and religious life.

*This article originally appeared in Review for Religious Vol. 50, no. 2 (1991) under the title, U.S. Hispanic Catholics: Trends and Recent Works.*

# 1991 IN REVIEW

## Statistics and the Census

The Associated Press reports that 90 percent of Hispanics live in only 11 states, chiefly in large urban areas. They face challenges common to other minorities. ABC News states that three of every five Hispanics live in a deteriorated environment. They have, too, a very high cancer rate. *The New York Times* (27 September, 1990) reports that poverty among Hispanics has climbed during the last 17 years, reaching almost 24 percent. It theorizes the causes to be that two thirds of the heads of Hispanic households do not have high school diplomas, that Hispanic women are less likely to work outside the home, that heads of households are young and therefore only beginning their careers, and that Hispanics face discrimination in the workplace. Large families may also contribute to the poverty rate. The same paper reports on 8 November that Hispanics are concentrated in blue collar jobs despite some success in their academic achievements. Likewise it reports on 1 September and 3 October respectively that Hispanics face discrimination in housing and in our criminal justice system.

There is, however, good news to report as well. The National Council de la Raza describes the continuing gains in the education of young Hispanics. Also, Latinos and Latinas are becoming more politically active. The National Association of Latino Elected and Appointed Officials (4 September, 1991) reports that the Latino/a vote increased by 30 percent in the last decade, and the number of Latino/a elected officials continues to climb. Such clout has given rise to a number of lawsuits concerning redistricting (*USA Today*, 12 September, 1991). On 30 December, 1991 the New York Times News Service reported political victories by previously under represented Hispanics in Bell Gardens, California—this after Los Angeles elected its first Latina alderwomen and Texas appointed some Hispanic judges. Such trends may also be occurring in the Church. Well known lay minister Olga

Villa Para has been appointed to the religious division of the Lilly Foundation. The foundation has already funded the Notre Dame study of Hispanic Catholic history (all three volumes are now being researched) and a project headed by Antonio Stevens-Arroyo to study the importance of religion to Hispanic culture. The next president of the Leadership Conference of Women Religious, Anita Deluna, is Hispanic, as is the new president of the Canon Law Society. Domingo Rodriguez was elected minister general of the Missionary Servants of the Most Holy Trinity, and Allen Ramirez was elected minister provincial of the California province of the Conventual Franciscans. CARA reports a slight rise in Hispanic religious vocations, and David Garcia, the vocation director of San Antonio, reports that for the first time the percentage of Hispanic seminarians in Texas is roughly equal to the percentage of Hispanics in the state (*National Catholic Reporter* [NCR], 11 November, 1991).

## More Church News

The recently reconstituted bishops' committee for Hispanic affairs includes Bishops Enrique San Pedro (new coadjutor of Brownsville), Joseph Madera, John Nevins, Seán O'Malley, Raymundo Peña, and Plácido Rodriguez. The National Association of Family Life has established an Hispanic caucus, as reported by *En Marcha*, the newsletter of the National Secretariat for Hispanic Affairs. Since 1974 Pablo Sedillo has headed the secretariat. He announced his retirement this year. He will be working with the bishops' committee for the Observance of the Fifth Centenary of the Evangelization in the Americas. The new director of the secretariat is Ronaldo Cruz, who, among other things, successfully convoked a national meeting of Hispanic diocesan directors and has helped compile valuable statistics on the United States Hispanic population. Other noteworthy events include the founding of a new Spanish diocesan newspaper (*Vida Nueva*, Los Angeles), the death of the renowned santería scholar Lydia Cabrera, and the 23 October funeral Mass in Palm Beach, Florida, for seven Guatemalan sugarcane workers who died in a car accident.

Hispanic bishops have been in the news. Bishop Agustín Román of Miami busily promoted his "Noche Familiar Cristiana" and has been instrumental in the Comité de Reflexión Cubana en la Diáspora. Bishop Joseph Madera of Fresno has been appointed auxiliary of the Archdiocese of the Military. Two Hispanic bishops have died: Retired Puerto Rican Bishop Rafael Grovas-Félix on 9 September of cancer, and the following month, Sacramento auxiliary Alphonse Gallegos in a car accident. When appointed, Bishop Gallegos became the first Hispanic bishop in California in 120 years.

The bishops have also been busy in groups. The five Hispanic auxiliary bishops of the Northeast published a joint letter, *At the Fifth Centenary's Threshold*, a call for renewed evangelization; and the bishops of both Alta and Baja California continue to meet to coordinate the interchange of clergy. Bishop Ricardo Ramírez of Las Cruces published a talk about the National Pastoral Plan for Hispanic ministry in the 14 March issue of *Origins*. Other bishops published talks in *Origins* concerning newly ordained Hispanic priests, inculturation, and evangelization.

The various Hispanic movements and organizations have been active. The National Catholic Council for Hispanic Ministry met in Irving, Texas, 18–21 October. For the first time, the national office of RENEW was represented. Carmen Cervantes, Roberto Piña, and Silvia Sanchez were elected to the board of directors. The main activity was the planning of a national gathering of Hispanics in Los Angeles 13–16 August to promote the new evangelization. The gathering hopes to provide an opportunity for Catholics who exercise leadership in the Church and society to dialogue and reflect on themes from the National Pastoral Plan. It will be the first time in years for such a national gathering to share and celebrate the gifts of Hispanic Catholics in the Church.

Auburn Theological Seminary of New York hosted the first ecumenical gathering of Hispanics. Noted theologians Virgil Elizondo and Justo González were among the many who attended.

The Academy of Catholic Hispanic Theologians of the United States (ACHTUS) met and inducted several new members and elected Arturo Bañuelas president. Bañuelas recently taught a course on United States Hispanic theology for which he prepared an excellent bibliography. The current secretary, Orlando Espín, is busy preparing for the publication of a new journal of Hispanic Catholic theology. Past president Allan Figueroa Deck, S.J., published an editorial in the spring issue of *Church*, and Virgil Elizondo was featured in the 24 February issue of London's *Tablet*. The ACHTUS gathering reflected on the importance of popular religiosity and on the methodology for doing theology. Its next meeting is set for June in San Diego, California. The National Association of Hispanic Priests (ANSH) held its annual convention in Washington, DC, 21–23 October. The theme was the anniversary of *Rerum Novarum*.

The Catholic Migrant Farmworkers' Network offered a series of evangelization workshops and retreats to its constituents throughout 1991. Its work in Yakima was recognized in the local paper, and the executive director, Dick Notter, was featured in the 15 September, 1991 edition of *Our Sunday Visitor*. The work is especially valuable during this time when César Chávez is being criticized. Both CBS News (19 September, 1991) and the *National Catholic Reporter* (19 September 1991) question the effectiveness of the United Farm Workers and its leader. For those interested in the issue of migrant health and ministry, a good resource is the National Migrant Resource Program in Austin, Texas.

The Conference on Religious in Hispanic Ministry (CORHIM) did not host a seminar this year, but was very active. Members published articles (and *Review for Religious* published an article about CORHIM), and the executive committee met three times to reflect and set new directions. Gary Riebe-Estrella and Verónica Méndez both offered courses at the Chicago Theological Union, and their newsletter, *Papelógrafo*, continues to inform members and invite them to social functions. LAS HERMANAS, the organization of Hispanic women religious, met in Albuquerque to celebrate their twentieth anniversary. *The National Catholic Reporter* (15 November, 1991) published an article on the convention and highlighted Aurora Camacho de Schmidt, Lucie Barrón, Yolanda Tarango, and Ada María Isasi-Díaz (see her article in *Christianity and Crisis*, 13 May).

In September in St. Augustine, Florida, the Instituto de Liturgia Hispana held its convention, on the fifth centenary theme (Tape Production of Phoenix, Arizona, has copies of the conferences). Two hundred seventy-three persons from twenty-one states and four countries participated, and twelve new members were added. The National Organization of Catechists for Hispanics (NOCH) announced that it had influenced the NCCD to open eight positions for Hispanics. NOCH has a new episcopal moderator, Bishop Manuel Moreno, of Tucson. It has been working with Mexican catechists on a pastoral approach for the border area, and several of its members were featured in the 1991 issue of *Catechetical Sunday*.

The Northeast Hispanic Catholic Center celebrated its 15th anniversary, at which its "Padre Bartolomé de las Casas" award was conferred. The center continues its many publications, including a new missalette, and its director has been actively writing about and promoting the fifth centenary celebration. Jacksonville, Florida, saw the meeting of the Southeast Regional Office of Hispanic Affairs, whose theme was small Christian communities. Jacqueline Manzo of Raleigh, Georgina Gamarra of Tampa, and Kenneth G. Davis of RENEW were among the speakers. The highlight was a Mass celebrated on the very spot of the first Mass ever celebrated in North America.

On 24–26 September RECOSS met; for the first time its various committees (for example, youth, migrants) talked over their works and activities. The meeting endeavored to coordinate this work with the call for a new evangelization in each diocese. Allan Figueroa Deck, Ph.D., was present along with many other Hispanic leaders of California.

The bishops' committee for the fifth centenary of evangelization has been quite active. It provides a fine resource in the newsletter *Aurora*. Another newsletter is available from the General Secretariat of the Organization of American States in Washington, DC, 20006. Many dioceses also offer fine resources—from newspapers and reflections on the National Pastoral Plan (for example, Sacramento, California) to newsletters such as *Caminantes* from the dioceses of Orlando, St. Petersburg, and Venice, Florida. Catholic Charities of San Francisco offers several resources for small Christian communities.

## Additional Resources

The most important resource may be Hispanic American Religious Publications, newly founded by Benjamín and Irma Alicea. It hopes to make books written by North American Hispanics more widely available, and indeed eventually to publish such works.

The Public Broadcasting System has become a rich resource for those willing to browse the listings. For example, this Christmas it featured a pastorela with Linda Ronstadt. Local museums, clubs, and organizations are often terrific. Program is a tape recording company in Washington, DC, that offers a catalogue with almost a dozen tapes of interest. They feature the conference "A Century of Catholic Social Teaching," with Elizondo and Ramírez, and the Jesuit conference "Faith Doing Justice," which was held in Detroit.

The Mexican American Cultural Center (MACC) offers a full line of workshops and seminars along with a bookstore, catalogue, and publications of its own. In 1991, for instance, it offered training on home visitation and on youth ministry and published a bilingual booklet titled *Manual for Basic Ecclesial Communities*.

Creative Communications in St. Louis, MO, offers calendars, booklets, and prayer cards in Spanish. Alba House (718–698–2759) has fine, inexpensive booklets for personal prayer and reflection. *Extension* magazine dedicated its June issue to Mexican Americans, and its information briefs often contain useful information. It and the *Maryknoll* magazine (available in Spanish as well as English) are free. Liturgical resources are proliferating (see NCR, 13 December, 1991). The Liturgical Press released *Rito de la Iniciación Cristiana de Adultos*, and GIA Publications has produced a new catalogue for Hispanics. Mark R. Francis published a series of three articles in *Modern Liturgy*, and, besides the usual (and helpful) reprints, *Liturgia y Canción* published an article by Jaime Lara in the May–August issue.

## Book Reviews

The Institute of Contemporary Art of Boston published *El Corazón Sangrante*, a 176 page bilingual catalogue of an exhibit of the same name. It endeavors to demonstrate the syncretic continuity between the pre-Columbian preoccupation with blood and the heart, baroque Christian representations of the Sacred Heart and the Immaculate Heart of Mary, and contemporary United States Hispanic art that uses the heart as a symbol of liberation. It contains eight full color plates and numerous small black and white photos, a good index, and excellent references. It provides some very interesting insights into the social, political, and gender implications of folk art and into the blood and heart symbolism that endures especially among the Mexican-descent population. While it is a rich resource for everything from Sor Juana Inés de la Cruz (see also George Tavard's new work about her from the University of Notre Dame Press) to contemporary gay Chicanos, the connections made are often forced, and no individual themes are dealt with in depth. Nevertheless, it raises a series of compelling questions and intriguing suggestions.

Martin J. Morgado's *Junípero Serra: A Pictorial Biography* is such a wonderful work that it is a shame that its publisher (Siempre Adelante; 1190 Alta Mesa Road; Monterey, CA, 93940) is not better known. Its 137 pages are crammed with dozens of color photos, maps and drawings, complete notes, and an excellent index. It is obviously a labor of love by a first-rate historian. Further information concerning the history of the United States Hispanic Church is available from Jaime Vidal at Notre Dame's CUSHWA center. Its newsletter reports on the Notre Dame study of United States Hispanic Catholics and on historical publications and it also provides news of grants and archival activities.

*Hispanic Devotional Piety: Tracing the Biblical Roots* by C. Gilbert Romero (Orbis Books, 1991) is an essential resource in the quest for a

United States Hispanic theology. Catholic Hispanic theologians now commonly use their peoples' devotional piety (often called popular religiosity) as the locus of their theology. This work seeks to put the practice on a scriptural foundation.

Fr. Romero, a New Mexican Chicano, works as both pastor and teacher in the Archdiocese of Los Angeles and also teaches in Trujillo, Peru. Writing for pastoral agents, (specifically but not exclusively those working with Mexican Americans of the United States Southwest), he combines scriptural insights, theological acumen, and pastoral advice.

Chapter One is an overview of the tension between "official" church structures and Hispanic Devotional Piety (HDP). Romero marshals Sacrosanctum Concilium, Evangeli Nuntiandi, Gaudium et Spes, Medellín, and Puebla to argue that HDP maintains and transmits the Hispanic culture, provides a necessary affective balance to an overly abstract Roman worship, and is a source of both theology and evangelization/catechesis. He concludes the chapter with a claim he repeats throughout: The "official" Church and HDP provide a needed mutual balance and therefore require a respectful ongoing dialogue.

Chapter Two introduces a three-step biblical approach to HDP, the author's premise being "an already existing relationship between the Bible and Hispanic devotional piety." First, biblical analogues are sought through a historical-critical look at Scripture. Next, these analogues are strengthened by an analysis of HDP using the disciplines of cultural anthropology (specifically structuralism), reader response criticism, and language theory. Lastly, pastoral suggestions make these insights practical. Pages 17–19 provide a definition of HDP and a critique of its wane. This careful and logical presentation characterizes the entire book.

Chapter Three intelligently argues that the "intuitive insight" of HDP can be considered dependent revelation (that is, dependent on the deposit of faith) and clarifies this by relating HDP to tradition (its content and the process of its being handed on), to history, and to symbol (as self-involving and transforming). The author's conclusion is that HDP "can be considered a locus of divine revelation" (see pp. 48–54).

Chapters Four through Seven then apply this biblical approach to four specific expressions of HDP: Ash Wednesday, the *quinceañera* (a religious rite of passage for young women), the home altar, and the Penitentes (a lay movement in New Mexico). Each chapter ends with an appeal for the pastoral agent to discover the "internal disposition" to appreciate HDP, to use an appropriate pedagogy in order to "unfold" its potential and correct its excesses, and to advocate a mutual dialogue with official church structures (see p. 119–121). The treatment of *quin-ceañera* is timely and especially good, (though obvious Marian parallels are neglected), and the political implications of the home altar are startling (p. 92). Because the Penitentes have been exhaustively studied and because they are geographically limited and arguably near extinction, focusing on a different devotion (a Cristo or a Virgen) would have been more helpful.

Other unfortunate oversights are the use of sexist language and the failure to mention the specifically feminist aspects of HDP (for example, Kay Turner's insights into the home altar). Inexplicably, there is no reference to either the National Pastoral Plan for Hispanic Ministry or the United States Hispanic theologians Virgil Elizondo, Orlando Espín, and Ada María Isasi-Díaz, who have all dealt extensively with HDP. Justo González and Michael Candelaria are mentioned, but González does not represent the majority of Hispanic Protestants (for example, Pentecostals), and Candelaria wrote about Latin American HDP, not the United States Hispanic experience.

In spite of these omissions, this is a foundational work by a fine biblical scholar and erudite author. It merits the attention not only of those pastoral agents serving Hispanics and constructing a theology about them, but also of any United States Catholics who wish to understand and dialogue with the signs of our times.

## Other Significant Writings

Buckley, Francis. "Popular Religiosity and Sacramentality: Learning from Hispanics a Deeper Sense of Symbol, Ritual, and Sacrament." *Living Light* 27, no. 4 (Summer, 1991): 351–360. While only repeating what Hispanics have said for decades, this and other articles by non-Hispanics suggest that the balance of the Church may finally be listening to the claim that Latinos have something to offer their Anglo counterparts.

Davis, Kenneth G. "On Being a Frog in My Field." *The Priest* 47, no. 10 (October, 1991): 6–7. The reflections of a non-Hispanic working with Hispanics; he feels himself to be an amphibian between two cultures.

_____. "CORHIM: Hispanic Seminars." *Review for Religious* 50, no. 6 (November/December, 1991): 881–887. A thematization of the written reflection of over ten years of seminars held by the Conference of Religious in Hispanic Ministry.

Espín, Orlando O. "The Vanquished, Faithful Solidarity and the Marian Symbol: A Hispanic Perspective on Providence." In *On Keeping Providence*, eds. Joan Coultas and Barbara Doherty, 84–101. Terre Haute, Indiana: St. Mary of the Woods Press, 1991. Dealing deftly with the scandal of providence among this minority, the author argues that popular religiosity (for example, Our Lady of Guadalupe and Our Lady of Charity) is the locus of the Hispanic experience and description of providence.

Goizueta, Roberto S. "The Church and Hispanics in the United States: From Empowerment to Solidarity." In *Theologies of Empowerment*, ed. Michael Downey, 160–175. New York: Crossroad, 1991. Using Catholic social teaching, liberation theology, theories of empowerment and solidarity, and United States Hispanic culture and popular religiosity, Goizueta argues that a preferential option for the poor and their consequent empowerment are preconditions for the Christian faith.

Hanlon, Don. "The Confrontation of Two Dissimilar Cultures: The Adobe Church in New Mexico." *Journal of the Interfaith Forum on Religion, Art, and Architecture* (Winter, 1991): 17–20. A fascinating account of how indigenous artisans and architects maintained much of their peculiar cultural insights in their production of Spanish American Christian art and churches.

Hinojosa, Juan-Lorenzo. "Formation in Hispanic Ministry." *Review for Religious* 50, no. 5 (September/October, 1991): 722–729. Using Ricoeur's study of symbolism, he argues that reevangelization must use popular religiosity in such a way that the leader of the community must become a learner, learning again the sacred myths and symbols of the people served.

Isasi-Díaz, Ada María. "Hispanic Women in the Roman Catholic Church." In *Women and Church: The Challenge of Ecumenical Solidarity in an Age of Alienation*, ed. Melanie A. May, pp. 13–17. Grand Rapids, Michigan: Wm. B. Eerdmans, 1991. A cogent analysis of challenges in contemporary church ministry; it concludes with a call for a recognition of ministry among Hispanics that is collegial and respects the culture, plurality, and religiosity of the people.

Matovina, Timothy A. "Liturgy and Popular Expressions of Faith: A Look at the Works of Virgil Elizondo." *Worship* 63, no. 5 (September, 1991): 436–444. A fine assessment of the internationally acclaimed Chicano scholar and his liturgical contributions. Matovina sees these contributions as an appropriate emphasis on popular religiosity to reinforce identity and community, to give meaning to suffering, and to celebrate hope. Matovina also published an excellent article on Hispanic identity in the 16 March issue of *America*.

Pulido, Alberto L. "Are You an Emissary of Jesus Christ?: Justice, the Catholic Church, and the Chicano Movement." *Exploration in Ethnic Studies* 14, no. 1 (January, 1991): 17–34. An admirable exploratory study of the clash between Católicos por la Raza and the diocese of San Diego, California. It concludes that the clash did not worsen the relationship between Chicanos and the Church; it initiated one, marking the beginning of the Church actually entering into a dialogue with this community.

Segovia, Fernando F. "A New Manifest Destiny: The Emerging Theological Voice of Hispanic Americans." *Religious Studies Review* 17, no. 2 (April, 1991): 101–109. Besides Bañuelas, Segovia emerges as the only United States Hispanic who offers a critique of the theologies of his colleagues. His critique of their use of Scripture is especially valuable. He identifies four common themes: (1) use of the methodology of liberation theology, (2) a trenchant indictment of the church establishment, (3) a retrieval of the historical, spiritual, and theological contributions of Hispanics to the United States Church, and (4) an appreciation of mission and the consequent insistence that no one culture can exhaust the manifestation of God.

Silva Gotay, Samuel. "El Partido Acción Cristiana: Transfondo Histórico y Significado Sociológico del Nacimiento y Muerte de Un Partido Político Católico en Puerto Rico." *Cristianismo y Sociedad* 108: 95–108. An instructive account of how the Catholic Church reacted to the "invasion" of Protestantism. Gotay argues convincingly that reactions based on presumptions (for example, that Hispanic Catholics have not been affected by modernity) rather than on analysis have resulted in hierarchical decisions completely out of touch with the reality of the laity.

*This article originally appeared in Review for Religious Vol. 51, no. 2 (1992) under the title, "U.S. Hispanic Catholics: Trends and Works 1991."*

# 1992 IN REVIEW

## Migrants and Immigrants

One half of all immigrants entering the United States are Latinos/as. The September issue of *Hispanic* reports that changing United States policies and priorities have left up to 100,000 Nicaraguans in legal limbo. *El Visitante Dominical* (VD, 5 April, 1992) says that the United States and Salvadoran Catholic hierarchies have interceded for Salvadoran exiles and won an extension of terms from the Bush administration. *The New York Times* (NYT, 7 October) quotes the Coast Guard as recording the highest number of Cuban refugees since the Mariel boatlift of 1980. Puerto Rico is concerned about the influx of Dominicans to the island, according to VD, 11 October.

The Center for Immigration Studies relates that about 24 percent of Hispanic immigrants are from Central and South America and the Caribbean, but the majority are still Mexicans; indeed, the Immigration and Naturalization Services (INS) estimates that there was a 25 percent increase in Mexican immigration in 1992 (Mexico: *El Excelsior*, 25 July). However, the Colegio de la Frontera Norte believes that the flow of undocumented Mexicans leveled off in 1991 because of the United States recession and border security (Associated Press, 27 December). The character of Mexican immigration seems to be changing. After seventy years of mainly male immigration, more single women and women with children are crossing the border (NYT, 7 June). Perhaps, with generations of Mexican men far from home, women have had to fill traditionally male roles, one of which was emigration.

Emigration has drastically affected not only the Mexican family, but also its economy. Mexico's *El Universal* (6 June) reports that Mexicans in the United States sent four billion dollars home that year. Over time this influx of dollars has created inflation even in small villages. This inflation increases the Mexican economic crisis, which in turn creates more pressure to emigrate. A cycle of greater and greater dependence on emigration to the United States develops which has a long-range impact on the family, economy, religion, culture, and politics of Mexico. Countries just beginning to see greater emigration to the United States may do well to study this mixed blessing.

Likewise the 1986 Immigration Reform and Control Act seems to have had ambivalent effects. Although some 900,000 Mexican immigrants (and millions of others) became legalized and have translated that status into greater strength at the ballot box (see the November poll conducted by the Midwest-Northeast Voter Registration Education Project), the consensus of most experts is that the law was a failure. Congress's Commission on Agricultural Workers admits that it neither curtailed undocumented immigrants nor improved the lot of United States migrant workers; in fact, the opposite occurred (22 October and 4 November).

Moreover, the abuse of both migrants and immigrants rose. The organization Americas Watch has accused the Immigration and Naturalization Service (INS) of routinely beating immigrants, as well as of shootings, torture, and sexual abuse. Mexican police on the other side of the border also rob, kill, and extort from their emigrating compatriots, according to Mexico's Comisión Nacional de Derechos Humanos. The *National Catholic Reporter* noted that similar problems are recorded in Florida (NCR, 6 March). United States organizations such as the Mexican American Legal and Defense Fund (MALDEF) and several local bishops and Catholic charities have addressed these problems. Similarly, the Mexican government is energetically aiding the 16 Mexicans on death row.

Sister Eleace King, I.H.M., of the Center for Applied Research in the Apostolate, found in her study of eight dioceses that the Catholic Church has not been welcoming of Hispanic immigrants, often failing to address either their social or their spiritual needs. In contrast, groups such as the Jehovah's Witnesses seek out and strongly encourage Hispanics; indeed NCR reports an increase in Hispanic Protestant ministers immigrating to proselytize in the United States. Similar findings appear in a study of religious leadership (*Origins*, 24 September); likewise an earlier study of newly ordained priests found that great numbers felt ill prepared to deal with persons of other cultures. Ecumenical leaders of the organization "La Frontera" lament the absence of United States bishops' participation (NCR, 16 October). This is particularly disconcerting considering the continued influence religion has on Hispanics: The 1992 *Hispanic Monitor* reports that, next to the Spanish language, maintaining their religion is the most important thing mentioned by Hispanics who take pride in their cultural ancestry.

Despite this, there are valiant ministers struggling to meet migrant needs. *Hispanic Link* (HL) highlighted the work of the Reverend Joseph Gallegos in Chicago, and likewise the June issue of *Hispanic* highlights Marlene Barrera and her founding of the Organization of the Latin Americans, which helps immigrants with housing, education, and employment.

The Church's ministry to migrant workers is more encouraging. César Chávez seems to have been rehabilitated in the secular press. NBC (10 October) reported positively on his organizing efforts in Delano, California, and a report in the 26 February edition of *U.S.A. Today* appears to support his claim that hundreds of thousands of migrant workers suffer from severe pesticide exposure. The Union of Farm workers mourned the loss and celebrated the achievements of co-founder Fred Ross, who died 27 September in San Rafael, California. Other lay people such as Luis Magaña and Carlos Rivas were also recognized for their ministry to migrants (*Noticias*, April). Zeferino González has worked almost four years for the migrants of Fresno, California, without remuneration of any kind (VD, 24 May). The Catholic bishops' Campaign for Human Development awarded Baldemar Velásquez their Development of People Award for his work as founder and president of the Farm Labor Organizing Committee. And the USCC Publishing Services now offers Adán Medrano's video and bilingual study guide *Yo Trabajo la Tierra* (13 minutes, $18.20). Moreover, three border bishops (Peña of El Paso, Ramírez of Las Cruces, and Juan Sandoval Inigues of Ciudad Juarez) signed a joint statement insisting on migrant workers' rights to fair wages, health care, and collective bargaining (NCR, 6 November). *Newsweek* (9 November) highlighted a study by sociologist David Hayes-Bautista which shows that Latinos have an "extraordinary work ethic," stable homes, and low use of welfare, all of which could strengthen our economy and social values."

## More Church News

The Comisión Episcopal de la Alta y Baja California continues to coordinate ministry on both sides of the border, maintaining ongoing collaboration on evangelization and catechesis. Sister María de la Cruz Aymes works with its members on a catechetical project (*Noticias*, February/March). *En Marcha* reports that Bishops Sánchez, Ramírez, and Pelotte have formed a New Mexico Catholic Conference coordinated by Antonio Luján. The continued local and national organizing of Hispanic ministry was evident also in the May meeting in Illinois of the diocesan coordinators of Hispanic ministry. Along with the Bishops' Committee for Hispanic Affairs, they decried the debilitating effect of the mentality that sees Hispanics as a needy minority even in those twenty large dioceses where they now constitute the majority (*Catholic Voice*, 15 June). Similar sentiments were expressed by Dr. Marilyn Aguirre-Molina, Ph.D. in the New Jersey gathering of Hispanic leadership. Father Ramón Gaitán brought these ideas to the attention of the National Conference of Catholic Bishops during its 18–21 June meeting in South Bend, Indiana.

Bishops and their dioceses have been active during the beginning of this decade of evangelization. Newark plans a synod, and Austin concluded one that recommended opening a diocesan office of Hispanic ministry (*Crux*, 20 April). The dioceses of San Diego, Fresno, Dallas, Phoenix, and Boise all held conferences on Hispanic evangelization.

Gerald R. Barnes was named auxiliary bishop of San Bernardino, California, bringing the number of United States Hispanic bishops to 21 (of whom only five are ordinaries). This is still nowhere near representative of the numbers of United States Hispanic Catholics. Auxiliary Bishop Carlos Sevilla of San Francisco was named the chair of the Bishops' Commission on Religious Life. Bishop René Gracida of Corpus Christi wrote in the *South Texas Catholic* about the dangers of Masonry. Bishop Ricardo Ramírez, of Las Cruces, New Mexico, continued to be a frequent speaker. He delivered lectures at the Perkins School of Theology in early February and gave a widely publicized address at the 5 May Denver Workshop on Christian Unity in which he called for an ecumenical Hispanic summit (*Origins*, 28 May). Bishop Agustín Román, after recovering from hospitalization, continued his work on behalf of Cubans in the Diaspora (CRECED). Fellow Cuban Enrique San Pedro of Brownsville, Texas, accompanied Bishops David Arias (Newark), Raymundo Peña (El Paso), and Roberto González (Boston) to the meetings in Santo Domingo with Pope John Paul and the episcopal conference of Latin America. Bishop Peña must also be excited about the beatification of one of El Paso's first priests, Pedro de Jesús Maldonado Lucero. Bishops Donald Wuerl of Pittsburgh and Enrique San Pedro issued a joint statement, "The Support of Newly Ordained Hispanic Priests" (*Origins*, 7 November), a timely piece because the increase in Hispanic seminarians continues (VD, 1 November). Frater José Rivera, C.S.S.R., writes from Washington, DC, about the founding of a regional union of Hispanic seminarians called Asociación de Seminaristas Hispanos.

Father Virgil Elizondo continues his prolific writing and speaking. Orbis has translated his previous book and released it as *Way of the Cross: The Passion of Christ in the Americas*. Elizondo also made the news for suggesting that an ecumenical prayer gathering be held at the pyramids outside Mexico City for both repenting the past and dreaming about the future (NCR, 6 November). He spoke at the Berkeley Earl Lecture series and appeared with Father Allan Figueroa Deck, S.J., on Univision's "Voces del Pueblo." Deck, president of the National Catholic Council for Hispanic Ministry, has begun a Hispanic ministry program at Loyola Marymount University in Los Angeles. (A review of his new book appears below). Likewise, the University of San Diego has begun a series of both graduate and undergraduate courses on United States Hispanic Catholicism and theology. Fordham University underscored its commitment to Hispanic ministry by sponsoring a bilingual conference on the five hundred years of Hispanic religious experience in the Americas. One hundred and fifty participants heard remarks by Maruja Sedano and Roberto Gutiérrez, among others (*Catholic New York*, 9 July). A conference on the evangelization of the Hispanic family was held at Notre Dame in June, and that month the National Catholic Council for Evangelization considered the same theme. Sister María de la Cruz Aymes, Bishop Ramírez, and Carmen María Cervantes were featured speakers.

The winner of Notre Dame's dissertation fellowship in the history of Hispanic Catholics is Timothy Matovina, who is working on *Spanish Speaking Catholics in San Antonio, Texas, 1821–1860: A Study of Religion and Ethnicity*. Matovina also delivered lectures at the South-West Liturgical Conference and at the National Association for Chicano Studies. Other Hispanic scholars have been busy. Indeed, the Fund for Theological Education reports that twenty Hispanic Catholic scholars won funding. This is second only to Presbyterians, but still proportionately low considering that more than 70 percent of United States Hispanics are Catholic. Jaime Vidal spoke at Augusta College in Georgia and at the National Conference of the Holy Cross Hispanic Ministries. Antonio Stevens-Arroyo gave a conference on the Catholic philosophy of Pedro Albizu Campos, continues to plan the very promising spring symposium on Latino/a religious experience to be hosted at Princeton, and was featured in HL, 2 November.

Other Hispanic lay people were very much in the news. Juan José Gloria was named director of Hispanic affairs for the California Catholic Conference. Under his direction, this region has given even more emphasis to the development of base communities (*Noticias*, August). Also from California, Cuco Chávez has been instrumental in exploring a possible national organization of Hispanic pastoral musicians. Gelasia Márquez addressed the 23–27 September National Association of Catholic Family Life Ministers conference at Dallas; this was the first address ever delivered to the group by someone from the association's Hispanic caucus (NCR, 9 October). Benito López, Jr. was appointed executive director of the Association of Catholic Colleges and Universities; María Teresa Garza was named director of the Midwest Hispanic Catholic Commission; Alejandro Aguilera has been named temporarily to the Northwest Hispanic Pastoral Center.

Sister Dianna Ortiz continues her heroic search for justice by returning to Guatemala, where she testified against those who kidnaped, tortured, and raped her. In the face of governmental outrages, she has spoken out not only for herself, but also for all Guatemalan survivors of state terror (*Catholic Trends*, 11 April).

The National Catholic Education Association awarded the United States Surgeon General Antonio Novello the 1992 Seton award, and Rafael Peñaler of Miami received the pope's *Pro Ecclesia et Pontifice* medal (HL). Los Angeles had something to be proud and happy about when Oscar De La Hoya won a gold medal at the summer Olympics in Barcelona and parlayed that into the largest contract ever given an amateur boxer (HL, 28 September).

The year 1992 was, of course, the fifth centenary of Columbus' arrival in the Americas. It was the occasion of great controversy and historic interest in the Church. Arguably, it was the cause of the explosion of Hispanic writings this year (see bibliography below), which marks the beginning of true acceptance of Hispanic contributions to mainstream Catholic publishing. It is noteworthy that the Lilly Endowment has given two awards to further these endeavors. The Academy of Catholic Hispanic Theologians of the United States received $99,000 to found the new *Journal of Hispanic/Latino Theology*; Orlando Espín will be the first editor. And the Catholic Book Publishers Association received $108,000 to direct a nationwide market analysis for the religious reading needs of the United States Hispanic Catholic. The head of the steering committee is Frank J. Cunningham of Ave Maria Press.

The 500th anniversary itself, however, will probably have much less effect on Hispanics than the North American Free Trade Agreement (NAFTA), and, curiously, while the former was the occasion of great hierarchical and scholarly debate within the United States Church, the latter merited barely a polite comment. The balance of opinion among United States Hispanics (with the notable exceptions of the Labor

Council for Latin American Advancement and the National Puerto Rican Council) seems to be that they will benefit from NAFTA (Vista, 5 April). The Southwest Voter Research Institute, for example, estimates that Hispanics in the border area will gain nearly 11,000 jobs (HL, 12 October). The best books on the subject may be *The Disappearing Border: Mexico–United States Relations in the 1990s* ($4.25 from the Stanford Alumni Association, 415–723–2021) and *The Mexican–U.S. Border Region and the Free Trade Agreement* ($10; San Diego State University, 619–594–5423).

Some Mexican bishops have frequently and energetically opposed the agreement, arguing that it would widen the gap between the immensely rich and the miserably poor. The Canadian Catholic Conference also opposes the agreement. Curiously, the United States Church has had little to say although Cardinal Mahoney is supportive of the current version of NAFTA for reasons others cite: The jobs which will move to Mexico would move out of the country anyway, probably to Asia, and free trade and competition would eventually help everyone. Cincinnati's Bishop Daniel Pilarczyk suggested that NAFTA be a subject at the inter-American meeting of bishops proposed by the Holy Father at Santo Domingo (*Origins*, 5 November).

## News from National Hispanic Organizations

The most important event of the year was the National Congress "Roots and Wings," sponsored by the National Catholic Council on Hispanic Ministry, an organization which now coordinates the efforts of 43 participating regional and national Hispanic Catholic organizations. The congress was the first national meeting of Hispanic leadership since the Tercer Encuentro, and despite a lower than expected attendance and some logistical problems, it was a success for both the council and the participants.

The congress specifically wanted to reach second and third generation Hispanics and to bridge the gap between ecclesial and secular Hispanic leaders. Lines of action were developed around five themes based on the pope's call to a new evangelization, and the congress included both lectures and work in groups. The Very Reverend Domingo Rodríguez, S.T., was the keynote speaker, and a lengthy cable from the Holy Father pleasantly surprised the participants. The evaluation of the congress was quite positive from both the participants and the press, as related in the council's annual meeting in Denver. At that time it was also announced that all the Hispanic bishops had approved of the congress' lines of action. The Denver meeting also decided to continue the congress every three years, identifying the theme through grass roots consultation and bringing the conclusions back to member organizations for their implementation. The council has begun to promote its work through a newsletter called *Puentes*, edited by José A. Amorós Alicea.

The third convention of the National Association of Hispanic Priests was held in St. Augustine and also focused on the new evangelization. Present were Bishops Ramírez (episcopal moderator), Román, and San Pedro, all of whom gave talks (*El Heraldo Católico*, 9 August). The Academy of Catholic Hispanic Theologians of the United States (ACHTUS) met in its third annual colloquium in San Diego in June and inducted seven new members. The Virgil Elizondo award was given to the co-founders of the academy, Msgr. Arturo Bañulas and Father Allan Deck, S.J.

The seventeenth meeting of the Comunidades de Reflexión Eclesial Cubana en la Diáspora (CRECED) in Miami saw 150 delegates from nineteen countries consider the very impressive "Documento de Consulta," which included pastoral suggestions (a popular version of the document was separately published). The reflection continues on local, regional, national, and international levels. The Conference of Religious for Hispanic Ministry (CORHIM) plans its seminar in Denver, 5–23 July, 1993.

The Hispanic Telecommunications Network (HTN) now offers a series of thirty six video cassettes, both interactive catechesis material and themes from its television series "Nuestra Familia." Broadcast information and updating are available in HTN News from P.O. Box 15248, San Antonio, Texas 78212. HTN also offers its production services to other nonprofit Catholic organizations.

The Instituto de Liturgia Hispana held its sixth conference in Miami in April. Jaime Lara and José Menéndez were among the speakers. The Instituto also was charged with the very impressive liturgies celebrated at the Los Angeles congress. Many of its members took part in an October meeting at which they considered the second revision of the *Misal Romano* and spoke eloquently in favor of popular religion (*La Voz Católica*, 23 October). The Mexican American Cultural Center (MACC) commemorated its 20th anniversary with a Mass celebrated by San Antonio's Archbishop Patrick Flores. Among the speakers were Rosa Guerrero and Edmundo Rodriguez, S.J. The convention of the National Association of Pastoral Musicians in Albuquerque, New Mexico, in July was a bilingual celebration of the gifts of Hispanics, especially musicians. More than just an "Hispanic Day," it was a great achievement by Hispanic liturgists.

The National Organization of Catechists for Hispanics (NOCH) held its fourth annual meeting in conjunction with the Los Angeles congress. Eduardo Salazar, S.J. spoke, and the organization considered its relation to the USCC department of education. Its project "Semillas del Reino" has received widespread support and interest. The organization is also preparing a common curriculum for the training of catechists throughout the nation. The Catholic Migrant Farmworker Network received a matching grant of $20,000 from the American Board of Catholic Missions and was featured in Toledo's *Catholic Chronicle* and Alabama's *Blount County Magazine.*

The National Office of Renew continues its innovative work among Hispanics, providing both training and materials for gathering adolescents and children into small Christian communities. It is the first group to do this, a very important step when one considers the youthfulness of the Hispanic communities. Kenneth Davis, O.F.M.Conv., and Sister María Stella Herrera, R.J.M., addressed the Bishops' Committee on Hispanic Affairs concerning these outreaches (*En Marcha*, Winter). There have also been some efforts to organize Hispanic youth ministry. Rosa Guerrero addressed the National Conference on Catholic Youth Ministry at its December meeting in Houston; Modesto García was one of the five award winners at that meeting. Conventions on regional levels (West and Southwest) have met with success, and the young people themselves have asked for help. The best source of information on the subject is still the St. Mary's Press newsletter *Construyendo Nuestra Esperanza* (800–533–8095).

## Resources

The Claretians' newsletter *Nuestra Parroquia* now includes homily helps. *Ecos Cristóferos* is the Spanish edition of Christopher Newsnotes. Likewise *CareNotes* (Abbey Press) are now available in Spanish. The Eternal Word Network continues to add programs in Spanish, and some Catholic publishers are slowly adding Spanish titles (for example, Paulist Press now offers six).

For youth, the Eaton Publishing Company (Box 1064, Jefferson City, MO 65102) offers four pamphlets in Spanish concerning life decisions, and Life Directions (4418 W. Walton St., Chicago, IL, 60651) publishes fourteen bilingual guides to the National Pastoral Plan for Hispanic

Ministry. The Rogatian Fathers are offering a large Vocation Awareness Package in Spanish ($35), as are the Sisters of the Company of Mary. Father Gary Riebe-Estrella, S.V.D., wrote an article in the July/ September issue of *Vocation and Prayer* called "Why Target Latinos in Vocation Ministry?" The Washington Theological Union has begun to look into the formation of Hispanics beginning with Marina Herrera's *Strategic Plan to Prepare Ministers for the Multi-cultural Church.* Franciscan Communications (now part of St. Anthony Messenger press) offers two new Bible study tools: Robert Delaney's series *Vivamos las Escrituras*, and Carlos Mesters' six new books for the formation of Bible circles. All their Spanish language materials are excellent values.

Liturgists may have noted the articles concerning Hispanics in the November–February edition of *Today's Liturgy*. Homilists will welcome Alba House's *Bilingual Homilies for Feast Days and Other Occasions* by Frederick Murphy, and the pastoral Spanish program developed by Father Romuald Zantua ($195; 55 Grand Street, Newburgh, NY, 12550). Also for preachers is the Northeast Pastoral Center's *Announcing the Gospel Every Day* ($5). Word Graphics (Box 850, Flanders, NJ, 07836) offers bulletin graphics in Spanish. Musicians ought to note the GIA publication of new songs by Donna Peña, Gregory Norbert's Spanish endeavors with Oregon Catholic Press (which now offers prayers of the faithful in Spanish), and Ariel Ramírez's *Misa Criolla* on Palisades Home Video (800–229–8575).

Historians should take note of Bishop David Arias' *Spanish Roots of America*, with bibliography and index ($9.95; Our Sunday Visitor); this is the English translation of the Spanish original, one of 278 titles published in Spain (Mapfri) concerning Spain's encounter with the Americas. See also William Wroth's *Images of Penance, Images of Mercy: Southwestern Santos in the Late Nineteenth Century* (University of Oklahoma Press) and the 1992 issue of the *Journal of Texas Catholic History and Culture*, which was devoted to Catholic evangelization since the conquest. The events surrounding the arrival of Columbus were the subject of a debate between María Luisa Gastón and Marina Herrera on the January/February edition of Paulist Press's cassette journal, *Overheard*. Because of the 500th anniversary, many books were published about Bartolomé de las Casas. The best is Paulist Press's *Bartolomé de las Casas: The Only Way*, with an introduction by Helen Rand Parish. A more popular version is Orbis' *Witness: The Writings of Bartolomé de las Casas*, edited by George Sanderlin, with a foreword by Gustavo Gutiérrez.

Fortress Press reprinted Ada María Isasi-Díaz and Yolanda Tarango's pioneering work *Hispanic Women: Prophetic Voice in the Church*. Also available is Electa Arenal and Stacy Schlau's *Untold Stories: Hispanic Nuns in Their Own Words* (University of New Mexico Press), a retrieval of the life and writings of religious women of Latin America and Spain.

Both Catholic and Protestant scholars are included in Justo González's *Voces: Voices from the Hispanic Church* (Abingdon Press). Besides an excellent foreword and afterword, it contains reprints of some of the best articles in *Apuntes*. Interested readers are encouraged also to look at the NCR Fall books edition of 11 September. Of interest also is NCR's story about Richard Rodriguez and the review of his *Days of Obligation: An Argument with My Mexican Father* in the 20 November issue.

## Significant Books

*Nuestro Clamor por la Vida: Teología Latinoamericana desde la Perspectiva de la Mujer.* María Pilar Aquino. San José, Costa Rica: Editorial DEI, 1992. Bibliography and notes. Paper. 224 pp. Translation forthcoming from Orbis Books.

Aquino's book, part of her dissertation, is a "liberating theological epistemology" whose goal is to "find the principal nuclei, essential categories, basic theoretical structures, originating experiences, spiritual itinerary, and internal unity which characterize the theological thought of women in and from Latin America." This is a daunting task since much of this theological output is not transcribed, but is the fruit of reflection in ecclesial base communities. The reflection of Latin American (LA) women in these contexts (marked by poverty, suffering, and often mortal danger) energizes Aquino. She divides her study into two parts: First, a history of how LA feminist theology came about and a discussion of how it differs from other theologies. She examines a diversity of works by women and about women in LA. She looks at Medellín and Puebla's pronouncements about women, statements by the Ecumenical Association of Third World Theologians, and the works of three male LA liberation theologians concerning women. The second part is a synthesis of the methodology and content of LA feminist theology. Aquino draws on the work of LA feminists such as María Clara Lucchetti Bingemer, Tereza Cavalcanti, Ivone Gebara, Carmen Lora, and Elsa Tamez and on statements produced by meetings of women theologians at Buenos Aires (1985) and Oaxtepec (1986).

She does not, however, adequately describe what is uniquely LA about feminist theology being done by these thrice-oppressed women. Aquino herself recognizes this, but never really develops it.

It cannot be said that even today Latin American liberation theology from a women's perspective has developed a coherent analytic tool capable of dealing with the problem of women. In addition to indicating an internal methodological flaw, this fact reveals the great challenge which lies ahead: To achieve its own methodological coherence. (p.197). She does provide clues to this uniqueness. Two sections are particularly suggestive: Chapter Three of Part 1, "Women in the Church of the Poor," and the section on women and popular religiosity in Chapter Three of Part Two. Unfortunately, Aquino does not analyze either of these situations in detail. What she clearly establishes is that there is a corpus of theological reflection in LA that is in keeping with North American and European feminist theology. Her extensive and pain-staking citations from such theologians as Elizabeth Schüssler-Fiorenza, Rosemary Radford Ruether, Anne E. Carr, and Lisa Sowle Cahill indicate the close relationship between their work and that of their LA counterparts.

But there are other difficulties. On several occasions it is evident that what has been published has been extracted from the original disser-tation. This makes for a choppy presentation. For example, in the intro-duction Aquino writes that the book is divided into three parts: It is actually divided into two. She mentions that she intends to critique LA feminist theology, but her only theological critique is that of what she calls "traditional theology" and the writings about women by the three male liberationists. More importantly, the inclusion of some chapters of the original has not really contributed to a smooth exposition. This is the case with Chapter Two in Part One, "The Discovery of Causality in Latin American Women," which deals with the general theory of how sex/gender exploitation came about. The reader could have been spared this without losing Aquino's principal argument. Greater care by the editors was needed.

At times Aquino's analysis is reductionist. For example, in her critique of what she calls "traditional theology," she ascribes to it the pejorative label "logocentric." She distinguishes between theology done by women—which is more concerned with poetry, play, and painting—and this logocentric theology, which became a reasoned word which clarifies and defines truths, next to which all other human accesses to truth . . . turned out to be false and inconsistent, closing the possibility of other forms of knowing (pp. 119–120). The "traditional theology" which encompasses the mystical poetry of John of the Cross and the scholasticism of Thomas Aquinas are too diverse to be lumped together as simply logocentric. Throughout the book, one is barraged by the injustices committed by men against women; no mention is made, however, of women's equal ability, as equally free agents, to sin. Aquino's discourse paints an unrealistic picture of women, whose only sin seems to be allowing patriarchal structures to continue. One could easily assume that all women have, like the Blessed Mother, escaped the ravages of original sin. Such a depiction detracts from Aquino's plea that the theological community consider men and women equals.

Be that as it may, the comprehensive bibliography of LA feminist output provides reason enough for any student of feminism to be familiar with Aquino's work.

*Reviewed by Claudio M. Burgaleta, S.J.*

*We Are a People! Initiatives in Hispanic-American Theology,* Roberto Goizueta, ed. Minneapolis: Fortress Press, 1992, pp. 144. Paper. $10.95.

This book takes its stance on the communally manifested faith practices of the people. Its context is the Hispanic people "struggling to find acceptance as Christians and Americans without having to deny their Hispanic identity" (p. xvii). In the preface Goizueta identifies the *mestizaje* essence of the Hispanic American, that is, the experience of being racially and culturally—and, I would add, psychologically—mixed. The contributors are one female and five male theologians, all Hispanics and all members of the Academy of Catholic Hispanic Theologians of the United States.

I found Goizueta's article, "Rediscovering Praxis: The Significance of U.S.–Hispanic Experience with Theological Method," to be the most intriguing in the book. His question is that of the relationship between praxis and theory. We must ground our reflection in the experience of our own communities, he contends, but the path confronting us is neither assimilation nor repudiation but critical appropriation. He warns of the tendency to identify practice with technique. He argues that the relationship between the two dimensions of praxis—as intrinsically liberative and as a liberative result—needs to be addressed more systematically.

Orlando Espín's "Grace and Humanness" is a striking example of an earlier chapter's call for a poetic theologian or a theological poet. Espín's presentation of what it means to be human as an image of God is both poetically written and theologically sound. Espín speaks of God's presence in the world and identifies culture's role as a mediator of grace. He further argues that if grace can be experienced only through one's culture, then any dehumanization of the people and their culture is active opposition to the God of love and salvation, "and to deculturalize or to trample on culture is dehumanizing." Espín challenges us by asking, "How does the Hispanic individual and community encounter 'the God for us' in a culturally authentic way?" He argues that popular religiosity is a locus for Hispanic self-disclosure and is a vehicle of manifestation of God's grace. He understands what it means to be human for the Hispanic community as familial and communal, namely, that the individual is valued and important "because he or she is a member of family and of community." Of utmost importance for this community are the dimensions of solidarity and mutual trust. Justice and liberation, argues Espín, are other names for love. This love includes the worlds of private individuals and the public worlds of socioeconomic and politics. Human reconciliation can come about only if it is present in all these places.

María Pilar Aquino's article, "Doing Theology from the Perspective of Latin American Women," critiques both Latin American liberationist and feminist theologies (as dominated by white Anglo women), the former for its male-centeredness and the latter for its weak link between sexism and classism. Aquino argues that our creation, as Scripture says, in God's image demands a total break from the prevailing patriarchal system leading to global liberation. Of primary focus for Aquino, however, is the ecclesial reality that most women find themselves excluded from decision making in theological formation and in sacred ministry. Theology from the perspective of women, therefore, demands a new way of being Church that must be profoundly ecumenical and ecological. Theology from the perspective of women recovers the oldest and most liberating tradition of the Scriptures and of the Church, and that is what the Church is called to be: A community of disciples who are equal.

Sixto J. García, writing about the role of the Hispanic theologian, roots his Trinitarian theology in its Christocentric dimension and reintroduces Mary as the key to this Trinitarian experience. Allan Figueroa Deck, S.J., discusses the complex matter of the marginality of the Hispanics in North America and argues that Hispanics will ultimately be able to unite and integrate only from a position of strength—in his example, when we have our own parishes. And Fernando Segovia draws on the work of four Hispanic American theologians who reflect the influence of liberation theology as a methodology.

*Reviewed by Jeanette Rodriguez.*

*Frontiers of Hispanic Theology in the United States* 'Allan Figueroa Deck, S.J., ed. Maryknoll: Orbis Books, 1992. Index, notes, bibliography. pp. xxvi + 174. Paper. $16.95.

In his excellent introduction, Deck explains that this anthology of essays heralds the advent of professional United States Hispanic theology and its challenge to the Church to reconsider its own self-understanding in the light of the Hispanic presence and contributions. He provides a brief history of United States Hispanic theology and explains their three unique contexts: First, United States Hispanics encounter themselves in the source of world modernity with its plurality and secularity. Second, Hispanic women have been co-constructors of this theology since its beginning. Third, the cultural and sociopolitical atmosphere of the United States Hispanic is unique. I would add two more: Unlike even United States Hispanic Protestants, Catholic theologians include many lay people. Four of the ten contributors to this work are lay. Also significant is their youth, especially if contrasted to colleagues, for instance, of the Catholic Theological Society of America. Doubtless their context is unique and their contribution essential.

While the founding authors of this theology are of course represented (that is, Elizondo not only has his own contribution, but also is referred to by others), refreshingly we hear the voices of relative newcomers as well. Gloria Inés Loya continues the best of feminist inquiry in her deft analysis and reflection on Californian Chicanas as passionate pastors to their families and communities. Juan-Lorenzo Hinojosa develops a theme that has captivated him for years, the retrieval of Hispanic spirituality in the face of increasing modernity. Their presence proves Deck's thesis that this book is only the advent of a new theological voice because they represent a new generation.

Sixto García and Orlando Espín, who have collaborated in the past, both have contributed to this text. This is Espín's best development yet of his contention that Hispanic popular religion is a cultural expression of a *sensus fidelium*. He presents three excellent criteria for studying popular religion and a good explanation of the role of inculturation, concluding that popular religion is a necessary area of theological reflection. García agrees, insisting that an Hispanic Trinitarian theology must be based on reflection on this and on the kenotic and pastoral dimensions of Christology and liturgy.

The Mexican American Cultural Center's Rosa María Icaza also writes on liturgy and spirituality, drawing from them key values of the Hispanic communities. These she addresses in reference to the liturgical year, with practical suggestions on how to celebrate faith in the context of culture. C. Gilbert Romero has written the book on Hispanic popular religion from a Scriptural perspective, and in his essay he continues to develop his thesis that the symbols and traditions of this faith expression can elucidate the Bible. Like Justo González, he believes that Hispanics have a peculiar insight into the Bible because they are an oppressed minority.

María Pilar Aquino, like a number of Latinas who are not included in this work, questions the importance of popular religion in Hispanic theology. She wishes to break clearly with what she sees as an endocentric, patriarchal, and neocolonial past found in the liberal/ modern theology with which her fellow essayists dialogue. She seems to fear that too exclusive attention to popular culture will deter us from the hard work of analyzing and solving the real world problems of Latinas. Precisely by standing in contrast to others, Aquino shows the maturity of the United States Hispanic theological enterprise. This book is not the work of fearful novices, but of professionals who welcome debate and critique. And this is where the chapter by Roberto Goizueta may be most helpful. With evident care for a feminist perspective, he bridges the gap between popular and "official" religion and deals with the co-option of modern/liberal theology.

*Frontiers* continues the Hispanic tradition of collaborative theology, but has the limitations of any anthology. There are too few contributors, and there is not much room for them to really develop their thought. Considering the explosion of United States Hispanic theological output, perhaps now is the time to consider a series of complete volumes each developing and dialoguing with others as a way to continue this valuable collaboration without the constraints of a single anthology. Here we have only a taste of what could be a feast of complementary theological courses.

*Prophetic Vision: Pastoral Reflections on the National Pastoral Plan for Hispanic Ministry.* Galerón, Soledad, et al., eds. San Antonio: MACC, 1992. Bilingual. Notes and bibliography. pp. 360. Paper. $19.95.

This uneven collection seems to lack a defined audience. Some chapters are obviously written for novices while others assume not only a working knowledge of theology but also the specific United States Hispanic contexts. Scholars would welcome certain chapters while others certainly are aimed at a less sophisticated audience. Moreover, the book begins badly. The first chapter, "Recent History of Hispanic Ministry in the United States," starts with the first conquest. That is not recent history, and it does not even mention the work of contemporary historian Moises Sandoval. Likewise, the second essay, while presenting some excellent sociological analysis and ecclesiological reflections on the Tercer Encuentro, deals with its topic, "A Theological Reflection," almost as an afterthought in the last two pages. Elizondo as the third essayist follows up with a poignant reflection on this sociological analysis, eloquently reflecting on what it means to be a "pueblo," a people of God.

The editor does a good job of pointing out some key aspects of the pastoral plan in her chapter, distilling its ecclesiology and presenting its challenges. Juan Alfaro also sticks to his topic and presents a good biblical reflection on what it means to be prophetic. Ricardo Antoncich, S.J., reflects on the role of social justice in the context of *mística*, a concept also broached by Rosa María Icaza.

Dominga Zapata gives a taut and concise theoretical and practical summary of the term *pastoral de conjunto*, and Juan Díaz Vilar, S.J., offers the best explanation of why the ecclesiology of the plan is valid for the entire United States Church.

The model of base communities is referred to throughout the book. Taken together, the contributions of Rosendo Urrabazo, C.M.F., and John Linskens, C.I.C.M., are quite informative. The former offers a wealth of statistics to ground his emphasis on community organization, and the latter offers an ecclesiology built on base communities that are constituted by, among other things, grass roots organizing for justice.

The different priority groups identified by the plan are represented. A couple from the Christian family movement speaks of the fissures that erupt in families when they are not supported by society, and of the importance of church as an extended family. José Morán presents a manifesto of youth who were involved from the plan's inception. And María Pilar Aquino's essay, simply titled "Women," is the lengthiest one and the only one that critiques the plan (its social analysis is fearful and inconsistent). Urrabazo's contribution deals with an option for the poor.

There is much to recommend this work. It is the only text of its kind to appear in an English/Spanish format. That and its diversity mean that there is something for everyone. It also offers a good appendix of resources and publications. And doubtlessly it includes some excellent reflections by leading thinkers; no one could argue that Mario Vizcaíno, SchP., lacks the experience and education to write well about "Christian Leadership as Service," nor does he disappoint us. Perhaps most striking is the obvious ardor and dedication so many of its authors display. No one who reads this book could complain that the National Pastoral Plan simply served to fill shelves. These are participants for whom the Encuentros were paradigm-shifting experiences.

My quarrel is that these golden nuggets are not easily accessible. Some of the authors strayed from their topics; essays that are logically linked are not placed together, nor does any introduction point out either this complementariness or the variant (and therefore interesting) points of view. The chapters are very brief and sometimes cover overly ambitious topics. It is a pleasure to uncover a nugget of pastoral or theological gold, but when I buy a book I prefer not to have to pan out the sand and gravel myself. This is a good book that could have been much better with tighter organization, more logical presentation, and a more helpful introduction.

## Other Noteworthy Writings

Aquino, María Pilar, "The Challenge of Hispanic Women," *Missiology* 20, no. 2 (April 1992): 261–268. Author of the new book *Nuestro Clamor por la Vida* enumerates some of the elements for a Latina feminist liberation theology. These include egalitarianism, inclusiveness, and participation by poor women themselves, such that theology becomes faith seeking liberation.

Bañuelas, Arturo, "U.S. Hispanic Theology," *Missiology* 2 (April 1992): 275–300. A survey of seven Catholic and Protestant United States Hispanic theologians with a helpful assessment of their commonality and a critique of their limitations.

Davis, Kenneth G., "A Return to the Roots: Conversion and the Culture of the Mexican-Descent Catholic," *Pastoral Psychology* 40, no. 3 (January 1992): 139–158. Description of the experience of conversion in this community based on an analysis of their popular spirituality.

_____, "Child Abuse in the Hispanic Community: A Christian Perspective," *Apuntes* 12, no. 3 (Fall 1992): 127–136. Explores the causes of physical child abuse and neglect within this community and Parents Anonymous as a possible pastoral approach to it.

\_\_\_\_\_, "Preaching in Spanish as a Second Language," *Homiletic* (Fall 1992): 7–10. A veteran of cross-cultural preaching offers personal insight into the challenge with a helpful bibliography.

Deck, Allan Figueroa, "Popular Culture, Popular Religion: Framing the Question," *Way Supplement* 73 (Spring 1992): 24–35. Argues for a serious discussion of popular religion, spirituality, and affectivity as a remedy for the "serious limitations that social class and cultural location place on our understanding of how God works."

Elizondo, Virgil, "Méstissage: La Naissance d'une Nouvelle Culture et d'une Nouvelle Chrétienté," *Lumière et Vie* 208 (July 1992): 77–90. Latin Americans are a mixture of black, indigenous, and Europeans, a painful but unique cultural, racial, and physical mix which must be recognized as a distinct ethnicity worthy of appreciation and study.

Espín, Orlando, "Trinitarian Monotheism and the Birth of Popular Catholicism: The Case of Sixteenth Century Mexico," *Missiology* 20, no. 2 (April 1992): 178–204. Shows that art, catechisms, and popular religion were early, native, and sometimes subversive hermeneutics of the Christian message.

\_\_\_\_\_, "The God of the Vanquished: Foundations for a Latino Spirituality," *Listening* 27, no. 1 (winter 1992): 70–84. The symbols of popular Catholicism portray God in solidarity with the vanquished victims of society. Hence our spirituality must evoke a solidarity with victims, and our symbols effectively remind the vanquished that Christ and the Church suffer and hope with them.

Gabriel, Rosemary, ed. *Santos de Palo: The Household Saints of Puerto Rico*. New York: Museum of American Folk Art, 1992. A brief but important work because it adds to the small number of studies of popular religion among Puerto Ricans.

Goizueta, Roberto, "Nosotros: Toward a U.S. Hispanic Anthropology," *Listening* 27, no. 1 (Winter 1992): 55–69. For the Hispanic, the understanding of the human is born out of the conflictual experience of *mestizaje*. This means that the Hispanic theologian must be able to deal with mixtures/dialogues between seeming opposites (men and women) and that the Hispanic is in a unique position to midwife the birth of a polycentric United States Church.

Herrera, Marina, "Meeting Cultures at the Well," *Religious Education* 87, no. 8 (Spring 1992): 173–180. Uses John 4:41–45 as a model for intercultural, interracial, and intergender communication.

Hughes, Cornelius, "Views from the Pews: Hispanic and Anglo Catholics in a Changing Church," *Review of Religious Research* 33, no. 4 (June 1992): 364–375. Suggests that the exodus of Hispanics is due more to their nominal relation to the Church and less to ecclesiastical failure as others have insisted.

Isasi-Díaz, Ada María, "Mujerista Theology's Method: A Liberative Praxis, a Way of Life," *Listening* 27, no. 1 (Winter 1992): 41–64. Presents this method with its goal of liberation through enhanced moral and historical agency that has been effective for the struggle of poor Latino/as to survive and thrive.

Pierce, Brian, "Bartolomé de las Casas and Truth: Toward a Spirituality of Solidarity," *Spirituality Today* 44, no. 1 (1992): 4–19. Reflects on the new evangelization based on this Dominican's dedication to the truth, solidarity with the poor, and readiness to risk martyrdom.

Pineda, Ana María, "Evangelization of the 'New World': A New World Perspective," *Missiology* 20, no. 8 (April 1992): 151–161. Builds on her fascinating study of the effects of the encounter in the Americas between a literate and an oral culture and its consequence for evangelization. Pineda was one of the guest editors for this special edition of *Missiology*.

Ramírez, Ricardo, "The Challenge of Ecumenism to Hispanic Christians," *Ecumenical Trends* 21, no. 8 (1992): 1, 11–14. Ecumenism among Hispanics has yet to be a priority, but ought to be because any unity within a culture requires family and community collaboration.

Riebe-Estrella, Gary, "The Challenge of Ministerial Formation," *Missiology* 20, no. 2 (April 1992): 269–274. The seminary education system must be willing to be transformed and restructured in order to appreciate and learn from the richness Latinos bring.

Segovia, Fernando F., "Two Places and No Place on Which to Stand: Mixture and Otherness in Hispanic American Theology," *Listening* 27, no. 1 (Winter 1992): 26–40. The beginnings of an autochthonous, self-conscious, and critical Hispanic hermeneutic and theology based on the painful yet liberating experience of both otherness and mixture. Segovia was the guest editor for this issue of *Listening*.

Urrabazo, Rosendo, "Pastoral Education of Hispanic Adults," *Missiology* 20, no. 2 (April 1992): 258–260. Focuses on the content and direction of this education and sees that a culturally sensitive, participative learning model is most apt.

_____."Pastoral Ministry in a Multi-cultural Society," *Origins* 22, no. 23 (19 November 1992): 386–391. The text of his 29 September talk to the Texas Catholic Conference, in which he laments the under-counting and discounting of Hispanics, reiterates the need for small Christian communities imbued with justice, and closes with an elegant meditation on the Mass.

*This article originally appeared in Review for Religious Vol. 52, no. 2 (1993) under the title, "U.S. Hispanic Catholics: Trends and Works 1992."*

# 1993 IN REVIEW

Among Hispanic Catholics who made the secular press this year are astronaut Mario Runco; deceased salsa great Héctor Lavoe; Wilfredo Mercado, who died in the World Trade Center bombing; and the late Jesse Sepulveda, Jr., whose heart transplant some seven years ago led to the implementation of a new Federal organ donor system. Also much in the news was Colombia native William Lozano, a Miami police officer, whose conviction of killing two African Americans was overturned on appeal (*New York Times* [NYT], 6 June). Of note also was the unanimous Supreme Court ruling that recognized the legitimacy of animal sacrifices such as those practiced in Santería, whose rituals are also practiced by many Catholics.

The late activist, writer, and labor organizer César Chávez, during his last year (along with Dolores Huerta and Victor Salandini), pushed for a thorough investigation of child labor laws on United States farms. Events commemorating him included an exhibit of art works at Center Becas Artes in Fresno, California, that featured him and his work (*Hispanic Link* [HL], 1 November). And the premier issue of *The Journal of Hispanic/Latino Theology* was dedicated to his memory.

Chicano students at the University of California at Los Angeles successfully organized in Chávez's name for education reforms. Some headway was made in Catholic educational institutions. Notre Dame University and St. Edwards in Austin, Texas, are among those who successfully used financial aid, campus cultural support, remedial tutoring, and travel allowances to attract and retain Hispanic students (NYT, 24 February). And Sister M. Isolina Ferré won the 1993 Hispanic Achievement Award for her dedication to education.

## Migrants and Immigrants

Roger Cardinal Mahoney has been perhaps the most consistent and vocal member of the hierarchy to support immigrant rights. He has insisted that the universal insurance coverage apply to them (*Catholic Trends* [CT], 9 October) and has promoted their right to seek dignified work (*El Visitante Dominical* [VD], 22 August). Bishops John Quinn of

San Francisco and John Cummins of Oakland also criticized the new wave of anti-immigrant sentiment, especially in California. Likewise, ecclesial leaders (VD, 11 April and 23 May) have criticized the threatened execution of nineteen Mexicans now on death row. See the *National Catholic Reporter* (NCR) report Church Immigration View: Countercultural (10 September).

Migrant workers, especially the United Farm Workers, have been much in the news because of the sudden death of founder César Chávez. Unfortunately, very few reports in the secular press recognized the spiritual roots of his work (see *Newsweek*, 3 May). Chávez's son-in-law Arturo Rodríguez is now the president, and apparently the union is functioning well under his direction. (Another tragedy that affected farm workers, of course, was the terrible flooding in the Midwest.) Chávez's work is far from over. Disunity confronts migrants and immigrants (*Washington Post*, 12 September). Univision reports that migrant children suffer more accidents and worse education than any other group in the country (28 May).

Chávez helped galvanize and organize migrants not only in the fields, but also in the Church. The National Catholic Charities has championed their cause (NCR, 15 October), and although their voice is not always heard, migrant ministries began in such disparate places as Owensboro, Kentucky, and the Twin Cities of Minnesota. The Franciscan International Award, the oldest Catholic award ceremony in the United States, will confer the honor next year on Carolina Mata-Woodruff for her work on behalf of migrants. For more migrant information, consult the newsletter Catholic Migrant Farm Worker Network (419–243–6608).

## The North American Free Trade Agreement (NAFTA)

This very complex treaty will remove tariffs and other trade barriers over the next fifteen years between the three nations of this continent. The Church has been cautious in its appraisal. Both the Mexican and United States conferences of bishops understand that projected good or ill resulting from NAFTA is widely disputed. What is not in dispute is the moral grounding of any government policy. Hence, they have raised questions apart from the agreement itself, insisting that governments protect human dignity, workers rights, the environment, and holistic communities. Mexican bishops have especially questioned the lack of popular representation in the negotiating process and have noted the probable dire effects on rural people.

However, some segments of the Church have been more critical. The National Catholic Rural Life Conference, for instance, has condemned the accord. The Conference of Major Superiors of Men published a balanced assessment, but asked why the entire negotiating process has not been more open and democratic and why reams of paper cover the needs of the economic elite (for example, trademarks, royalties) and so little covers the rights of workers, their communities, and the environment. The United States Catholic Conference has circulated several press releases on the issue. Now that side agreements, pledges to clean up the environment, financing infrastructure, worker retraining, new banking systems, and other complex issues are completed, it will forward to Congress a letter which will probably repeat its April pronouncement that nations should be guided by a priority concern for the poor in both lands and by a firm commitment to the dignity of work and the rights of workers.

## General Church News

The Bishops Secretariat for Hispanic Affairs helped convene a February meeting of diocesan directors of Hispanic ministry; regional meetings followed it. Among other agenda items is the planning for the fiftieth anniversary of organized, national, United States Hispanic ministry. The director, Mr. Ronaldo Cruz, has spoken on several topics, including base communities. He has also advised Latino/a leaders that the American Board of Catholic Missions is seriously considering cutting its long-standing funding of the Regional Offices of Hispanic Ministry.

On the other hand, the Campaign for Human Development gave $70,000 to the organizing committee of Agricultural Workers of Toledo, Ohio. The new president of this organization is Father Anthony J. Stubeda. An equal amount was also given to Proyecto Visión, based in Monrovia, California, and dedicated to help gang members (VD, 25 July). The Institute of Religion and Health will use $376,271 from the Robert Wood Johnson Foundation to train both lay and ordained New York Hispanics on how to make mental health referrals. In the West, Juan José Gloria, Luis Velázquez, and Rose Ann Rasic have cooperated with Californias Century Council in a campaign to curtail excessive drinking among Hispanics (VD, 5 September).

Father Phil Cioppa was named the new director of the Northwest Regional Office of Hispanic Ministry. The newly elected executive committee members of the National Association of Diocesan Directors of

Hispanic Ministry are Rudy Vargas IV, Esther B. García, Ronald J. Patnode, Gonzalo Saldaña, and Thomas W. Florek. Featured speakers for their February meeting in Houston, Texas, were Mario Vizcaino and Jeanette Rodríguez Ph.D.

Virgil Elizondo continues his frequent writing and lectures. He was featured at the Future of the American Church conference and at the National Association of Lay Ministry conference. Along with Tony Melendez, he animated Chicagos Jesus Day 1993. He spoke at the National Conference of Preaching and in May at a Washington, DC, workshop on The Catechism of the Catholic Church. Elizondo also taught a course, along with Yolanda Tarango, C.C.V.I., and Rosendo Urrabazo, C.M.F., at the Pastoral Institute of Incarnate Word College. Verbo Divino published a Spanish translation of Elizondos 1992 book Way of the Cross; he collaborated with Leonardo Boff on *Any Room for Christ in Asia?* (Orbis, 1993) and published articles in *Educación Hoy*. Along with Timothy Matovina, Ph.D., he will be studying the history of San Antonios cathedral (see U.S. Hispanic Catholics and Liturgical Reform, *America*, 6 November).

Fernando Segovia lectured at the now defunct Maryknoll School of Theology on the fiftieth anniversary of the Catholic Biblical Society. Joseph Fitzpatrick, S.J., Marina Herrera, and German Martínez, O.S.B., were featured at the July Multi-Culturalism: Perspectives for Ministers workshop held at Seton Hall University. Herrera also addressed faculty members from Boston College and the Weston School of Theology in November. Martínez mentored a Parish/Pastoral/Church ministry course in Fordham Universitys summer program. Allan Figueroa Deck, S.J., was featured on the Discovery Channels program Rediscovering America, which toured antique Spanish mission sites. Deck also presented a paper on Catholic social teaching at the Catholic Theological Society of America. Charismatic San Antonian Gloria Rodríguez was cited in the March issue of *Salt* for her work with Latino/a families. (In last years installment I repeated an erroneous press report that the National Association of Catholic Family Life Ministers meeting last year included consideration of Hispanic family life.)

Juan Díaz Vilar, S.J., Carmen María Cervantes, and Pedro Nuñez were among featured speakers at New Orleans first Catholic Congress on Evangelization. Ana María Pineda, R.S.M., was guest lecturer again at the Washington Theological Union. María de la Cruz Aymes spoke at the April National Convocation of Directors of Religious Education. Paula González taught at the Sacred Heart Summer Institute, while the same season saw Juan Lorenzo Hinojosa teaching at Loyola Marymount.

Cuban Silvia Bravo Camarza was given a special award by the National Catholic Education Association. This same association published a document called *Readiness for Theological Studies* that concluded, It is incumbent on all of those who are preparing for ministry to become educated about other ethnic, racial, and cultural groups (NCR, 5 February). Dominican Lucy Vazquez was elected the first female president of the Canon Law Society of America (CT, 10 April). The Dominicans of the Southern province elected their first Hispanic provincial, Alberto Rodríguez, O.P. Otto Maduro was interviewed in *America* (14 August), and Ursuline Sister Diana Ortiz continues her crusade for justice for herself and other survivors of torture in Guatemala. Benedictine Sister Theresa Torres and her colleagues in youth ministry were featured in NCR (17 December).

Glenmary Home Missioners sponsored a May workshop on coordinating shared information on migrants and immigrants in the southeastern part of the country (*Crux*, 8 March). Bishop Peña of El Paso, Texas, has been an outspoken critic of the new, harsher methods of controlling the international border of his diocese. He and other border bishops have challenged both the justice and economic wisdom of these initiatives. Due to unproven, extremist criticism, Bishop Peña has also had to deal with controversies surrounding El Pasos very successful and widely acclaimed Instituto Tepeyac.

Other bishops in the news include Michael Sheehan, who was appointed to the Archdiocese of Santa Fe after the controversial resignation of Archbishop Roberto Sanchez. James A. Tamayo was named auxiliary bishop of the diocese of Galveston-Houston, while auxiliary Bishop Juan Arzube retired from his post in Los Angeles. Bishop Ricardo Ramírez spoke at the Annual Conference on Lay Ministry, encouraging a growing recognition of the cultural diversity within the Church. Ramírez also published an eloquent eulogy to César Chávez in the 27 May issue of *Origins*. San Franciscos Auxiliary Bishop Carlos Sevilla has been appointed delegate to the World Synod on Religious Life. And Bostons Roberto Gonzáles, O.F.M., was instrumental in sending aid to Cubans suffering from their deteriorating economy (*Crux*, 22 February). Archbishop Patrick Flores of San Antonio has been one of the principal voices asking compassion for prisoners. Along with Domingo Rodríguez, S.T., and Joseph Fitzpatrick, S.J., he spoke at the Annual Summer Institute for Priests in New Jersey. And Joseph Cardinal Bernardin received praise from Rick Garcia, director of Chicagos Catholic Advocates for Lesbian and Gay Rights (NCR, 18 June).

Ecclesial changes of note include the appointment of Pedro Villarroya, C.M., to direct the Office of Hispanic Affairs for the Archdiocese of Los Angeles, and the sad deaths of Mr. José Ocampo of the diocese of Monterey, California, an indefatigable friend of migrants, and Claretian priest Luis Olivares, a peace activist. Domingo Rodríguez, S.T., continues his popular publications and dynamic speaking. He has recently been appointed to the Bishops National Advisory Council. Lourdes Toro, M.S.B.T., has been elected to her congregations general board. In July Father Tomás Marín was appointed Miamis first Hispanic chancellor. In September, Luis Ripoll, S.J., who dedicated his life to young, Cuban exiles, died (*Voz Católica*, 23 July and 24 September). The last 1993 report of note is the unlikely finding by the National Survey of Religious Identification that only 14 percent of Catholics identify themselves as Hispanics (NCR, 17 December).

## Organizations of Note

The Academy of Catholic Theologians of the United States held its annual colloquium in May, in San Antonio. The several papers presented, plus other articles and book reviews, will appear in the first issue of *The Journal of Hispanic/Latino Theology*. Information is available from the publisher, The Liturgical Press. Several new members were inducted at this meeting, and the new president, María Pilar Aquino, addressed the awards banquet where Dr. Espín received the Virgil Elizondo award, and the Mexican American Cultural Center (MACC) won the ACHTUS award. Immediately following this meeting, the Catholic Theological Association of America held its annual convention, also in San Antonio. Much attention was devoted to Hispanics this year; almost 20 percent of the workshops treated the issue, and Virgil Elizondo gave one of the keynote addresses.

Two ACHTUS members, Fernando Segovia and Ada María Isasi-Díaz, will host a conference in April, 1994 at Drew University titled Aliens in Jerusalem: The Emerging Theological Voice of Hispanic Americans. The conference papers will eventually be published through Fortress Press.

The Asociación de Sacerdotes Hispanos held its annual convention 11–14 October in New Orleans. The theme was The Hispanic Priest Confronting Contemporary Crisis, and Rosendo Urrabazo, C.M.F., gave the keynote. In attendance were Bishops Ricardo Ramírez of Las Cruces, New Mexico; Juan Arzube of Los Angeles, California; Jaime Tamayo of Galveston-Houston, Texas; and Manuel Romero of Nayarít,

Mexico. Several work groups considered talks such as that of their president, Juan Gonzales Castro, O.M.I., whose words on The Hispanic Priest Confronting His Sexuality were synopsized in *El Visitante Dominical*. This same publication has inaugurated a column concerning Hispanic priests. The association formally supported the letter of Cuban bishops directed at their government and a petition to pardon a young Latino on death row in Joliet, Illinois. They plan a 1994 convention in Houston and in 1995 another in Atlanta. Also organizing is the Asociación Occidental de Seminaristas Hispanos, which includes Latino/a religious. For information call the president.

The Catholic Book Publishers Association has released *A Study of Religious Reading Needs among U.S. Hispanic Catholics*, funded by Lilly Endowment. The document concludes that Latino/a want brief, handsomely bound, illustrated books in Spanish that cost five dollars or less. They prefer simple (not simplistic) writing by persons of authority on themes such as the Bible, doctrine, marriage and family life, and writing that offers help with personal problems. Personal contact is the best way to market these books, and they are interested in themes for or about children. Readers tend to be devout (predominantly Mexican) and frequently read other publications such as newspapers. See the NCR report of 17 December.

The Comisión Hispana de la Región XI held its annual meeting in Tijuana. Professors David Hayes Bautista, María Pilar Aquino, Orlando Espín, and Laura Velasco and composer José Antonio Rubio aided those attending. Comunidades de Reflexión Eclesial Cubana en la Diaspora (CRECED) released its final document, fruit of much study and discussion. It is available by calling 305–262–1727. Likewise, Miamis Bishop Agustín Román announced the annual meeting of the Fraternidad Clero y Religiosos de Cuba en la Diaspora for 27–29 June in Washington, DC. He and Bishop Enrique San Pedro of Brownsville, Texas, led a CRECED pilgrimage to meet Pope John Paul and present the final CRECED document.

The Conference of Religious in Hispanic Ministry held its 1993 seminar on 4–25 July at St. Thomas Seminary in Denver, Colorado. Sixteen religious attended, thanks to $11,600 in grants from various congregations. The 1994 seminar will be held from June 19 to July 8 in Boerne, Texas, at the Benedictines Omega Center. The new member of the executive committee is Ms. Benita Huerta of the Oblate Missionaries of Mary Immaculate.

Cursillistas can take pride in the results of a study done on their members in New York by the Center for Applied Research in the

Apostolate (VD, 9 May). The study concludes that some 84 percent of those who make a cursillo remain active in their parishes, and many exert significant leadership.

The CUSHWA center at Notre Dame awarded summer research stipends to Roberto Goizueta, Ramon Gutiérrez, and Alberto Pulido. Dissertation fellowships went to Virginia Bouvier, Grayson Waystaff, and Nancy Wellmeier. Joseph Bator received a research travel grant. Jaime Vidal delivered papers at William Paterson College and at the annual meeting of the Society for the Comparative Study of Civilizations. Unfortunately both the summer research grants and dissertation fellowships are being phased out. However, the centers three volume study of United States Hispanic Catholics should be available through Notre Dame University Press in fall 1994.

LAS HERMANAS gathered some two hundred Latinas at Fort Myers, Florida, to discuss Hispanic Women Are the Salt of the Earth. Sister Yolanda Tarango of the Sisters of Charity of the Incarnate Word was quoted concerning the meeting in the 29 October National Catholic Reporter. For more information call 210–434–0947.

El Instituto Hispano de Formación Pastoral celebrates its twentieth anniversary of service to Latino/a leadership in the New York area. It has grown to include sixteen professors who offer some twenty four courses to lay ministers and permanent deacons (VD, 8 August). The restored permanent deaconate, of course, celebrates its silver anniversary this year. This ministry is especially important to Hispanics because it is one of the few areas of leadership in which the percentage of Latino/a participation approaches the percentage of Hispanic presence in the Church. Fortunately, this trend is apparently, though slowly, becoming a reality among seminarians as well. In Texas, for instance, Hispanics account for 40 percent of seminarians (NCR, 22 October). Nationwide the 1993 increase in Hispanic seminarians was 2.8 percent (NCR, 16 April).

The Hispanic Telecommunications Network has begun a new initiative called the National Hispanic Catholic Media Center. It hopes to be a clearinghouse for adult evangelization and a research network that will include a database of pastoral programs for Hispanic Catholics. Call 210–227–5959 for more information.

The Instituto de Liturgia Hispana met in Orlando and St. Augustine, Florida, from 22–25 April to consider the theme: Liturgical Heritage for the Third Millennium. Besides several specialized workshops, major addresses covered the issues of The Impact of the Liturgy Among our People, The Beginnings of the Faith in Florida, and Liturgical

Challenges for the Third Millennium. The presentations were given in Spanish. The Instituto is planning the next gathering of its membership for 2–5 June in Mexico City around the theme Culture and Cult: Seed and Flower, which will deal with the inculturation of the liturgy.

MACC has a new president, Mercy Sister María Elena González. She is the first female to hold that post. Information concerning courses or publications can be had by calling 800–368–5445. Visiting professors during the summer included Edmundo Rodríguez, S.J., Mario Vizcaino with Lydia Menocal, Ninfa Garza, M.J., Allan Figueroa Deck, S.J., and Msgr. Arturo Bañuelas. MACC also hosted the July conference Bridges in Black and Brown, an inter-ethnic dialogue between Latinos/as and African Americans coordinated by Roberto Piña and Clarence Williams, CPPS (*Crux*, 4 October).

The fall edition of the newsletter *En Marcha* reports the first meeting of the Midwest conference on base communities. Six dioceses were represented along with Chicagos Bishops Plácido Rodríguez, Thad Jakubowski, and Raymond Goedert. November 4–7 saw the annual meeting of the National Catholic Council on Hispanic Ministry in Miami, Florida. Among other things, they considered the three regional consultations they had held throughout the year which endeavored to: (1) identify the need for leadership in nonprofit organizations, especially within the Church; (2) identify the successes, challenges, and deficiencies in current leadership; (3) develop a plan to respond creatively to those needs. The Lilly Endowment continues to aid them in this process. In January, the council released the conclusions and action lines of its 1992 Congress.

The National Organization of Catechists for Hispanics held its April, 1993 convention in Pasadena, California. Among other things, they discussed the response of eleven dioceses to a questionnaire concerning the catechesis of Latino/a. Great emphasis was placed this year on pastoral ministry to youth. Mary Lou Barba, M.C.D.P., was elected president (512–873–7771), and Cincinnati was selected as the site of its 14 April 1994 convention. Its members were instrumental in the publication of *Sin Fronteras: Lineamentos para Una Catequesis Evangelizadora*.

The National Pastoral Life Center has begun to investigate church-based Hispanic leadership development. Although it is obvious that Latino/as are under represented in Church leadership, and that projects to train them have been under funded, precise data is lacking. The project began by identifying as many good leadership development programs as possible and will proceed to assess them so as to recommend various models of formation. A report is due in June, 1994. Although begun under the direction of Teodosio Feliciano, Rudy Vargas now coordinates it. The center also sponsored a teleconference of the 4 November annual meeting of the National Catholic Council on Hispanic Ministry. Philip Murnion was the moderator; guests included Carmen María Cervantes, Ed.D., Allan Figueroa Deck, S.J., Juan Díaz-Vilar, S.J., and Mario Vizcaino, Sch.P.

Several new attempts at organizing Hispanic youth ministry have begun, perhaps spurred by the popes visit to Denver (see *En Marcha*, Fall 1993). Note the selection of Colombian Gloria Jarava by the Catholic Telecommunications Network to narrate its coverage of the popes visit (VD, 4 July). Over twenty five thousand Latino/a youth from around the world attended. Its workshops were coordinated in part by Cuco Chávez and Carmen Villegas.

Saint Mary's Press has received a grant to begin producing material for small group work with youth. Likewise, the International Office of RENEW will be offering a full line of training materials and faith-sharing booklets for Spanish-speaking youth (800–229–1232). The last meeting of CRECED included a group of youths who have since worked to organize themselves. Of interest particularly to the youth of the Southwest will be the Arizona bishops bilingual pastoral You Are Our Future.

The Program for the Analysis of Religion among Latinos (PARAL) gathered about thirty five psychologists, sociologists, anthropologists, theologians, and others at Princeton University in April to consider such topics as the shift of Latino/as to non-Catholic churches, and the catholization of the churches they join (VD, 21 May). The work continues, under the direction of Antonio Stevens-Arroyo (212–642–2950), with several task forces and a projected four volumes for publication by fall 1994.

During World Youth Day, a conference on Hispanic Youth and the New Evangelization was held under the auspices of several of the organizations mentioned above. And the last issue of *En Marcha* announced the reorganization of the Asociación Nacional Católica de Pastoral Juvenil Latinoamericana, mentioning Oakland, California, as headquarters.

## Resources

Although it is quite easy to find Spanish-as-a-second-language programs, one worth mentioning is aimed specifically at women. It is the

Intensive Spanish Language Program for Women of Faith Committed to Social Justice. Call 202–635–3118.

The diocese of Newark, New Jersey, offers small group discussion booklets by Father Hector Mazabel, available at one dollar each by calling 201–596–4200. The same office offers bilingual bulletin inserts based on the Sunday Scriptures. Also for small groups is *Simplemente Escritura*, from Twenty Third Publications (800–321–0411). The diocese of Miami, Florida, has a program called Systematic Training for Efficient Parenting that helps parents help children; call 305– 757–6241.

The Catholic Bookstore offers *Catecismo Popular: Saber y Vivir del Cristiano*; call 312–855–1908. It has expanded its fine newsletter, *Nuestra Parroquia*, to include articles called Notas para la Liturgia. World Library Publications offers *Cantos del Pueblo de Dios* and *El Pan de Cada Día*; call 800–404–3943. GIA has published Donna Peñas *A New Heaven, a New Earth* on cassette or compact disk as well as songbooks and a cassette titled *Roots and Wings*, both available at 708–496–3800. Cuco Chávez's *Mariachi* and Lorenzo Floristan's *En el Calvario* are also new GIA releases. Chávez, who performed at World Youth Day, has released *Misa Caribeña* too. New music is also available from SWLC Music by calling 817–560–3300. Oregon Catholic Press has begun to publish *La Oración de Los Fieles* in one year volumes: Call 503–281–1191.

Gale Research continues to offer good reference works including *The Hispanic American Almanac, The Hispanic American Information Directory 94–95*, and *Notable Hispanic American Women*. Call them at 800–877–GALE. Also in the area of research is the work of the Office of Minority Health Resource Center at 800–444–6472, and the National Coalition of Hispanic Health and Human Services Organizations (202–387–1401). The National Council de la Raza does much research and can be reached at 202–236–7782. On local issues the California Policy Seminar (510–642–5514) and Chicagos Latino Institute (312–663–3603) are good. For migrant issues see *Research in Rural Issues: An Annotated Bibliography*, from Western Illinois University, 309–298–1031. MACC publishes Rosendo Urrabazo's *Hispanic Catholics in Texas* (800–368–5445). His weekly column in the San Antonio Express News is also worthwhile, as is the article published by Antonio Stevens-Arroyo in *Hispanic Link*, 11 October.

Popular books in Spanish can be ordered from the Catholic Craftsmen Guild (800–874–8453) and The Saint Anthony Messenger Press (800–488–0488). The latter is publishing Kenneth Davis *Cuando el Tomar Ya No Es Gozar*. For Lenten and Easter meditation, see Archbishop Patrick Flores, *Caminando con el Señor* (512–922–2181). Liguori Publications (800–325–9521, ext. 999) has a new catalogue, *Recursos Valiosos para Parroquias Hispanas*. And Alba House is always a good source: 718–698–2759.

New videos are available from Don Bosco Multimedia (800–342–5850) and from Hispanic Telecommunications Network (210–227–5959). *Vocations and Prayer* devoted its July–September issue to Latino/as. Other resources for youth include *Celebration and Change*, a bilingual video of Denvers World Youth Day (800–225–5222), and the bilingual video *I Am Only a Child* (301–593–1066). Also available is the bilingual *Challenge of Catholic Youth Evangelization*, published by the National Federation of Catholic Youth Ministry, and available from 800–342–5850.

The United States Catholic Conference continues to improve its Spanish titles, this year releasing *En Marcha Hacia el Señor* for migrants. Call for a catalogue: 800–235–8722. Also for migrants is the booklet *La Violencia Doméstica*, available by calling 703–368–1171. For a brief work about violence against women call 914–561–8191 and ask for Rights and Remedies, in Spanish or English.

We highly recommend the 1993 Proceedings of the Catholic Theological Society of America and also the new *Journal of Hispanic/Latino Theology*. Since both were unavailable at press time, neither is annotated below.

Aquino, María Pilar. El Des-Cubrimiento, Colectivo de la Propia Fuerza: Perspectivas Teológicas desde las Mujeres Latino-americanas. *Apuntes* 13, no. 1 (Spring 1993): 86–103. Building on a historical over-view, cites creative tension as the context for this theology based on the particularities of its being done by women, its asking the questions they propose, its being relevant to their concrete struggles, and its being contextual, transformational, egalitarian, and inculturated.

Burgaleta, Claudio M. A Rahnerian Reading of Santería: A Proposal for a Christian Recovery of the Syncretic Elements of Latin American Popular Religiosity based on Rahners Concept of Anonymous Christianity. *Apuntes* 13, no. 2 (Summer, 1993): 139–150. A worthy summary of his attempt to do justice to the syncretic elements of Latin American popular religiosity while remaining committed to the normativity and definitiveness of the Christ event.

Davis, Kenneth G. What's New in Hispanic Ministry? *Overheard*, vol. 13. A work-in-progress report on the present article that incorrectly identified *En Marcha Hacia el Señor* as a catechism instead of a training manual for catechists.

Deck, Allan Figueroa. La Raza Cósmica: Rediscovering the Hispanic Soul. *Critic* (Spring, 1993): 46–53. Describes Hispanic spirituality as popular, communal, festive, and transcendent and as such a resource for our modern, secular world.

Elizondo, Virgil. Analyse de Racisme. *Concilium* 248, 1993: 69–77. An historic, cultural, socioeconomic, and phenomenological analysis of racism from the perspective of the *mestizo*. Continues his argument that differences ought not be abolished, but rather, as the source of our self-identity, are the foundation for respectful dialogue and mutual acceptance.

_____. Evil and the Experience of God. *Way* 33, no. 1 (January, 1993): 34–43. Describes the institutional evil of the contemporary world and the experience of God aroused when victims of injustice realize that suffering does not result from divine chastisement, but from human sin that must be confronted.

Engh, Michael E. Frontier Faiths*: Church, Temple and Synagogue in Los Angeles, 1846–1888.* Sante Fe: University of New Mexico Press, 1993. Deals with Los Angeles' Latinos/as, specifically comparing their treatment to New Mexican Hispanics under Bishop Jean Baptiste Lamy.

Espinosa, Manual J. The Origin of the Penitentes of New Mexico: Separating Fact from Fiction. *Catholic Historical Review* 79, no. 3 (July, 1993): 454–477. Argues that the Penitentes were a grass roots evolution of the Franciscan Third Order adapted to fill a civic and ecclesial leadership vacuum.

Goizueta, Roberto. Méstissage Hispanique et Méthode Théologique aux États-Unis. *Concilium* 248, 1993: 35–44. Critiques the methods of the theological elite and suggests that Hispanic theologians must serve justice by developing a communal, critical reflection on the particularity of their peoples.

Isasi-Díaz, Ada María. Defining Our Proyecto Histórico: Mujerista Strategies for Liberation. *Journal of Feminist Studies in Religion* 9, nos. 1–2 (Spring/Fall, 1993): 17–28. Argues that since liberation means constructing ones own history, it must include practical strategies for creating a more just, communal kingdom of God.

Martínez, German, O.S.B. Hispanic American Spirituality, in Michael Downey, ed., *The New Dictionary of Catholic Spirituality*. Collegeville, Minnesota: Liturgical Press, 1993: 473–476. After a brief historical overview, treats the popular forms of this spirituality as *sensus fidei*, the various apostolic movements, and modern challenges as reflected in contemporary church documents. Goizuetas Liberation Theology, Influence on Spirituality is also included in this dictionary.

_____. Hispanic Culture and Worship: The Process of Inculturation. *Catholic Historian* 11, no. 2 (Spring, 1993): 79–91. Promotes a renewed liturgy as the preferred vehicle of an evangelization of Hispanic cultures through a synthesis of their popular religion and elements of contemporary society that will ultimately transform and liberate both.

Matovina, Timothy. Ministries and the Servant Community. *Worship* 67, no. 4 (July, 1993): 351–360. Uses examples from popular, Hispanic rites to illustrate ministry as Christ-like service open to all.

McNamara, Patrick H. *Conscience First, Tradition Second: A Study of Young American Catholics*. Albany: State University of New York Press, 1993. Seems to suggest a positive correlation between maintenance of the Spanish language and orthodox Catholic belief and behavior. These few, intriguing pages merit further investigation.

_____. Researching Churches in the Southwestern Latino Community: How do the Assumptions, Theories, and Methods of Twenty Five Years Ago Stand Today? Paper presented at the 1993 Meeting of the Society for the Scientific Study of Religion, Raleigh, North Carolina. Assesses chapters on religion in the 1970 Grebler, Moore, and Guzman book *The Mexican American People* and suggests a renewed paradigm which would include a consideration of cultural and personal identity within any institutional analysis.

Muñoz Sepúlveda, Isidro. Puerto Rico: Idioma e Identidad. *Razón y Fe* (March, 1993): 227–287. Describes how language has always been both the symbol and tool of the various parties who have striven to win the soul of this people.

Novo Pena, Silvia. Religion, in Nicolás Kanellos, ed., *The Hispanic-American Almanac*. Detroit, Michigan: Gale Research, 1993: 367–387. An excellent, balanced introduction, although it contains minor inaccuracies and fails to attend fully to the experience of women.

Pulido, Alberto. The Religious Dimensions of Mexican Americans, in Julian Samora and Patricia Vandel Simon, *A History of the Mexican-American People* (revised edition). Notre Dame, Indiana: University of Notre Dame Press, 1993: 223–234. Not only provides a good overview of popular and institutional Catholicism among Chicanos, but is a prime example of how Latino scholars are finally giving serious attention to this often neglected aspect of their cultures.

Romero, Gilbert. The Bible, Revelation and Marian Devotion. *Marian Studies* 44 (1993): Argues that Hispanic popular devotions to Mary, as dependent revelation, have theological legitimacy and pastoral relevance.

## Notable Books

*Oxcart Catholicism on Fifth Avenue: The Impact of the Puerto Rican Migration upon the Archdiocese of New York.*. Ana María Díaz-Stevens. Notre Dame: University of Notre Dame Press, 1993. Pp. 293. Cloth. $34.95.

This balanced, readable history of Hispanic ministry in New York is perhaps the finest work yet available concerning Puerto Rican Catholics on the mainland. Díaz-Stevens speaks not only as a sociologist, but also as a witness to and participant in many of the events she narrates. She deals masterfully with such prominent figures as Félix Valera, Ivan Illich, Robert Fox, Robert Stern, and Joseph Fitzpatrick, without forgetting such discounted heroines as *Las Hijas de María*.

René Marquézs play *The Oxcart* acts as a metaphor for the popular religious expressions that Puerto Ricans brought to the automated streets of New York. The transformation this wrought upon the archdiocese and the changes that religiosity itself experienced are the subject of this book. Chapter One deals with both the history of Puerto Rican migration and various sociological constructs to help understand it. Chapter Two summarizes the historical and social forces that created this Oxcart Catholicism. Chapters Three and Four deal with a history of ministry to migrants in New York (especially during the time of Francis Cardinal Spellman) and argue that it was precisely this challenge that uniquely prepared the archdiocese for Vatican II. Chapter Five deals with the influence of such clerical intellectuals as Illich and Fitzpatrick, Chapter Six with the charismatic Fox, and Chapter Seven with Sterns successful institutionalization of some of Fox's best innovations. In Chapter Seven Díaz-Stevens introduces her own sociological typology to analyze this history and concludes that under Robert Stern, the archdiocese had begun to eliminate the social distance between the Puerto Rican and the Church, but that subsequent rejection of many of his policies has eroded that success.

Díaz-Stevens largely omits the writings and work of Bishop Roberto González and sometimes fails to properly annotate her sources (for example, Illich's, *The Vanishing Clergyman*). Nonetheless, it was a pleasure to read her work and an honor to be invited into her very fine history and innovative analysis of the Puerto Rican Catholic experience in New York.

*Strangers and Aliens No Longer, Part One: The Hispanic Presence in the Church of the U.S.*. Edited by Eugene F. Hemrick. Washington, DC: Catholic Conference Publishing Services, 1993. Pp. 136. Paper. $14.95.

This is the first in a series of publications by the United States Catholic Conference (USCC) on the multi-cultural phenomenon experienced by the Church. The editor is director of research for USCC and coauthors two of the seven chapters. Joseph Fitzpatrick, S.J., also writes two chapters, and Ronaldo Cruz, the director of the USCCs Office of Hispanic Affairs, coauthors chapter 5 along with Brian Jordan. The other five authors are relative newcomers to the field.

Fitzpatrick endeavors to identify good working models for Hispanic ministry and reviews the literature on the subject. Ecclesial pronouncements gleaned from *Origins* constitute one chapter, and a brief history and somewhat dated roster of Hispanic organizations constitute another. Good empirical data on the demographics of Hispanics in general, and priests and seminarians in particular, make up two chapters. The last identifies research priorities.

The books layout on large pages is quite reader friendly. The outside back cover provides a helpful list of related USCC publications. This first publication in the series achieves its modest goal, to serve as a useful resource readers can turn to as they explore the dimensions of multi-cultural ministry in local settings; hopefully, it and subsequent volumes will also lead to a new surge of research focusing on the multi-cultural experience.

*En la Lucha / In the Struggle: A Hispanic Womens Liberation Theology* Ada María Isasi-Díaz. Minneapolis: Fortress Press, 1993. Pp. 176. Paper. $13.

Isasi-Díaz has spent more than a decade defining and refining what she means by *mujerista* (womanist) theology. This book, based on her dissertation, is her most complete and compelling work yet. It is a remarkable achievement, especially when one recalls that she and her colleagues have had to construct their theology from virtually nothing, with little support, and often against prevailing prejudices.

Hers is a conscious, active, and reflective participation in the communal struggle for the fullness of life and self-determination for all Latinas, especially the poor. She rejects objectivity as humanly impossible and pretentiously oppressive and has therefore developed new methods and sources for theology. Even one who may disagree with her must respect her vast learning and intelligence, her unshakable commitment to her task, and her frankness and candor as well.

Chapter One looks at the particularity of Hispanic ethnicity as a vital social construct and identifies Hispanics struggle to survive and thrive, their socioeconomic reality, and their *mestizaje* (inclusiveness and diversity) as key elements in that self-identification.

Chapter Two expands this construct, explaining how the Latina *proyecto histórico* (the liberation struggle and the specific strategies needed to attain it), popular religion, and the Spanish language are essential components of *la lucha*. Note that while Isasi-Díaz deals with concepts common to other Hispanic theologians (such as popular religion and *mestizaje*), she painstakingly explains how she agrees with or differs from them.

Having explained the source of her theology, she moves in Chapter Three to describe her methods. She borrows the ethno-methodology of Harold Garfinkel and explains how she conducted ethnographic interviews (see her collaborative work with Yolanda Tarango, *Hispanic Women: Prophetic Voice in the Church*, also from Fortress, 1992) with a representative number of Latinas. Chapter Four presents the voice of these women and identifies the themes of praxis and moral agency as generative and germane. The next two chapters are devoted to elaborating these themes from historical and theological perspectives. The final chapter presents a summary and a symbol: *Mestizaje* is a call to recreate moral standards according to our daily struggle . . . a call for social change so we can embrace diversity and . . . our own moral value norms.

This fascinating and important work leaves me with questions about the method, namely, what checks and balances were placed on the interviews to insure that the author did not unknowingly elicit only those answers that the other women thought she wanted or would approve? For instance, on page 77 an interviewee mentions her preoccupation with giving good answers. Would not other sociological principles or even an ancillary quantitative analysis (such as that cited on page 23) make this good method better? Nonetheless, this is a welcome and overdue theological contribution.

*This article originally appeared in Review for Religious Vol. 53, no. 2 (1994) under the title, Hispanic Catholics: Trends and Works 1993.*

# 1994 IN REVIEW

There is good news and more good news to report in 1994. First, the field here covered continues to expand rapidly as more Latinos publish, organize, and take leadership in the Church. This welcome surge necessitates a happy collaboration on this report with one of these new voices, Eduardo C. Fernández, S.J.

## Migrants and Immigrants

Midterm elections once again played to xenophobia, especially in California. There, Proposition 187 purports to save taxes by denying basic human rights to the undocumented. Despite inevitable lawsuits and the unanimous and vocal opposition of California's Catholic hierarchy, the proposition won. Florida's church also has organized to help immigrants. Regarding the influx of Cubans, it has criticized both Castro and Clinton and has been operating refugee centers around the clock (*El Visitante Dominical* [VD], 11 Sept.). In Puerto Rico the church played a crucial role in defeating two proposed constitutional amendments which would have eliminated the right to bail and prejudiced the commonwealth's supreme court.

The Church of the Texas Valley has joined the secular press in criticizing the Immigration and Naturalization Service, especially its latest efforts around El Paso (*National Catholic Reporter* [NCR], 3 June). In September the *New York Times* (NYT) ran a series of articles describing the INS as "cold, rude, and insensitive." Church leaders have been neither naive nor provincial in their approach. The University of Santa Clara sponsored a symposium on worldwide immigration called "Ethics and Immigration" (VD, 12 June), and Notre Dame's CUSHWA Center reports on a Lilly Endowment grant which will encourage research into immigrant congregations. The Bishop's Committee on Migration continues to sponsor its National Migration Week in the nation's parishes as a way to bring the fruit of such insights to ordinary Catholics.

Migrant workers continue in the spirit of César Chávez, whose United Farm Workers now number 22,000, and have greater church support (VD, 22 May). These advances were recognized by Vice President Gore, as reported in *La Voz Católica* (LVC) of 18 March and 16 December. Migrants and other low-income Latinos continue to face ecological deprivation (NCR, 3 June). They have responded readily to initiatives such as the Mercy Sisters' mobile classrooms (*Crux*, 9 May) and cooperatives (VD, 11 Sept.).

## General Church News

Despite the modest achievements noted above, there are still many things to do and setbacks to report. The diocese of Brooklyn announced the closing of its newspaper *El Nuevo Amanecer*. Allan Figueroa Deck, S.J., notes that the church is not empowering nearly enough Hispanic leadership nor promoting intimate community experiences (*Catholic Trends*, 16 July). Sister Eleace King laments our failure to evangelize Hispanics in their "cultural idiom," which includes popular religion. At the conference where she and Deck spoke, Protestants claimed that their success was due to Hispanic members attaining financial and managerial control over their own ecclesial destiny, even if that means that they operate from storefronts rather than basilicas (VD, 21 August). Deck, writing in *America* (23 April), notes that Hispanics are not passive objects of pastoral care, but artisans of ministry both within and outside of the church. The church is embracing these views, but in a haphazard manner.

The good news includes the Church's continued support of community organizing in predominantly Hispanic neighborhoods (*Crux*, 27 June), the success of recent publications such as the *Journal of Hispanic/Latino Theology* (NCR, 26 August), and Miami's Radio Paz, which has increased its broadcasting to twelve hours daily (LVC, 23 Sept.). Also promising is the Archdiocese of Chicago's adaptation of the National Pastoral Plan for Hispanic Ministry, especially the local *encuentros* coordinated by Sister Dominga Zapata, S.H. The Archdiocese of Detroit is involved in a similar though less ambitious process, while the Archdiocese of Washington, DC, celebrates twenty five years of Catholic Hispanic ministry. Also heartening is the naming of two new Hispanic bishops, Placido Rodriguez to Lubbock and Gabino Zavala as auxiliary of Los Angeles. The death of Bishop Enrique San Pedro of Brownsville leaves it among other largely Hispanic dioceses awaiting new bishops. Whoever replaces them will hopefully be as loved as the late Bishop Alfonso Gallegos, to whose memory the faithful of Sacramento, California, are dedicating a $45,000 memorial.

Women religious have been in the news. Gloria Urrabazo, M.C.D.P., was named director of all campus-ministry programs in San Antonio. A coreligious, Anita de Luna, was interviewed in Human Development's spring issue. Yolanda Tarango, C.C.V.I., gave a workshop at the Chicago Call to Action conference. Verónica Méndez, R.C.D., was published in the bulletin of the National Religious Vocation Conference.

Lay women Marina Herrera and Ada María Isasi-Díaz taught at the Maryknoll Summer School of Theology. Maria Pilar Aquino graced the summer session of the Graduate Theological Union. Gabriela Santivañez won the J.C. Penney "Golden Rule" award. Juliana A. Perez was selected for a leadership development program sponsored by the National Hispana Leadership Institute, which also gave its "Mujer" award to Dolores Huerta (HL, 26 Sept.). Workshops on family life continued to be offered by Gelasia Marquez Marinas and Alicia Rivera.

Henry Cisneros has received high marks for using his cabinet office to combat racism. Frank Newton resigned as the director of the National Hispanic Leadership Agenda, but not before acknowledging that President Clinton has appointed twice as many Latinos to federal office as his predecessor (*Hispanic Link* [HL], 3 Oct.). Newton now serves as Southwest regional director of the Corporation for National and Community Service (HL, 14 Nov.).

Boxer Oscar de la Hoya has heart but lacks experience, according to *El Pregonero* (EP, 10 March). However, if he is as persistent as baseball great Roberto Clemente, someone may yet erect a statue to him as they did to Clemente in Pittsburgh (EP, 11 August). Even Clemente's homers did not fly as high as astronaut Sid Gutiérrez, who found a way to receive Holy Communion even when in space (VD, 14 August).

Other laity in the news were Jaime Vidal, who lectured at William Paterson College before accepting a position at the Pontifical College Josephinum. Vidal formerly worked with the CUSHWA Center, which awarded summer research stipends this year to Yolanda Prieto and Rev. Jean Pierre-Ruiz. Filling a new position is María Luisa Gastón, who was named executive director of the National Catholic Conference's interracial justice department. Luis Leonardo Beteta Escalante was named director of Hispanic ministries for the diocese of Grand Rapids, Michigan. Historian and journalist Moises Sandoval addressed a regional gathering of diocesan directors of Hispanic ministry. There is wonderful news for and about Manuel Salazar, who won a new trial from the Illinois supreme court after grass roots organization and appeals from Joseph Cardinal Bernardin and the Holy Father. Many feel

Salazar is innocent of the accusation that he murdered a Joliet policeman. Lastly, Ronaldo Cruz, director of the Secretariat for Hispanic Affairs, continues his energetic leadership. He is coordinating the 23–25 June 1995 commemoration of fifty years of nationally organized Hispanic Catholic ministry to be held in San Antonio. This will coincide with an NCCB pastoral statement called "Convocation '95: The Hispanic Presence in the New Evangelization in the United States" and will culminate in three monographs on Hispanics in the church funded by Lilly Endowment.

Claudio M. Burgaleta, S.J., was awarded a research fellowship from the Jesuit Historical Institute for study in Spain during the 1994–95 academic year. Msgr. Louis A. Gutierrez was murdered while on vacation (NCR, 20 May). Also, Puerto Rico's retired Bishop Antonio Parrilla-Banilla died.[1] Father Arturo Perez helped design a new certificate program focusing on an Hispanic-inculturated liturgy. While featured first in El Paso, it could be adapted to any diocese. Father Gilbert Romero spent a sabbatical in Spain and then was appointed visiting scholar of the Oxford University Center for Postgraduate Hebrew Study. On the basis of these studies, he offered a course through the Fund for Theological Education's Hispanic summer program called "Simbolismo en la Biblia: Pautas Hermeneuticas." Other faculty members for the program were Gelasia Márquez and Teresa Maya Sotomayor. This year the fund provided scholarships for some nineteen Hispanic Catholics. Virgil Elizondo spoke at the Collegeville symposium called "Toward the Year 2000" and at the National Association for Lay Ministry. He also taught at the summer session of Boston College as well as at the Mexican American Cultural Center (MACC). Orlando Espín was featured at the Los Angeles Religious Education Conference along with María de la Cruz Aymes, S.H., Domingo Rodriguez, S.T., spoke at the Seventh Annual Summer Institute for Clergy. Finally, Vicentian Prudencio Rodríguez was named vicar of Hispanic ministry for the diocese of Phoenix, and Ricardo Olona became chancellor of Sante Fe.

Hispanic youth are beginning to receive the attention they deserve. They were the subject of a talk given to the National Congress of the National Catholic Education Association by Allan Deck, S.J., and were featured as well in the songs at the convention. Also speaking and singing was Tony Melendez (VD, 1 May). Twenty three year old Frankie Rocha made the news because, despite his illness, he realized his dream of meeting John Paul II before his death. His demise brings to mind the insistence by the International Office of RENEW that, given the demographics, one cannot claim to do Hispanic ministry if one is not engaged in youth ministry.

## National Organizations

Since 1988, Saint Mary's Press's Hispanic Youth Ministry Project has studied this urgent ministry. They have founded the new Instituto de Fe y Vida with monies from a Lasallian Fund for Education. The instituto will offer training and resources in holistic Christian formation and in leadership in society and church. Initial faculty members include Carmen María Cervantes, Alejandro Aguilera-Titus, Juan Díaz-Vilar, S.J., Carlos Carrillo, and Rev. Juan Huitrado. Also of note for youth was the Fort Worth regional meeting of some 600 young people coordinated by Andres Aranda. María Cepeda of the diocese of Saginaw has also placed a priority on youth ministry. Last, the phenomenal program on teen virginity, "True Love Waits," is available now in Spanish (*Christianity Today*, 18 July).

Rev. Jean-Pierre Ruiz will succeed as president of the Academy of Catholic Hispanic Theologians of the United States (ACHTUS). Ada María Isasi-Díaz was granted the academy's Virgil Elizondo award, and the César Chávez honor went to the Fund for Theological Education. The bulk of the ACHTUS proceedings was published in the November issue of The Journal of Hispanic/Latino Theology. ACHTUS members María de la Cruz Aymes, S.H., and Allan Deck, S.J., were both featured this year on the cassette journal Overheard. Alejandro García-Rivera and Yolanda Tarango published in U.S. Catholic, and Isasi-Díaz had an earlier work reprinted in Ursula King, ed., *Feminist Theology from the Third World* (Maryknoll: Orbis Books, 1994).

The Asociación Nacional de Diáconos Hispanos celebrated its eleventh national convention in Orlando in June. Likewise the Asociación Nacional de Sacerdotes Hispanos met 17–20 October in Houston. Bishops James Tamayo of Galveston, Ricardo Ramírez of Las Cruces, Roberto González of Boston, and Agustín Román of Miami attended. ANSH continues to receive considerable news coverage, including its networking with the National Secretariat (VD, 17 April).

The Catholic Migrant Farm Worker Network announces the resignations of the director, Rev. Dick Notter, and of his interim replacement, William Moore, O.F.M. Notter will long be remembered for his tireless dedication to this most worthwhile apostolate. The Committee of Religious for Hispanic Ministry (CORHIM) held its annual seminar in Boerne, but will not have a seminar in 1995. Benita Huerta OMMI is a new member of the executive committee.

Comunidades de Reflexión Eclesial en la Diáspora (CRECED) has been using the media well. The organization is maturing, moving beyond solely intra-ecclesial concerns to the wider society (LVC, 18 March). The group has made public statements about Cuba, Cuban immigration, and the role of the family in society. The Jornada de Reflexión this year took place 4–7 July in Miami. LAS HERMANAS has published a history and current status report of the organization, along with a plebiscite about its future. Some people feel it has served its task and should disband.

The Hispanic Catholic Center of the Northeast, headed by Mario Paredes, hosted the second Hispanic ecumenical encounter on 6 April (VD, 15 May). Likewise, Ada María Isasi-Díaz and Fernando Segovia coordinated another ecumenical conference of Hispanic theologians at Drew University 15–17 April. Those proceedings, titled *Aliens in Jerusalem*, will be published next year. The Hispanic Telecommunications Network collaborates now on airing the Mass for the Faith and Values Channel. Call 800–841–8476 (ext. 106) for details. HTN has also developed a video and discussion guide concerning priestly vocations.

The Conferencia Nacional de Música Litúrgica Hispana is also becoming quite sophisticated. Their 13–15 October conference in Miami boasted nineteen workshops by various artists and experts. This is a fine compliment to the older Instituto de Litúrgia Hispana, which met 2–5 June in Mexico City. An excellent presentation on the pre-Tridentine roots of popular religion was delivered by Jaime Lara.

The Jesuit Hispanic Ministry Conference elected Luis Quihuis, S.J., as its new president. The conference's commitment to Hispanic ministry was again demonstrated by the successful conference held 1–2 June at Loyola Marymount University under the title "Evangelical-Pentecostal Protestantism: A Challenge and Opportunity for Hispanic Catholics." On 15 January, Mercy Sister María Elena Gonzalez became the third president of MACC. She has struggled valiantly, and apparently successfully, in the face of considerable financial strain. Despite its reorganization, MACC has continued to provide prophetic leadership; from 10 to 13 November "Building Bridges in Black and Brown" was offered, a joint effort with Rev. Clarence Williams of the group Racism and Renewal of the Mind. MACC received $30,000 from the W.K. Kellog Foundation for this second conference to bring together leaders from the Hispanic and black communities.

A grant from Lilly Endowment has allowed the National Catholic Council for Hispanic Ministry to hire Adela Isabel Flores as director of its Urban Leadership Project. The Catholic Telecommunications Network aired part of the 1993 NCCHM conference; this year's was held 3–6 November in Washington, DC. Cincinnati was the site of the 14–16 April conference of the National Organization of Catechesis for Hispanics. Catechesis is one of the great though little recognized successes of Hispanic Catholics. This group continues to be an important support network.

Rev. Philip Murnion, Mr. Teodosio Feliciano, and Mr. Rudy Vargas of the National Pastoral Life Center will soon complete their review of church based programs that foster Hispanic leadership. From eight on-site visits to date, they have a list of thirteen factors which seem to help make such efforts successful. The study should be complete in 1995; call 718–229–8001 for details. The Program for the Analysis of Religion among Latinos received a grant from the Pew Charitable Trust to publish a four volume social-sciences study of Latino religion. With a grant from Lilly, PARAL will publish a directory and newsletter. They also offer the Olga Scarpetta annual award for the best student paper.[2]

The Southeast Pastoral Institute (SEPI) has done so much to build community that it is fitting it now has a new building in which to house its offices, classrooms, library, and bookstore. It is a welcome home for the twenty six dioceses they serve. The Federación de Institutos Pastorales (FIP) published the results of its 25–26 May meeting in En Marcha (August). The Asociación Nacional de Directores Diocesanos held its third general meeting around the theme "Share the Light: Lead the Way." New executive committee members include Rudy Vargas, Gonzalo Saldaña, Miguel Ramos, and Terry Garza.

## Notes

[1] For an account of Bishop Parilla's life and death, see National Jesuit News 23, no. 4 (February 1994).
[2] Write: Scarpetta Award; PARAL, Bildner Center; Graduate School and University Center, CUNY; 33 West 42nd Street; New York, New York 10036.

## Resources

Bibliophiles will rejoice in Latino Books (817–923–2440) and Libros de España y América (718–291–9891).Migrant resources include *New Beginnings*, written to guide immigrant parents (212–355–3992), *A Migrant Ministry Directory* (202–541–3035), and the CMFM video and study guide *Seasons of the Migrant.*

A Spanish booklet for ministry to persons with AIDS is available for one dollar from Catholic AIDS Ministry; 910 Marion Street; Seattle, Washington 98104. Twelve other Spanish pamphlets on a variety of ministerial topics are available by calling 301–853–5335. The Florida Catholic Conference produced a bilingual flyer called "Catholic Declarations on Life and Death," available from 904–222–3803. Call 414–259–0688 for a free, 36 page bilingual prayerbook titled *Prayers for '94.* *My Daily Bread* is now available in Spanish by faxing 718–854–6058. The United States Catholic Conference published a bilingual planning kit for catechetical Sunday: Call 800–235–8722. Also for catechism is the bilingual *A People on the Way* from CMFM and *Harvesting Hope / Cosechando Esperanza* from 312–243–3700. Sadlier continues to lead this field; for information call 800–221–5175.

Liturgical Press has released several new works in Spanish including a children's hymnal called *Canten con Gozo* and a translation of the Little Rock Bible Study program. They now also offer the complete three volume lectionary in Spanish; call 800–858–5450. Paluch has several new releases from Lorenzo Florián; call 800–621–5197. Oregon Catholic Press continues its commitment; call 800–548–8749 for new titles such as *Oraciones de los Fieles.* All of these companies also offer regular workshops. GIA released new recordings by Donna Peña and Cuco Chávez; order through 800–442–1358.

Marriage preparation is aided by Liguori (800–325–9521) with the translation of the famous *Together for Life.* Call for a catalogue and other titles including Vacation Bible School works. Scripture sharing is made easier with newsletters and pamphlets from Twenty Third Publications; call 800–321–0411. For Spanish Bibles and study tools, call 800–322–4253. For stewardship resources in Spanish, call 202–289–1093. New videos are available from The Christopher (212–759–4050) and the Catholic Video Club (800–545–2846).

Resources for youth include *El Verdadero Amor Espera* (202–636–3825), *You* magazine (305–569–0093), and *El Desafío de la Evangelización Juvenil* (800–328–6515). For educational opportunities consider the new Bilingual Undergraduate Studies for Collegiate Advancement through La Salle University of Philadelphia; call Brother Pat Duffy at 215–951–1234. And, for a free computer search on scholarship information, dial 800–EXCELDC. Claretian Publications offers a children's newsletter called *El Momentito de Fe* (800–328–6515).

Next year look for U.S. Hispanics to be published in Concilium and Religioni e Società (Italy). The latter, like the winter issue of Living Light (dedicated to the fiftieth anniversary of national Hispanic ministry), while dated 1994, will reach subscribers only in 1995. Both therefore were unavailable for inclusion in this article.

## Significant Works

Aquino, María Pilar. *La Teología, La Iglesia, y la Mujer en América Latina.* Santa Fé de Bogotá, Colombia: Indo-American Press Service, 1994. pp. 132. Paper. $6. Available from Gethsemane Bookstore of Los Angeles, this work looks at the Latin American church since Medellín and, while questioning why women are not included in decision making, concludes that they have been the hub around which more creative, participative, equal, and responsible ecclesial communities have been built.

Cervantes, Carmen María, Ed.D., et al., eds. *Prophets of Hope*, vol. 1, *Hispanic Young People and the Church's Pastoral Response.* Winona: Saint Mary's Press, 1994. Notes, bibliography, index, glossary. Paper. $14.95. Published in both Spanish and English, this series is a worthy contribution to this critically important ministry. The best yet of this length from a Catholic publisher.

Davis, Kenneth. "The Hispanic Shift: Continuity Rather than Conversion?" *Journal of Hispanic/Latino Theology* 1, no. 3 (May 1994): 68–79. Examines the appeal of Pentecostalism to Hispanics and the consequences of such a massive shift in religious affiliation. Surmises that one of the major reasons is Pentecostalism's similarities to popular Catholicism. The references, as well as the closing suggestions for dialogue between Hispanic popular and mainline United States religion, are noteworthy.

Deck, Allan Figueroa. "Latino Theology: The Year of the 'Boom.'" *Journal of Hispanic/Latino Theology* 1, no. 2 (February 1994): 51–63. Sees 1992 as a watershed in the emerging movement known as United States Hispanic theology. Aside from its descriptive qualities, raises some pertinent questions regarding ecumenism, the wider academy, and Hispanic theology vis-à-vis present Latino sociopolitical and cultural movements.

_____. "Trends in Latino Religion." In *Yearbook of American and Canadian Churches.* Edited by Kenneth B. Bedell. Nashville: Abingdon Press, 1994. Pp. 1–4. Makes apt observations regarding two current trends: (1) growth of Latino Hispanic evangelicals and Pentecostals and (2) increasing socioeconomic diversity among Latinos. Presents evidence of how the two trends may be possibly linked.

Díaz-Stevens, Ana María. "Ministerio y cambio institucional." *Cristian-ismo y Sociedad* 93–94, 31/4–32/1, nos. 118–119 (1994): 29–42. Digressing from the tendency in United States Catholic sociology to study immigrant groups from the point of their adaptation to life in the United States, this article uses a Latin American approach; that is, it focuses instead on the institutions involved. The case study is that of the effect of Puerto Rican immigrants in recent history on the Archdiocese of New York.

Elizondo, Virgil. "Cultural Pluralism and the Catechism." In *Introducing the Catechism of the Catholic Church*. Edited by Berard Marthaler. Mahwah: Paulist Press, 1994. pp. 142–180. Argues that just as the nature of the church is one of communion between particular churches, so the catechism will promote both ecclesial unity and the lived tradition only to the extent that it is adequately incarnated into the reality of those particular racial, cultural, and socioeconomic groups which will receive it.

Espín, Orlando O. "Popular Religion as an Epistemology (of Suffer-ing)." *Journal of Hispanic/Latino Theology* 2, no. 2 (November, 1994): 55–78. Dialoguing with other theologians and the social sciences, presents a hypothetical position in search of an authentic Latino epistemology. "The problem . . . is how [Latinos] explain their suffering, know it as suffering, and make sense (at least some sense) of it." Argues that popular religion plays an important role.

Feliciano, Juan G. "Suffering: A Hispanic Epistemology." *Journal of Hispanic/Latino Theology* 2, no, 1 (August, 1994): 41–50. Drawing heavily on the thought of Gustavo Gutiérrez, especially his pub-lished reflections on the Book of Job, presents the Latino com-munities' experience of suffering as a potential epistemological tool.

Fernández, Eduardo C. "Reading the Bible in Spanish: U.S. Catholic Hispanic Theologians' Contribution to Systematic Theology." *Apuntes* 14, no. 3 (Fall, 1994): 86–90. Gives a brief background of the theological context within which Hispanic theology is currently emerging. Concludes that presently its contribution is chiefly one of method. Vast bibliography.

Flores, Maria T. "The Latino Seminarian." In *Psychology, Counseling, and the Seminarian*. Edited by Robert Wister. Washington, DC: National Catholic Education Association, 1994. pp. 153–168.

Counsels the psychotherapist to approach the Latino as a man in transition who can be helped to navigate between various cultures in the construction of a new identity and greater self esteem.

García-Rivera, Alejandro. "A Contribution to the Dialogue between Theology and the Natural Sciences." *Journal of Hispanic/Latino Theology* 2, no. 1 (August, 1994): 51–59. Author draws from his own background as a physicist-theologian to demonstrate how one has shaped the other historically. An excellent piece which brings together the popular imagination and the specialist.

———. "San Martín de Porres: Criatura de Dios." *Journal of Hispanic/Latino Theology* 2, no. 2 (November, 1994): 26–54. In the words of Orlando Espín, the journal's editor, García-Rivera "offers us a very interesting 'reading' of the life of Martín de Porres, by applying the methods of R. Schreiter's semiotics of culture (assisted by A. Gramsci) to Martín's beatification process. The result is a stimulating, fresh, and thought provoking understanding of de Porres and of his challenging 'anthropology of creatureliness.'"

Goizueta, Roberto S. "*La Raza Cósmica?* The Vision of José Vasconcelos." *Journal of Hispanic/Latino Theology* 1, no. 2 (February, 1994): 5–27. Situated within the thought of the twentieth century Mexican philosopher/educator José Vasconcelos, Goizueta calls for a critical appropriation of the history of the term *mestizaje*; demonstrates why terms must be nuanced.

Isasi-Díaz, Ada María. "A *Mujerista* Perspective on the Future of the Women's Movement and the Church." In *Defecting in Place: Women Claiming Responsibility for Their Own Spiritual Lives.* Edited by Miriam T. Winter et al. New York: Crossroad, 1994. Calls on feminist believers to become action groups by praying and working against all injustice, including sexism in the church, with economic boycotts and a constant vocal challenge.

———. "'By the Rivers of Babylon': Exile as a Way of Life." In *Readings from This Place.* Edited by Fernando Segovia and Mary Ann Tolbert. Minneapolis: Augsburg/Fortress, 1994. pp. 148–163. From the perspective of a bilingual Cubana, offers an exegesis and a personal reflection, ending in a bilingual rewriting of Psalm 137.

———. "La vida de las mujeres hispanas: La fuente de la Teología Mujerista." *Cristianismo y Sociedad* 93/94, 31/4–32/1, nos.

118–119 (1994): 43–62. A summary of "mujerista theology," a Latina's theology of liberation. Against a background of economic and racial/ethnic oppression in the United States, sin and grace as experienced by Latinas serve as living sources for this emerging theology. Besides presenting a good summary of their socio-economic reality, the article is rich in actual quotes from United States Latinas.

Jackson, Robert H. "Congregation and Population Change in the Mission Communities of Northern New Spain: Cases from the Californias and Texas." *New Mexico Historical Review* 69, no. 2 (April 1994): 163–183. Compares changes in Native American populations at various mission sites, how they affected frontier policy, and how diverse peoples responded differently to these *congregaciones*.

Leon, Luis D.G. "Somos Un Cuerpo en Cristo: Notes on Power and the Body in an East Los Angeles Chicano/Mexicano Pentecostal Community." *Latino Studies Journal* 5, no. 3 (September, 1994): 60–86. Argues that Chicano Pentecostalism provides "an interactive, perhaps dramaturgical space for discrete Chicano and Mexican cultural traditions" in the face of an increasingly desperate situation in the barrios.

Matovina, Timothy M. "Lay Initiatives in Worship on the Texas *Frontera*." *U.S. Catholic Historian* 12 (Fall, 1994): 107–120. Highlights laity's role, especially women's, in maintaining vital religious rituals despite conquests and limited clergy. Uses examples from both rural and urban settings. See also the article by Michael Engh, S.J., in the same issue.

McGuire, Meredith B. "Religiosidad, Sí: Marginalidad, No: Porque la sociología de la Religión no puede permitirse el lujo de marginar la Religión Latina." *Cristianismo Y Sociedad* 93/94, 31/4–32/1, nos. 118–119 (1994): 9–18. Noting that the sociology of religion has impoverished itself by focusing too much on the institutionalized forms of religion, proposes a broader coverage which would account for other religious expressions, for example, Latin American religiosity, which is rich in analytical possibilities.

Medina, Lara. "Broadening the Discourse at the Theological Table: An Overview of Latino Theology 1968–1993." *Latino Studies Journal* 5, no. 3 (September, 1994): 10–36. An ecumenical summary of major works which ends with a call for greater emphasis on indigenous theologies and analysis of and strategies to overcome other oppressive social realities.

————. "*Dias de Muertos* da Puebla a Los Angeles: Migrazione e regenerazione identitaria di un complesso rituale." *Religioni e Società* [Italy] 18 (1994): 6–23. Tracing the Mexican celebration of the dead, describes and highlights its importance and development from pre-Columbian times to the present. An excellent example of the type of nuanced writing necessary to begin to understand the function and complexity of ritual among modern day urban Latinos in the United States.

Mendez, Veronica. "Sometimes Even God Needs Help." In *The On-going Journey: Awakening Spiritual Life in At-Risk Youth.* Edited by Thomas J. Everson. Boys Town, Nebraska: Boys Town Press, 1995. Discusses important cultural values such as spirituality and religion, as well as the problem of phenotyping. Was available in November 1994.

Pérez, Arturo, Consuelo Covarrubias, and Edward Foley, eds., *Así Es: Stories of Hispanic Spirituality.* Collegeville: Liturgical Press, 1994. pp. 111. Paper. $8.95. Also available in Spanish. Compilation of fifteen diverse Hispanic voices reflecting on the Latino school of spirituality. Helpful introduction and conclusion puts this in context.

Pulido, Alberto L. "Searching for the Sacred: Conflict and Struggle for Mexican American Catholics in the Roman Catholic Diocese of San Diego, 1936–1941." *Latino Studies Journal* 5, no. 3 (September, 1994): 37–59. Using case studies of two parishes, shows how differing interpretations of sacred symbols led to cultural conflicts between Mexicans and their bishop which ultimately denied the latter the power of the Mexican symbol system. Pulido and David Abalos, guest editors of this special issue, wrote the introduction.

Rosado, Caleb. "El papel de la Teología de la Liberación en la identidad social de los Latinos." *Cristianismo y Sociedad* 93/94, 31/4–32/1, nos. 118–119 (1994): 63–78. Drawing from the thought of Karl Marx and Max Weber, argues that liberation theology has raised the social consciousness of United States Latinos as well as aided them in their search for identity. Uses William E. Cross's model for studying the process by which a person goes from total self-rejection to total self-acceptance.

Ruiz, Jean-Pierre. "Beginning to Read the Bible in Spanish: An Initial Assessment." *Journal of Hispanic/Latino Theology* 1, no. 2 (February 1994): 28–50. One of the first articles to synthesize United States Hispanic theology within a certain area, namely, Sacred Scripture. Good summaries of Justo. L. González, Allan Figueroa Deck, and C. Gilbert Romero. Demonstrates well the dialogical bent of *teología de conjunto* and *pastoral de conjunto.*

Segovia, Fernando F. "Reading the Bible as Hispanic Americans." In *The New Interpreter's Bible,* Vol. 1. Edited by Leander F. Keck et al. Nashville: Abingdon Press, 1994. pp. 167–173. Provides several examples of the "reading strategies" employed by United States Hispanic theologians in their approach to Scripture. Two other Latinos published in this volume.

————. "Theological Education and Scholarship as Struggle: The Life of Racial/Ethnic Minorities in the Profession." *Journal of Hispanic/Latino Theology* 2, no. 2 (November, 1994): 5–25. A personal reflection from twenty years' experience in theological education and scholarship. The journal's editor comments: "An incisive reflection on the realities faced by racial/ethnic minorities in the world of professional theology, his address will hopefully lead to honest evaluations of schools, programs, and attitudes."

————. "Toward a Hermeneutics of the Diaspora: A Hermeneutics of Otherness and Engagement." In *Readings from This Place* Edited by Fernando Segovia and Mary Ann Tolbert. Minneapolis: Augsburg/ Fortress, 1994. pp. 58–74. Offers a new hermeneutics based on the social location of an Hispanic American diaspora or "otherness." Here and in the introduction, which he also wrote, Segovia builds on his other recent reflections on contextuality and its importance in analyzing a text. Justo González also published a chapter in this book.

Stevens-Arroyo, Anthony M. "How Latino/Hispanic Identity Becomes a Religious Reality." In *Yearbook of American and Canadian Churches.* Edited by Kenneth B. Bedell. Nashville: Abingdon Press, 1994. pp. 5–6. Just as in the case of other immigrant groups who came together under a common religious name, notes that "Latino" is "an extremely important notion to produce political and social unity." Although brief, succeeds in demonstrating the numerical importance of the growing Latino population in the United States.

Traverzo, G. David. "A Paradigm for Contemporary Latino Thought and Praxis: Orlando E. Costas' Latino Radical Evangelical Approach." *Latino Studies Journal* 5, no. 3 (September, 1994): 108–131. The title is an excellent summary of the article, which revolves around the three key elements to this theology: Praxis, holistic evangelization, and a fundamental option for the poor.

————. "La religión latina en Estados Unidos: luchas pasadas y tendencias presentes." *Cristianismo y Sociedad* 93/94, 31/4–32/1, nos. 118–119 (1994): 79–94. Demographic data on the United States Latino is coupled with a historical summary. Attempts to answer the question "Has religion assisted the struggle of the United States Latino against various types of oppression?" Good summary of recent ecumenical advances along with a bibliography.

Treviño, Roberto R. "In Their Own Way: Parish Funding and Mexican American Ethnicity in Catholic Houston 1911–1972." *Latino Studies Journal* 5, no. 3 (September, 1994): 87–107. Shows how Chicanos indeed have supported their parishes, but through *jamaicas* and other community based means which "melded spiritual and material consciousness into a singular expression of ethnoreligious identity."

Wright, Robert E. "If It's Official, It Can't Be Popular? Reflections on Popular and Folk Religion." *Journal of Hispanic/Latino Theology* 1, no.3 (May, 1994): 47–67. Draws from history and his own experience in Hispanic ministry to critique the way in which some United States Hispanic theologians have defined popular religion. Proposes his own definition. Excellent references.

**Notable Books**

*Hispanics in the Church: Up from the Cellar.* Philip E. Lampe, ed. San Francisco: Catholic Scholars Press, 1994. Paper. $29.95.

This publisher is certainly not scholarly and, if Catholic, has committed a mortal sin. Not only is it at fault for the many typographical errors, but also for the production and presentation, which leaves the book with several blank pages as well as a dull design and colorless cover. This is especially sad considering that Lampe is a scholar of merit, as are two of his contributors: Yolanda Tarango and Timothy Matovina. Their chapter on "Las Hermanas" may be the best in the book.

Lampe uses a metaphor from a 1983 article that characterized Hispanics in the church as relegated to the basement. The argument here is that in the last decade Hispanics have been moving into the front room. Lampe combines sociological analysis and an interesting interview with San Antonio's Archbishop Patricio Flores to argue (quoting Virgil Elizondo's preface): "The United States Catholic Church is making great efforts to respond to the challenge of the Hispanic presence, but in relation to the rapidly growing needs and numbers, it often appears to be doing little or nothing."

Lampe is to be commended for his continued interest in this area, but his expertise deserves better treatment and presentation.

Jeanette Rodriguez. *Our Lady of Guadalupe: Faith and Empowerment Among Mexican American Woman.* Austin, TX: University of Texas Press, 1994. Illustrations, bibliography index. Cloth, $35. Paper. $13.95.

Given the centrality of Our Lady of Guadalupe to Mexican Americans in general and Chicanas in particular, it is amazing that this work can truly claim that it is "unique primarily because no one had ever asked Mexican American women what they thought about the image of Our Lady of Guadalupe."

Chapters One through Three deal with the Spanish conquest of Mexico, the narrative of the Guadalupe event along with the image itself, and the psychological and religious impact of the experience, using James Fowler's developmental faith model to analyze Juan Diego.

In Chapter Four Rodriguez's own voice begins to come through most clearly, and her peculiar contribution is made clear. She deals adroitly with the themes of sexism, machismo, acculturation, and the family. While she appreciates the work of Evangelina Enríquez and Alfred Mirandé, she also points out their limitations, especially their neglect of the religious dimension of Chicanas.

Chapter Five presents her study of twenty Chicanas. Through a questionnaire and interviews, she sought to ascertain the perceptions these women have of Guadalupe and what kind of relationship exists between them and the Virgin. In Chapter Six the women themselves give voice to those very perceptions and relationships, and Rodriguez uses lengthy quotes. She concludes that their assumptive worldview includes complex relationality, an affective relationship with Guadalupe, and different stages of psychological and religious development based on their different needs. Chapter Seven is a theological reflection on the above; its keenest insight may be that, "as a universal symbol, Our Lady of Guadalupe bridges cultures: For Mexican American women she affirms them because she looks like them and is a woman and a mother, and she affirms their Anglo-educated side, challenging sexism."

Rodriguez's original research is unique and compelling. When dealing with psychology and sociology, she is particularly perceptive. One may argue with her about history: Is the internal-colony theory sufficient to understand the conquests of the United States Southwest? Is William Madsen an adequate source for understanding the adaptation of Catholicism by the Aztecs? Her work, however, adds much to the still very small corpus on the religious experience of Chicanas.

*Mexican Americans and the Catholic Church, 1900–1965.* Jay P. Dolan and Gilberto M. Hinojosa, eds. Pp. 352. Cloth. $29.95

*Puerto Rican and Cuban Catholics in the U.S., 1900–1965.* Jay P. Dolan and Jaime R. Vidal, eds. Pp. 256. Cloth. $24.95

*Hispanic Catholic Culture in the U.S.: Issues and Concerns.* Jay P. Dolan and Allan F. Deck S.J., eds. Pp. 480. Cloth. $32.95.

Notre Dame: University of Notre Dame Press, 1994.

It is impossible to do justice to this monumental, three volume series in this slight space. A glance at some of the contributors, however, will show that this is the most ambitious project of its kind: David Badillo, Jeffrey Burns, Ana María Díaz-Stevens, Orlando Espín, Marina Herrera, Joan Moore, Arturo Perez, Lisandro Pérez, Edmundo Rodríguez, Moisés Sandoval, and Anthony Stevens-Arroyo. Both Lilly Endowment, which funded this research, and the CUSHWA Center at the University of Notre Dame, which gave it form, are to be highly commended for this achievement.

The first two volumes are penned by just five authors, making for a unified textual treatment of the subject. They both deal with the antecedents to the clash between Anglos and these "newcomers" to the church of North America. Likewise, both treat the weakness of the church's institutional response to these particular needs. What is more fascinating, however, is the vast differences not only among the Cubans, Puerto Ricans, and Mexican Americans, but also in the experiences they have had of the church in the United States.

Volume Three has ten authors and therefore is more an anthology of themes such as ecclesial leadership, Latinas, and youth. This last chapter is of particular import, although for both liturgy and apostolic movements these chapters represent the first formally published historical works on the subject. Curiously the volume lacks an index, which would have made this unprecedented work much more helpful. But these are quibbles about handsome, durable volumes. United States church history is often presented as a movement westward from Baltimore. Now, however, this impressive work makes it impossible for any thoughtful teacher to begin anywhere other than at the beginning: The most ancient, enduring, and once again dominant group in the United States Catholic Church is the people whose faith and fight for it are chronicled in these pages.

*An Enduring Flame: Studies on Latino Popular Religiosity.* Anthony M. and Ana María Díaz-Stevens, eds. New York: Bildner Center for Western Hemisphere Studies, 1994.

First volume of the four volume PARAL (Program for the Analysis of Religion Among Latinos) Series.

This collection is excellent in every way. It is collaborative and ecumenical, yet not disjointed. It deals with the theoretical aspects of popular religiosity, but also with its very concrete manifestations. Its authors demonstrate convincingly that popular religiosity is not just a style of prayer, but a phenomenon linked to political and economic realities. One quickly realizes the profundity of this task which many United States Hispanic theologians are now tackling. This work is a quantum leap in the right direction.

The editors are commended for the design. They have provided for a focus on popular religiosity as practiced by specific Hispanic communities (for example, Virgilio's treatment of the Mexican American experience) as well as for coverage of specific practices, for example, Richard R. Flores's work on the *Pastorela.*

In writing about Puerto Ricans in New York, Ana María Díaz-Stevens's piece not only covers historical aspects, but keenly observes urban-rural differences. Gustavo Benavides "focuses on popular religiosity in Latin America as a form of resistance and accommodation by the indigenous peoples." Jaime R. Vidal studies popular religiosity from the angle of a continuity and new synthesis of Iberian practices. Luis N. Rivera Pagán deals not with specific practices but rather takes a general liberationist approach. It is refreshing to see more scholarly material on popular religiosity in Puerto Rico such as Samuel Silva Gotay's good historical summary and explanation of a new "Pentecostal era" for the island. From a Roman Catholic perspective, Kenneth Davis's "Brevia" summarizes some of the reasons given for the appeal of Pentecostalism to Hispanics. Finally, Meredith McGuire's essay presents some good questions for furthering the dialogue in this area between theology and the social sciences. This collection will greatly aid the exploration of popular religiosity among Latinos, obviously a phenomenon much more important, and therefore more in need of serious attention, than we ever imagined.

*This article originally appeared in Review for Religious Vol. 54 (1995) under the title, "U.S. Hispanic Catholics: Trends and Works 1994."*

# 1995 IN REVIEW

Without a cohort of dedicated helpers, this article would not have been possible, and so we name them before we do report or say anything else: Carmen María Cervantes Ed.D., Allan R Deck, S.J., Angela Erevia, M.D.C.P., Victoria Pastrano, M.D.C.P., and Anthony Stevens-Arroyo Ph.D.

## Migrants and Immigrants

Immigration to the United States—in absolute numbers, though not as percentages—is at a record high and continues to accelerate. California and New York receive the most immigrants. New York City, for instance, has the highest concentration of Dominicans outside of Santo Domingo, reports *El Visitante Dominical* (VD, 29 January). The top four sources of immigrants are Mexico, the Philippines, Cuba, and El Salvador, according to the *New York Times* (NYT, 30 August). For a closer look at this heterogeneous group, see Tim Stafford's article "Here Comes the World" (*Christianity Today*, 15 May).

San Salvador's *La Prensa Gráfica* estimates that almost four million Salvadoreños are in the United States *El Pregonero* (EP, 15 June) reports that the majority of them are quite young. Bishop Ricardo Ramírez, C.S.B., of Las Cruces, New Mexico, is among the members of the United States hierarchy who have publicly committed themselves to help this population (VD, January 15).

Some 200,000 Nicaraguans live here legally but tenuously as the Congress and commentators debate various proposals concerning both documented and undocumented immigrants (NYT, 21 March). Like virtually all before them, these "Nicas" are building a self-help network such as "La Fraternidad Nicaraguense" directed by Nora Britton Sándigo, featured in *La Voz Católica* (VC, 19 May).

Guatemalan Bishop Leonel Ramazzini rues the deterioration of traditional values suffered by immigrants to this country (VD, 3 September). However, this view may be a little naive. Modernity and foreign influences begin to erode those values even in their home countries. Moreover, sometimes those far from home are more likely to

79

hold to traditional practices precisely because they have a greater need to maintain contact with their heritage. See "Halloween's Popularity in Mexico Spooking Traditionalists" in the *San Antonio Express News* (SAEN, 29 October).

The composition of these immigrants continues to change, a constant challenge to pastoral agents. A growing number of indigenous people immigrating from Spanish-speaking countries do not speak Spanish but a variety of native languages (NYT, 24 August).

As with other countries, Cuba's internal situation and its relations with the United States affect emigration. And squabbles between local and federal authorities too often leave these same immigrants without adequate government support or protection and with the undeserved reputation of draining the economy. Note the quotation from Miami's mayor in the *St. Anthony Messenger* (AM, July). Even the term immigrant is eschewed for exile by Havana's Cardinal Jaime Ortega Alamino, who has presided over a church increasingly active both in Cuba and in the United States (AM, June and August).

Could this acrimony be increasing the violence against both border-patrol agents and detainees of the Immigration and Naturalization Service? Widespread press coverage deplored the maltreatment of such detainees in New Jersey, and *USA Today* ran a 28 March report on the increased danger of patrolling the country's borders. While many organizations such as the Mexican American Legal Defense and Educational Fund (AIALDEF) continue to fight such measures as Proposition 187, is there not a role for the Church in bringing some civility and justice to this critical combination of both growing immigration and xenophobia?

That seems to be the policy of the United States Catholic Conference's Committee on Migration (VC, 14 July). Thankfully, both the United States Catholic hierarchy (see Origins, 10 August) and the pope himself during his recent visit have reminded us of our obligation to be a moral superpower.

Unfortunately, we need to be reminded. *Vida Nueva* (VN, 215 June) reported that the FBI had fruitlessly investigated and suspected César Chávez of having been a communist. The 26 March edition of the same paper listed an impressive number of events commemorating this deceased leader of the United Farm Workers. Voters in San Francisco refused to change the name of the street which honors him. Friend and colleague Dolores Huerta continues to voice the cause of farm workers, reports *El Heraldo Católico* (HC, 5 November). Chávez's other successors can be also proud. This year they have won impressive victories and have extended their organization, says *Hispanic Link Weekly Report*

(HL, 11 September). For other reflections on being an Hispanic Catholic and on support for peoples on the move, consult the article about Linda Chávez (VD, 16 July) and her own article in the November 1995 Commentary. Another Catholic migrant leader has died, 58 year old Dolores Silha (HL, 8 May).

## General Church News

Perhaps the most important event was Convocación '95 held in San Antonio, Texas, on 23–25 June. Organized by the National Secretariat for Hispanic Affairs, it gathered several hundred Latinos and Latinas to celebrate fifty years of organized, national pastoral care of United States Hispanic Catholics. The Bishops' Committee on Hispanic Affairs published a program for the event which offered photographs of the secretariat's members (Ronaldo Cruz, Irma Nolla, Rosalva Castañeda, Leonor Castro) and the winners of the Patrick Flores Medals (Rev. Virgilio Elizondo, Sister Angela Erevia, Joseph Fitzpatrick, S.J., Mr. Eduardo Kalbfleish, Mr. Mario Paredes, Mr. and Mrs. Roberto and Rosie Piña, Bishop Agustín Román, Mrs. Olga Villa Parra, Rev. Mario Vizcaino Sch.P., and Msgr. Bryan Walsh). The apostolic nuncio delivered a message from Pope John Paul II. The keynote speaker was Msgr. Lorenzo Albacete. In addition to the golden anniversary, the convocación sought to celebrate the Hispanic Catholic presence in the United States, stress communion among church members, and commit itself to the New Evangelization (VC, 16 June). *Origins* (14 December) carries the United States bishops' conference's response to the convocación's statement of commitment, "The Hispanic Presence in the New Evangelization in the United States." What fruit may come from this? Perhaps more meetings such as the first statewide encuentro of Hispanic ministry held in October for the five dioceses of Indiana.

San Antonio also hosted a visit from the image of Nuestra Señora de San Juan de los Lagos and relics of St. Anthony of Padua on the 800th anniversary of his birth.

Boston's auxiliary Bishop Roberto O. González was appointed co-adjutor to Bishop René Gracida of Corpus Christi, Texas (VC, 10 May). Bishop Raymundo Peña moved from the diocese of El Paso to Browns-ville, Texas (HL, 5 June). Other bishops in the news: Deceased Bishop Alfonso Gallegos was honored by a play based on his life; Boise, Idaho, Bishop Tod Brown has asked that Celine Caufield begin to direct efforts toward a diocesan pastoral plan for Hispanic ministry; Bishop John Myers of Peoria, Illinois, has inaugurated a diocesan Pastoral Plan for

Hispanics; Bishop Dale Melczek of Gary, Indiana, has appointed Angel Torres director of the diocese's Office of Hispanic Ministry. Archbishop Patrick Flores of San Antonio not only celebrated 25 years as a bishop, but was honored by the ecumenical Distinguished Churchman Award (SAEN, 21 January and 6 May). Bishop Ramírez's continued eloquent plea for greater ecumenism among the Nation's Hispanics was featured in Our Sunday Visitor on 18 June. The bishops would seem to agree with evangelicals like George Barna, who was quoted in *Current Thoughts and Trends* (March 1995) saying that, in the competition by Christians for Hispanics, "the biggest winner will be agnosticism." An important ecumenical endeavor, the Hispanic Summer Program is an annual two week accredited conference held at rotating sites where Latino professors and faculty gather for curriculum and community. Two of the sponsoring seminaries are Catholic: Mundelein of Chicago, and the Oblate School of Theology in San Antonio.

Some important investments were made by Catholics in Hispanic ministry this year. President Clinton sent a congratulatory letter to the Campaign for Human Development which, in its 25 years, has spent $250 million dollars on projects such as restaurants run by farm workers and houses purchased by the poor (*Frente a Frente*, March). The diocese of Sacramento founded a lay ministry institute (VC, 16 June). The diocese of Miami opened new elementary schools specifically for the children of immigrants (VD, 7 May). Loyola Marymount University's Hispanic Pastor I Ministry Program graduated its first Spanish language certificate class. Allan Deck, S.J., is the director and has attracted faculty such as Verónica Méndez, R.C.D., Teresa Maya Sotomayor, Carmen María Cervantes, Eduardo Fernández, S.J., and Claudio Burgaleta, S.J. Maruja Sedano reports the first graduates (English and Spanish) of the Los Angeles Instituto Biblico. The Jesuits of Chicago opened a new high school that includes a work-study plan for Mexican Americans of low and moderate incomes (*Catholic Trends*, 18 November).

Other ecclesial news of note: Philip J. Murnion, of the National Center for Pastoral Life, continues to affirm the importance of Small Christian Communities, especially for Latinos (VD, 18 June); the Center for Applied Research in the Apostolate reports a 40 percent rise in Latina vocations to religious life and an 18 percent rise in Hispanic seminarians; Auxiliary Bishop of New York Francisco Garmendia was recognized for his attention to Hispanic priestly vocations.

Lay people in the news include mambo artist Sonny Melendez, "El Cachao," who was inducted into the Rock and Roll Hall of Fame (VD 12 January), and boxer Oscar de la Hoya, who won $1.72 million dollars along with his International Boxing Federation crown (HL, 15 May). The late Willie Velásquez, founder of the Southwest Voter Registration and Education Project, received the Presidential Medal of Freedom Award (SAEN, 29 September). Alejandro García-Rivera gave conferences in Metz, France, and to the College Theological Society. He was also published again in *U.S. Catholic*. Gilbert F. Casellas, president of the Equal Employment Opportunity Commission, reminisced that his Catholic education opened doors of opportunity for him (EP, 4 May). Tejano star Emilio Naviara was featured witnessing to his Catholic faith (VD, 26 November).

Puerto Rican Catholics may have more difficulty obtaining a Catholic education in the future, now that the island's supreme court declared the school voucher program unconstitutional (*Christianity Today*, 6 February). Also in Puerto Rico, the Arizmendi Center at Bayamón Central University received the papers (almost fifty bound volumes) of the late Bishop Antulio Parrilla Bonilla. Other Puerto Ricans in the news include Jaime Vidal, who was commissioned by the Bishop's Committee for Hispanic Affairs to produce one of a three volume series on United States Catholic Hispanics. Dr. Vidal also coordinated the 1995 Encuentro of the Midwest Conference of Seminarians for Hispanic Ministry. Anthony Stevens-Arroyo won the Harold Eugene Davis award for his article "The Inter-Atlantic Paradigm: The Failure of Spanish Medieval Colonization of the Canary and the Caribbean Islands;" this article was placed in the canon of Latin American colonial studies by the National Endowment for the Humanities. Dr. Stevens-Arroyo was also named visiting fellow at the Center for the Study of American Religion at Princeton University and was featured in several Spanish-language broadcasts as a commentator on the pope's visit.

Juan José Gloria retired for health reasons from his post as director of Hispanic Affairs for the California Catholic Conference (HC, 13 August). Roberto Goizueta taught "U.S. Hispanic Popular Catholicism" at the summer session of the University of Dayton. And Communities Organized for Public Service (COPS) was honored as "Friends of the U.N." for its 21 years of community organization.

Rev. Jean-Pierre Ruiz taught this summer at St. Charles Borromeo Seminary in Pennsylvania, and Gary Riebe-Estrella, S.V.D., and Teresa Muñoz did also at Loyola Marymount University. Riebe-Estrella addressed the joint assembly of the Conference of Major Superiors of Men and the Leadership Conference of Women Religious and also the Southern Province of Dominicans. Sister Anita de Luna, M.D.C.P., was the keynote speaker at the 24th annual gathering of the National Assembly of Religious Brothers. Joseph Esparza, C.S.C., just resigned after years of fine service to this group.

Several Latina religious made headlines. Sister María Elena González, president of the Mexican American Center, was honored by the Texas Catholic Conference. María Cevallos, O.P., will take her medical skills from Washington, DC to Brownsville, Texas (EP, 20 April). Ursuline Sister Diana Ortiz continues to campaign for justice for survivors of human rights abuses in Guatemala, according to the *National Catholic Reporter* (NCR, 5 May and 13 October). Sister Marilú Covani, S.T., was featured in *Vida Nueva*'s report on International Women's Day.

Also featured were lay women Rosario Marín and Mayra Fernández (VN, 10 March). Some of our finest bilingual composers are also lay women. Donna Peña was well known even before being featured in the 12 March NCR. Marta Reyes is now also gaining rightful recognition. Singer, musician, and composer Rosa Marta Zárate contributed to the November Women's Ordination Conference (NCR, 16 June).

Another artist honored was Cecilia Gonzalez Martinez. She has been named first director of Latino programming by Family Theater Productions (NCR, 17 October). Poet and novelist Sandra Cisneros won the $255,000 MacArthur Foundation Award (SAEN, 13 June), and New York's Museo del Barrio sponsored "Reaffirming Spirituality," under the direction of Susana Torruella Leval. Rosalinda Zapata Moreno was given the Pro Ecclesia et Pontifice medal, the highest papal award given to lay persons. Prolific María Pilar Aquino lectured at Pacific Lutheran University and the Congreso Diocesano of Oakland, California. She also offered reflections at the 1995 plenary session of the Catholic Theological Society of America and a conference for the Sisters of St. Joseph of Carondolet. Other Latinas recognized by the press include: Mercy Rodríguez, winner of the Miss America of Wheelchair award; Sara Luna Corral, who claims to be the oldest person alive at 126; Rita Barros Uriburu, who attended the Beijing Conference of Women; Verónica Méndez, R.C.D., and Paula Gonzalez, featured speakers at the Great Lakes Pastoral Ministry Gathering; Sylvia Sánchez, whose talk given at the Notre Dame Center for Pastoral Theology will be included in a forthcoming book; Benedictine Evangeline E. Salazar, who volunteered to care for Cubans held at the Guantánamo Naval Base; Alejandrina Vera, elected to the national council of the National Pastoral Musicians; Mary Francis Reza, a speaker at the Southwest Liturgical Conference's gathering. Women in the news must include singer Selena, who, although not Catholic, was remembered by Catholics in Masses, with candles, and in prayer (VD, 14 May).

A directory called Hispanic Alumni of Notre Dame, compiled by the university, lists about 1200 living Latino and Latina professionals. Notre Dame also offered a course in Hispanic theology by Miguel Diaz, and its CUSHWA center sponsored a lecture by Roberto R. Treviño, "Faith and Justice: The Catholic Church and the Chicano Movement in Houston," highlighting the positive role such individuals as Father Antonio Gonzales played. It is part of the center's worthwhile Working Papers Series; see also its newsletter.

One could fill this article with the 1995 activities of Virgilio Elizondo. He delivered over fifteen major addresses to groups as diverse as Brazilian bishops, Harvard Divinity School, and the Native American School of Ministry in Edmonton, Canada. In addition to his publications, he also helped produce three video series in conjunction with the USCC, the Mexican American Cultural Center (MACC), and the television channel Univision. He was featured in many articles such as El Visitante Dominical's 19 November piece.

Professor Fausto Avendaño won the prize for Chicano Letters given by the Universidad Autónoma de Ciudad Juárez. Mujerista theologian Ada María Isasi-Díaz spoke at the Maryknoll School of Theology, at Fordham University, and at a conference on minority scholars funded by Lilly Foundation and gave a summer course at Union Theological Seminary. She also delivered keynote addresses at Chestnut Hill College and at "The Tail of the Tiger" conference at Sinsinawa, Wisconsin.

Youth and youth ministry has also been in the news. The National Catholic Conference for Hispanic Ministry has received a grant from Lilly Foundation to host a day dedicated to youth ministry leaders at its August 1996 Congreso Nacional. Cristina Pita and Nelson Rodríguez were featured in an article about the Covenant House in Broward, Florida (VC, 20 October). The annual religious education conference in Anaheim, California, included special workshops for youth and young adults and music composed by Jaime Cortez. Ondina Cortés, R.M.I., has become the first female director of Miami's Office for Youth and Young Adults (VC, 19 May).

Instituto Fe y Vida held its first symposium from 3 to 9 July in Winona, Minnesota, giving special attention to the creation of small Christian communities for young people. Additionally, the Instituto held workshops in sixteen dioceses around the country.

Youth are slowly gaining more prominence in Hispanic ministry, thanks to groups like the Instituto. Some examples: (1) the interview with Martín Rosales Torres in the newsletter Senderos; (2) the report on young immigrants in EP, 20 April; (3) in EPs 9 February issue, a feature on Rosa Delmy Alvayero; (4) Ana Herrera's smiling face and biography in the 26 March issue of HC; (5) Felipe Salinas, recognized, at a conference on youth ministry in Colorado Springs, for his work with Hispanic youth; (6) Gina Maria López, featured in HC, 26 February, for winning a Knights of Columbus trophy; (7) full color full page articles, in January and March issues of VN, on the groups "Esperanza de la Juventud" and "Jóvenes, Inc.;" (8) a two page color roundup of work by and for youth, in EP on 13 April; (9) in VC, 19 May, a two page article with photos on El Centro Varela and Christie Arias, who gave a concert to benefit this resource for young people.

One of the goals of this annual article is to highlight often unknown successes by Hispanic Catholics. One certainly is that of the Spanish-language Catholic press. While secular papers are reducing their Spanish-language circulation (NYT, 16 October), well run Catholic newspapers like Washington DC's *El Pregonero* are actually adding to their press runs. It won nine national awards from the Asociación Nacional de Publicaciones Hispanas. Four awards from the same group, including best bimonthly, were given to Los Angeles's *Vida Nueva*. It and the *Heraldo Católico* of Sacramento won several awards this year from the Catholic Press Association.

The keys to success, in addition to a commitment to quality and initial support from a diocese, appear to be: Rely on financing from advertisers, not subscribers; give the paper away free, but place it where the Spanish-speaking gather; be clearly Catholic, but not unduly "churchy." Successful papers cover not only national and international news, but local *ligas* of sports and cultural events and practical stories like how to get a home loan or what to do about discrimination on the job. These papers are seen as part of the community. *El Pregonero*, for instance, has held annual job fairs for its constituents. *La Voz Católica* published a very complete and helpful history of United States Hispanic pastoral care, while always covering issues close to the heart of Cubans and Nicaraguans in Florida.

National Catholic journals in Spanish include *El Mensajero*, *El Visitante Dominical*, and the new *Nosotros* (call Deacon Alberto Romero at 201–854–7694). Videos, music, and books are available also. The Liturgical Press's *Así Es*, edited by Arturo Pérez et al., won first prize for the best Spanish-language book in the Catholic Press Association's 1995 competition. Note also the expansion of radio broadcasts such as "Hombre Nuevo," which reaches three million listeners, and "Radio Paz," which now broadcasts in three languages. The Spanish Mass in San Antonio's cathedral is watched faithfully by millions around the world, and that city's Hispanic Telecommunications Network has been so successful it is looking to build new quarters.

As Virgilio Elizondo pointed out (HC, 22 October), a sane and respected voice is needed when Hispanics are often portrayed in stereotypical ways in the media and when the nation is debating such issues as the English-only movement and denying services to immigrants. Despite scarce funds and dismal forecasts, the Catholic Spanish-language press has survived and in many areas thrived.

The *National Catholic Reporter* continues to provide the best English language coverage of Catholic Hispanics. See the articles of 17 November and 15 December. Perhaps the most renowned Hispanic Catholic journalist, Moisés Sandoval, publishes there regularly.

## National Organizations

The Academy of Catholic Hispanic Theologians of the United States (ACHTUS) met in New York. A dialogue was held with black Catholic theologians which may yet lead to a joint statement on theology.

Houston, Texas, was the site of the 12–14 July annual convention of the Asociación Nacional de Diaconos Hispanos. Details are available from the president, Deacon Ray Ortega (305–557–8898). CARA Report (Fall) states that 13 percent of the Nation's permanent deacons are Hispanic.

The Asociación Nacional de Sacerdotes Hispanos held its sixth annual conference in Orlando. VD printed on 4 June a statement by them concerning immigrants, as well as a lengthy article and a list of their executive board.

The Catholic Migrant Farm worker Network's interim director, Adela Gross, O.S.F., helped win a Lilly Endowment grant that was used for the first national consultation ever planned. Over one hundred participants came to the consultation in Techny, Illinois. CMFN continues to produce many helpful resources, among them a revised bilingual prayer book. For information write 3211 Fourth Street, N.E., Washington, DC 20017.

The Conferencia Nacional Carismática Católica held in Orlando in July began a dialogue between this movement and some sixty theologians, as reported 18 August in VC.

Comunidades de Reflexión ecclesial Cubana en la Diáspora (CRECED) gathered over thirty young people under the direction of Ondina Menocal to continue their reflection on the life and faith of this community (VC, 15 September).

Some 750 people who gathered 9–13 August in Denver for the Cursillo Nacional heard Cardinal Bernard Law praise their devotion to Scripture as the reason they have reached over four million Catholics (HC, 10 September).

HERMANAS published the results of their survey in *Informes* 9, no. 2. Strong support for the continuation of this group was reported, along with notes from Dolores Florez and reports on member activities. The National Assembly held 6–8 October in McAllen, Texas, reflected on the theme "Envisioning a Future without Violence." HERMANAS in 1995 not only considered the International Women's Conference in Beijing, but asked members to support CMFN and MACC. Past activities and current members of HERMANAS, like Yolanda Tarango, C.C.V.I., are featured in Rosemary Radford Ruether and Rosemary Skinner Keller, eds., *In Our Own Voices: Four Centuries of American Women's Religious Writings* (San Francisco: Harper Collins).

The weekly television series "Nuestra Familia" was presented for the first time in English by its producer, the Hispanic Telecommunications Network (HTN). Airing on the Faith and Values Channel, it reaches over 25 million homes. HTN also produced a thirty minute multimedia production for Convocación '95 and hosted two interns from the Pontifical Gregorian University: Father Sady Espinel and Ms. Daisy Orozco.

The Instituto de Liturgia Hispania dedicated its seventh national conference held in Houston to "Youth: Promise and Hope." Several workshops were offered in addition to general conferences given by Bishop Ricardo Ramírez, Dr. Virgilio Elizondo, Dr. Carmen María Cervantes, and Angela Erevia, M.D.C.P., Doris Turek, S.S.N.D., is the new executive director of the institute's offices, now located at the Catholic University of America.

The Mexican American Cultural Center's summer faculty included Angela Erevia, Anita de Luna, M.D.C.P., and Andres Aranda. The center continues to attract adjunct faculty of the quality of Virgil Elizondó and Eduardo Fernández, S.J. In addition to translating the Collegeville Bible Commentary and offering bilingual homiletic notes,

MACC has increased and updated its workshops. For instance, the language program has added a new cultural/pastoral dimension. MACC continues to host such important events as the founding of Encuentro Internacional de Catequesis. Present at this new beginning were catechists from the United States as well. Such meetings will be coordinated by Rudy Vela, S.M., who was appointed the new program director.

The Midwest Hispanic Catholic Commission, along with other regional offices of Hispanic ministry, collaborated on Convocación '95. Specifically they are helping with the bilingual monographs tracing the history of Hispanic ministry and a guide booklet for the New Evangelization based on the statement on evangelization which emerged from the convocación.

The National Catholic Association of Diocesan Directors of Hispanic Ministry (NCADDHM) met in conference as part of Convocación '95. The more than one hundred members heard talks by Virgilio Elizondo, Luis Velázquez, Elizabeth Hernández, Sister Teresa Gómez, and Bishop Geraldo Barnes.

The Organización Nacional de Catequistas para Hispanos held its ninth annual reunion in New Orleans. The keynote speaker was Dr. Alejandro García-Rivera. Honored for lifetime achievement in the area of religious education were María de la Cruz Aymes, Carmen María Cervantes, and María de los Angeles de García.

The Program for the Analysis of Religion Among Latinos (PARAL), while not Catholic or affiliated with any denomination, is important for its scholarly inquiry into all aspects of Hispanic religion. It not only completed the publication of a four volume study, but continues to network scholars and to hold seminars such as the one 11–14 April in Santa Barbara, California. This year it was featured prominently in international conferences, as well as at the Latin American Studies Conference, the Society for the Scientific Study of Religion, and the Religious Research Association. PARAL's first Olga Scarpetta Award went to Kathleen Sullivan. Member David Abalos won *Choice* magazine's Outstanding Academic Book award for his work, *The Latino Family and the Politics of Transformation.*

The Southeast Pastoral Institute (SEPI) continued its commitment to youth ministry and to the organization of Hispanic Catholics on diocesan and provincial levels. Its summer courses this year featured Casiano Floristán, and their publication arm continues to offer resources such as Miriam Codias's *La Renovación Carismática y La Iglesia Posconciliar.*

The National Catholic Council on Hispanic Ministry (NCCHM) seeks to serve and coordinate the efforts of these many groups, most of which are members of NCCHM. Three major efforts are underway in this umbrella organization. First, Adela Flores is coordinating a pilot program on Hispanic Catholic leadership both within and outside of the Church. Second, many members are donating great efforts to the planning of the second national congreso to be held at Loyola University in Chicago 8–11 August 1996. Some thirty models of leadership identified by the efforts of Flores and others will be showcased and discussed. Since the National Pastoral Life Center reports that only four percent of Church lay leadership is Latino (VC, 15 December), these efforts are crucial.

Other conferences of note this year included (1) the third International Marian Conference held 16–18 February in Miami; (2) the 19–20 May Congreso de Evangelización Hispano in New Orleans; (3) the Festival Católico Internacional, which took place in Orlando 7–9 June and featured Tony Meléndez, Martha Reyes, Ricardo Catellanos, and Wilfredo Peña; (4) that same month in the city of Queretaro, CEHILA's (Comisión de Estudios de la Iglesia en América Latina) symposium on "Cristianismo y Sociedad Estados Unidos y México," which featured among others Moisés Sandoval, Alberto Pulido, Juan Romero, Robert Wright, Timothy Matovina, Gilberto Hinojosa, David A. Badillo, Guadalupe Lozada León, María J. Rodríguez-Shadow, Silvana Forti Sosa, and María Alicia Puente de Guzmán; (5) the Ninth Annual Summer Hispanic Institute held at the Jesuit School of Theology at Berkeley, California; (6) a meeting in Dallas between Bishop Roberto González and representatives of the Movimiento Familiar Cristiano, Movimiento Shoenstatt, Encuentro Matrimonial Mundial, Movimiento Renovación Charismátic, and Talleres de Oración. It provided an opportunity for each group to know the others and promote greater unity of efforts.

## Resources

Liguori offers a long list of books, booklets, cassettes, and videos in Spanish; call 1–800–325–9521, ext. 343.

Tabor's line is especially good in catechetics, guided by María de la Cruz Aymes, S.H., call 1–800–822–6701. Other catechetical resources include *Conozca Primero Su Fe Católica* (504–943–5566), Sadlier's bilingual *Our Catholic Faith* (1–800–221–5175), and a full line of resources offered by the Missionary Sisters of Divine Providence (210–432–0113).

Videos for children are among new offerings from the United States Catholic Bookstore (312–855–1908). Sister Mary Elizabeth Tebo offers a children's book, *Mi Amigo Jesús,* available from 617–522–8911. For other young people, see the new, second volume by Saint Mary's Press, *Evangelización de la Juventud Hispana* (1–800–533–8095). Fax the Arlington, Virginia, diocese at 703–524–4261 for various manuals in Spanish on youth ministry.

Liturgists can took to the J.S. Paluch's two new recordings in Spanish by Lorenzo Florián (1–800–566–6150). Florián is also available for workshops such as those he gave in Anaheim, California, and in Cuba. Especially interesting is his *Salmos Responsoriales y Aclamaciones.* Ask, too, about their missalette. Oregon Catholic Press offers new music ranging from *cumbias* to *rancberas;* this material and their magazine Liturgia y Canción are available from 1–800–548–8749. GIA has new Christmas carols and a recording by Donna Peña; call 1–800–421–7250. The Cana Conference of Chicago (312–751–8201) has a new marriage-preparation manual, *El Pan Nuestro de Cada Día.*

One can get a list of USCC documents available in Spanish, as well as video cassettes, by calling 1–800–235–USCC.

Other companies: (1) St. Anthony Messenger Press continues to produce Hispanic resources and will inform callers of 1–800–488–0488; (2) *Alabemos Jubilosos: Himnos y Cánticos is* new from the San Ignacio Music Company at 505–831–2739; (3) call 505–344–9382 for LPD's series about contemporary Hispanic art and artists; (4) mission education is the point of *Vengan y Vean* from the Columban Fathers at 402–291–1920; (5) Miami's Ministry of Worship and Spiritual Life offers the bilingual booklet *Santa Barbara y San Lazaro* to callers of 305–757–6241, ext. 351; (6) *El Evangelio según María is* available from Twenty Third Publications at 1–800–321–0411.

Want information about how to ride the information highway into barrios of information? Consult "Olé: Latin America's Net Presence Is Growing" by Rosalind Resnick in April's Internet World. Or read Derly Andre Tijerina's "Exploring the Internet" in the March issue of "Hispanic."

## Significant Writings

Aquino, María del Pilar. "Including Women's Experience: A Latina Feminist Perspective." *In the Embrace of God. Feminist*

*Approaches to Theological Anthropology,* ed. Ann O'Hare Graff, pp. 51–70. Maryknoll: Orbis Books, 1995. Examines the theoretical categories used in some documents sponsored mainly by the Ecumenical Association of Third World Theologians. "These documents not only reflect the anthropological models at work in Christian discourse but also have a share in the intellectual and symbolic construction of social relations, with direct implication for women's lives." Her objective is "to find those intellectual elements that can help us confront and advance the struggles of women for social transformation leading to justice."

Boff, Leonardo, and Virgil Elizondo, eds. "Editorial." In *Concilium: Ecology and Poverty: Cry of the Earth, Cry of the Poor*, pp. ix–xii. Maryknoll: Orbis Books, 1995. Speaks of today's quest for an "integral ecology," one forming a "new alliance between societies and nature, which will result in the conservation of the patrimony of the earth. . . . Today, nature's most threatened creatures are not the whales or the giant pandas of China, but the poor. . . ."

Cunningham, Hilary. *God and Caesar at the Rio Grand: Sanctuary and the Politics of Religion.* Minneapolis, University of Minnesota Press, 1995. Her dissertation surveys the ideologies controlling the anthropological study of religion, and the Sanctuary movement, to argue that religion does not necessarily support the status quo but can challenge the power of civil authority.

Davis, O.F.M.Conv., Kenneth G. "Encuentros, National Pastoral." In *New Catholic Encyclopedia,* Volume 19 (Supplement 1989-1995), pp. 117–119. History and significance of three national conventions of United States Hispanic Catholics, 1972, 1977, and 1985. Provides a context for under standing present national Hispanic ministry initiatives.

———. "Pointers for Presiders, Spanish as a Second Language: Part I" *AIM: Liturgy Resources* (Winter 1995): 22–24. Reminds presiders of some basic *dos* and *don'ts* to keep in mind when presiding before a Hispanic community, particularly when the presider is not native to the culture. Among the topics discussed are the role of popular religion, a liturgical voice for the people, and the need for planning.

Deck, S.J., Allan Figueroa. "Chávez, César Estrada." In *New Catholic Encyclopedia,* Volume 19 (Supplement 1989–1995), pp. 77–78. Biography of "arguably the single most significant United States leader of his time."

———. "'A Pox on Both Your Houses': A View of Catholic Conservative-Liberal Polarities from the Hispanic Margin." In Mary Jo Weaver and R. Scott Appleby, eds., *Being Right: Conservative Catholics in America,* pp. 88–104. Bloomington: Indiana University Press, 1995. "Explores the relevance and significance of conservative-liberal polarizations from within an emerging new perspective, that of the burgeoning Hispanic Catholic communities. Their distinctive heritage and style of acculturation, occurring at this moment and not some other in United States history, make past interpretations of the immigrant reality, the so-called immigrant analogy, inadequate for grasping the meaning and import of their presence."

Durand, Jorge, and Douglas S. Massey. *Miracles on the Border: Retablos of Mexican Migrants to the United States.* Tuscon, New Mexico: University of Arizona Press, 1995. Over 75 full color retablos are catalogued along with interpretive essays, bibliography and index. Elizondo, Virgilio. "Guadalupe, Our Lady of." In Richard P. McBrien, ed., *The Harper Collins Encyclopedia of Catholicism,* pp. 594–595. Harper San Francisco, 1995. Summarizes the historical, anthropological, and theological implications of the apparition. "In the mestizo Mother of the Americas, irreconcilable differences are not only reconciled but a new 'beyond exclusion existence' is introduced, one that will destroy the very basis of cruel violence produced by any exclusion-based existence." See also brief entries by Jaime Vial on "Santería" and "Voodoo."

———. "Letter to the Church in Italy." Adista (Italy) (14 October 1995): 92–95. Highlights the rich spiritual traditions which characterize Italy, yet also challenges moderns to live the faith in a climate of growing nationalism and immigrant bashing. Appeals to gospel values such as openness to other cultures and other religions, as well as care for the increasing foreigners in the country. Published in Italian.

Espín, Orlando O. "Pentecostalism and Popular Catholicism: The Poor and Traditio." *Journal of Hispanic/Latino Theology* 3, no. 2 (November, 1995): 14–43. Argues that, given their shared sense of Christianity as *traditio* and their common central concern for the empowerment of the poor, popular Catholicism and Pentecostalism in the United States have the promise of developing an authentic dialogue, probably more conducive to full communion than previous denominationally sponsored ones.

Garcia-Rivera, Alejandro. "The Cosmic Frontier: Toward a Natural Anthropology." *Journal of Hispanic/Latino Theology* 3, no. 1 (August, 1995): 42–49. Advances the discussion of the consequences of modernity and postmodernity, especially as related to the development of a synthesis of both the religious and scientific imagination. Within this context, discusses the possibility and need for a natural anthropology.

Goizueta, Roberto S. "The Preferential Option for the Poor: The CELAM Documents and the NCCB Pastoral Letter on U.S. Hispanics as Sources for U.S. Hispanic Theology." *Journal of Hispanic/Latino Theology* 3, no. 2 (November, 1995): 65–77. Examines the notion of the preferential option for the poor by "briefly analyzing its role in (1) the documents of Medellín, Puebla, and Santo Domingo and (2) the United States National Catholic Conference of Bishops' (NCCB) pastoral letter on United States Hispanics." Suggests "that the more recent documents reflect a 'new distinction of planes' epistemological model which threatens to undermine the option for the poor as articulated in the earlier documents." Closes with some "possible avenues for avoiding that danger."

González, R.S.M., María Elena. "Parish Restructuring in Multi-Cultural Communities." *Origins* 24, no. 46 (4 May, 1995): 781, 783–788. Text of keynote address given at the 2–5 April convention in Newport, Rhode Island, of the Conference for Pastoral Planning and Council Development. Focuses on the challenge of the multi-cultural parish, explores the meaning of the terms "culture" and "inculturation," and analyzes the "mindsets that are barriers to restructuring parish living."

Isasi-Díaz, Ada María. "Elements of a *Mujerista* Anthropology." In Ann O'Hare Graff, ed., *In the Embrace of God: Feminist Approaches* to *Theological Anthropology"*, pp. 90–102. Maryknoll: Orbis Books, 1995. Centers on three Spanish phrases "as elements that need to be considered when elaborating a mujerista anthropology, which must have as its source the lives of Latinas and as its goal our liberation." The three are *la lucha* (the struggle), *permítame hablar* (allow me to speak), and *la comunidad/la familia* (the community/the family).

————."*Mujerista* Theology's Method: A Liberative Praxis, A Way of Life." In James D. Whitehead and Evelyn Eaton Whitehead, eds., *Method in Ministry: Theological Reflection and Christian Ministry*, pp. 123–132. Kansas City: Sheed and Ward, 1995. Discusses two qualitative research methods that she has used to "gather the voices and lived-experience of Hispanic Women. *Mujerista* theologians must present in our writings particular voices from the communities in which our theology is rooted. Otherwise we will run the risk either of objectifying grass roots Hispanic women by talking about 'them' and for 'them,' or we will speak exclusively for and by ourselves instead of providing a forum for the theological voice of our communities."

————. "*Mujerista* Liturgies and the Struggle for Liberation." Chauvet and François Kabasale Lumbala, eds., *Concilium: Liturgy and the Body*, pp. 104–111. Maryknoll: Orbis Books, 1995. Illustrates how "*mujerista* liturgies are born out of and become expressions of Hispanic women's determination to be self-defining women. . . . And, though the Church continues to deny Hispanic women, in fact all women, full participation, *mujeristas* believe that the reappropriation of the sacred that happens through our rituals ultimately does contribute to change the social order."

————. *Women of God, Women of the People*. St. Louis: Chalice Press, 1995. A series of biblical meditations first delivered at the Tenth International Christian Women Fellowship Quadrennial Assembly held at Purdue University in June, 1994, printed as a small book. Looks at three women found in the Bible from a *mujerista* perspective.

Jiménez, Pablo A. "In Search of a Hispanic Model of Biblical Interpretation." *Journal of Hispanic/Latino Theology* 3, no. 2 (November, 1995): 44–64. Part of the emerging commentary and synthesis of the thought of United States Latino theologians, compares the use of the Bible by both Virgilio Elizondo and Justo L. González, identifying key similarities and differences in their hermeneutics and providing some insights into pastoral applications.

Levada, William. "Hispanic Ministry's Changing, Face." *Origins* 25, no. 3 (1 June, 1995): 46–48. Text of the then Archbishop of Portland's talk at a clergy in-service assembly for priests of the archdiocese. Speaks of a model for ministry that "integrates Hispanics into the Church and overcomes their being viewed as a separate community, as 'those others.' Such integration, it should be clear, is not the same thing as assimilation."

Macy, Gary. "Demythologizing 'the Church' in the Middle Ages." *Journal of Hispanic/Latino Theology* 3, no. 1 (August, 1995): 23–41. A study on the use and abuse of such terms as "church" and "theology" in current academic literature on the European Middle Ages. Closes with an explanation of how such an unnuanced treatment has been detrimental to United States Hispanics/Latinos, who are in many ways heirs to this tradition.

Maldonado, Roberto D. "La Conquista? Latin American *(Mestizaje)* Reflections on the Biblical Conquest." *Journal of Hispanic/Latino, Theology* 2, no. 4 (May, 1995): 5–25. Compares some aspects of Israel's multi-cultural history to aspects of Latin America's *mestizaje.* Particularly highlighted for their use of the symbol of La Guadalupe are two United States Latino authors: Virgilio Elizondo and Gloria Anzaldúa.

Matovina, Timothy M. "Lay Initiatives in Worship on the Texas Frontera, 1830–1860," *U.S. Catholic Historian* 12 (Fall, 1995). Highlights the role of laypersons, especially women, in maintaining religious ritual vitality despite conquests and limited clergy. Uses both rural and urban examples.

Ramirez, Ricardo. "Prison Reform and the Ideals of Justice." *Origins* 24, no. 37 (2 March, 1995): 612-615. Text of the homily given at the annual Red Mass in Phoenix, Arizona. Punishment "is but one part of justice; rehabilitation has to accompany that penal aspect." Contains some practical suggestions.

———. "The Crisis in Ecumenism among Hispanic Christians." *Origins* 24, no. 40 (23 March, 1995): 660–667. His address to a meeting of representatives of the National Conference of Catholic Bishops' committees for ecumenical and interreligious affairs and for Hispanic affairs and to the ecumenical section of the Latin American bishops' council, in Washington, DC. Discusses historical factors that have "contributed to the hostility, suspicion, and mistrust between Hispanic Protestantism and Roman Catholicism." Gives reasons for hope.

Romero, C. Gilbert. "Hispanic Theology and the Apocalyptic Imagination." *Apuntes* 15, no. 4 (Winter, 1995): 133–137. Maintaining that one of the principal resources for a Hispanic theology in the United States is devotional piety *(religiosidad popular),* argues that it "provides a broad framework for a solid theological investigation which includes postulating the use of an apocalyptic imagination."

Ruiz, Jean-Pierre. "Contexts in Conversation: First World and Third World Readings of Job." *Journal of Hispanic/Latino Theology* 2, no. 3 (February, 1995): 5–29. Uses Gustavo Gutiérrez's *On Job: God Talk and the Suffering of the Innocent* and William Safire's *The First Dissident: The Book of Job in Today's Politics* to compare first and third world understandings of Job, attempting to discover commonalities and differences of critical exegesis.

———. "New Ways of Reading the Bible in the Cultural Settings of the Third World." In Wm. Beuken and Sean Freyne, eds., *Concilium: The Bible as Cultural Heritage,* 73–84. Maryknoll: Orbis Books, 1995. Presents a "sampling of ways in which third world interpreters are presenting new readings of the Bible." Addresses "some of the ways in which [it] has begun to make a difference in the Church and in the academy in the first world."

Segovia, Fernando E, and Mary Ann Tolbert, eds. "'And They Began to Speak in Other Tongues': Competing Modes of Discourse in Contemporary Biblical Criticism." In Segovia and Tolbert, eds., *Reading from This Place.* Vol. 1, *Social Location and Biblical Interpretation in the United States,* pp. 1–32. Minneapolis: Fortress Press, 1995. Introduction to the text they coedit, outlines the recent shift away from the historical-critical model to one which allows "for incredible diversity in models of interpretation as well as for a thoroughgoing reformulation of the role of culture and experience in the task of criticism." They also edited the international project entitled *Social Location and Biblical Interpretation in Global Perspective,* Vol. 2 of *Reading from This Place,* 1995.

Stevens-Arroyo, Antonio M. "Latino Catholicism and the Eye of the Beholder: Notes Towards a New Sociological Paradigm." *Latino Studies Journal* 6, no. 2 (May, 1995): 22–55. Reviews important survey and interpretive works over the past fifteen years. Shows that survey data has been more inclusive than general studies of United States Catholicism. Particular studies and authors are cited to show the poor understanding of Latinos generally found in the sociology of United States Catholicism. A new paradigm is suggested along the lines of the internal colonialism model.

United States/Latin American Bishops, "Fostering Ecumenism. in the U.S. Hispanic Community." *Origins* 24, no. 40 (23 March, 1995): 657, 659–660. A statement issued by bishops representing the United States National Conference of Catholic Bishops' ecumenical and Hispanic affairs committees as well as the ecumenical section of the Latin American bishops' council (CELAM). At the first working session, the bishops commented that ecumenism will assume "different forms in different cultural situations, with ecumenical partners who have different priorities."

## Book Reviews

Tejano Religion and Ethnicity: San Antonio, 1821–1860. Timothy M. Matovina. Austin: University of Texas Press, 1995. Cloth. $24.95.

This is not just another history book, but a narration of the origins, formation and molding of the living memory of today's San Antonio. It takes one far beyond the surface of statistical history or the walls of historical buildings and into the intimate struggles and decisions of ordinary people whose lives and efforts have contributed to making San Antonio the vibrant, multi-cultural city that it is today.

While the flags of Spain, Mexico, the Republic of Texas, and the United States have flown over San Antonio, the Tejanos and their families (Texans of Spanish or Mexican descent) evolved as a distinct ethnic group, providing continuity and welcome to the newcomers, and, through the religious-cultural life in and around San Fernando, strengthened the mestizo roots and character of San Antonio.

Matovina reveals the violence and social upheaval that Tejanos suffered during national changes, but he emphasizes their valor and strategies for physical and ethnic survival as well as the determination to build a new alliance and fellowships. What emerges is a portrait, not of a sad, victimized, and defeated people, but of an enduring community filled with joy, faith, and pride in the mestizo heritage combined with a deep spirit of respect and openness to the heritage of newcomers.

*Virgil Elizondo*

*St. Martin de Porres: The "Little Stories" and the Semiotics of Culture.* Alejandro García-Rivera. Maryknoll: Orbis Books, 1995. pp. 142. Paper. $16.95.

Through the method of semiotics of culture as developed by Robert Schreiter, the author finds a vehicle to retrieve popular religion in the context of theology. The canonization process of Martín de Porres provides the semiotic whole for the development and meaning of *mestizaje* in the construction of New World identity, and the particular meanings of the little stories of eyewitnesses to the saint's life. It is the story of the crossing of major boundaries of politics, philosophy, the institutional church, and popular religion in the creation of new meaning and the restoral of older, lost meanings.

Martín de Porres as African, Spaniard, and Indian embodies the new identity of *mestizo* and represents a solution to the conundrum of the identity and humanity of the African and Indian for European theological, philosophical, and political categories. The construction of this saint became the mosaic of a new reality and meaning which García-Rivera suggests is actually a return to an "anthropology of creatureliness," that is, "an act of symmetry, of *subsuming of differences for the goals of a personal freedom.*"

The book was his doctoral dissertation. Its style is at times confusing, especially if one is unaccustomed to the language of the semiotics of culture. More problematic is a lack of a critical analysis of the canonization process itself. While the semiotic method certainly helps to retrieve the articles of popular religion for theological reflection, it should be accompanied by a greater evaluation of the material evidence of cultic practice. There is no doubt, however, that Alex García-Rivera has produced an exciting new approach to theology, and a way to utilize popular religion for theological investigation and reflection.

*Joseph M. Palacios, S.J.*

*Caminemos con Jesús: Toward a Hispanic/Latino Theology of Accompaniment.* Roberto S. Goizueta. Maryknoll: Orbis Books, 1995. pp. 224. Paper. $16.95.

Since its beginnings, liberation theology has looked with disfavor on popular piety as an ideological form of control and/or a fatalistic quietism. United States Hispanic theology, on the other hand, has always explored popular piety as *locus liberationis*. Goizueta articulates the theoretical foundation for a liberation theology of Hispanic popular religion. His brilliant and courageous insight emerges from his revitalization of an almost forgotten branch of theological method: Theological aesthetics. Reflecting on his personal experience of Holy Week as practiced at the San Fernando Cathedral of San Antonio, Texas, he makes the distinction between aesthetics as an intrinsic praxis of relationships between subjects rather than a poiesis or instrumental praxis of a subject creating an object of value. Borrowing and critiquing the aesthetics of Vasconcelos, Goizueta forges a new theological aesthetics of praxis, aptly named *accompaniment.*

*Alex García-Rivera*

*Dialogue Rejoined: Theology and Ministry in the United States Reality.* Ana María Pineda and Robert Schreiter, eds. Collegeville: Liturgical Press, 1995. pp. 187. Paper. $15.95.

The early attempt at dialogue between the Franciscan missionaries and the Aztec-Nahuatl leadership resulted in mutual misunderstanding and the replacement of native religion and culture with Spanish. Moisés Sandoval, in his overview of the current Hispanic membership in the United States Church, and Paul J. Wadell, in his treatment of Hispanics' narrative approach to ethics, acknowledge that this conquest is a living memory; the exclusion from dialogue with the dominant culture has significantly shaped the Hispanic view. The CTU faculty has reinitiated a dialogue between the United States Church's established membership and the growing Hispanic constituency which is reshaping it; the present collection is its early fruit.

First, it identifies the generic "Hispanic" people. Carlos B. Córdova addresses the various sociopolitical backgrounds of immigrants from Central America. Dominga Zapata describes the Puerto Rican experience from its pre-Hispanic background to its current status within the United States Guillermo Fernández-Toledo relates the unique situation of the Cuban population and its religious idiosyncrasy. Except for a brief mention by Sandoval, South Americans are not considered.

Second, the work looks at how the above realities affect theology, ranging from a liberation biblical exegesis by Barbara E. Reid to Mark R. Francis's assessment of the Hispanic liturgical experience. Gary Riebe-Estrella challenges theological education to move from articulating the deposit of tradition to "doing theology." Closely related is Pineda's treatment of ministerial formation. John E. Linnan asks if base communities' attempt at "a new way of being" church is being realized in this country.

It is remarkable how many disciplines and perspectives are considered in this small, thought-provoking volume. While each essay in the second part is outstanding, the predominant concern with the Mexican American experience does not sufficiently take into account the multicultural makeup of the United States Hispanics described in the first part.

*John Stowe, O.F.M.Conv.*

*César Chávez: A Triumph of Spirit.* Richard Griswold del Castillo and Richard A. Garcia. Norman: University of Oklahoma Press, 1995. pp. 224. Cloth. $19.95.

This book is unique because it brings into focus Chávez's life in the context of Chicano and American history. Well written and readable, it provides a brief history of César's early life, the years of involvement with Fred Ross and the Community Service Organization in California, and the establishment of the United Farm Workers of America. The bibliographic essay provides future researchers with an excellent source.

The most important aspect of the book is the recurrence of the theme identified by its subtitle, "Triumph of Spirit." Chávez's life was a triumph for all people. His personal commitment to farm workers and his conviction that the poor should have more control over their lives were the chief motivating factors for all that he did. His life of self-sacrifice and of commitment to nonviolence serves as an example for all.

*Barbara Jenkins, S.C.*

*Mestizo Christianity: Theology from the Latino Perspective.* Arturo. J. Bañuelas, ed. Maryknoll Orbis Books, 1995. pp. 278. Paper. $16.95.

Though the articles in this anthology are reprints, Bañuelas has selected an excellent representative sample of Latina and Latino writings that address, from Catholic and Protestant perspectives, the theological significance of *mestizaje.* Bañuelas points out that *mestizaje* is more than a mixing of cultures, blood, and religious traditions. It is a dynamic reality that births forth a new race, a cultural paradigm through which one understands Hispanic Christianity. Within Hispanic culture it is a key *locus theologicus* for human and divine self-disclosure.

While *mestizaje* serves as the overarching context, the articles are arranged according to seven topics: (1) the theological significance of cultural identity, (2) methodology, (3) popular religiosity, (4) Latinas' voices, (5) social ethics, (6) spirituality, and (7) ecumenism. With its comprehensive bibliography, this is an excellent introduction to Hispanic theology.

*Miguel H. Diaz*

*Our Lady of Guadalupe: The Origin and Sources of a Mexican National Symbol, 1531–1797.* Stafford Poole, C.M. Arizona: University of Arizona Press, 1995.

Poole does not present substantial new evidence, but his comprehensive and systematic approach to the known sources provides a new framework for this study.

Distinguishing between a sixteenth century shrine devotion and a later apparition is the heart of the book: "The devotion at Tepeyac prior to 1648 and the apparition devotion after that are two distinct entities." The only thing that can be said with historical plausibility is that the apparition stories were chiefly constructed as an explanation for a devotion that already existed. Poole addresses the lack of definitive evidence for these apparitions, the problems with dates, the character of native sources, and the undue weight given to tradition despite the lack of documentation from the very beginning. The silence of 16th century sources lies at the core of his argument. There is no convincing explanation why such an event did not generate any manuscripts.

Guadalupe was fundamentally a criollo construct and remained so for the larger part of the colonial period. In fact, the only reason we know anything about her is due to her criollo devotees. Indian devotion since the 16th century was always "tangential" and difficult to assess. This devotion became popularized among the native population in the 18th century and only after direct evangelization. Poole contests the connection that has been made between an Indian goddess and Guadalupe, insisting that there is no reason to propagate a theology based solely on the arguments given by Bernardino de Sahagún.

Poole's revisionism is forceful, bold, indeed even judgmental. He concedes, for example, that it is "plausible" that Juan Diego existed and has some relation to the original devotion, but feels there is insufficient evidence to affirm resolutely that he was involved. Furthermore, he is extremely critical of the "canonization" of the Nican Mopohua. He calls it "one of the greatest errors in the development of the Guadalupe tradition" and questions its uncritical use.

The consequences of this study could be serious; yet, as Poole himself affirms, the symbol of Guadalupe has taken a religious significance of its own independent of its historical origins and continues to be interpreted to suit the ideology in vogue. The popularity of the myth will stand despite history. This book represents a ground-breaking accomplishment, a veritable tour de force in Guadalupe scholarship.

*Teresa Maya Sotomayor*

*Old Masks, New Faces: Religion and Latino Identities.* Anthony M. Stevens-Arroyo and Gilbert R. Cadena, eds. New York: Bildner Center for Western Hemisphere Studies, 1995. Vol. 2 of the four volume PARAL series. pp. 196.

*Enigmatic Powers: Syncretism with African and Indigenous Peoples' Religions among Latinos.* Anthony M. Stevens-Arroyo and Andres L Pérez y Mena, eds. Vol. 3 of the PARAL series. pp. 208.

This series is proving to be a significant contribution to PARAL's objective to address Latino issues in religion from a national perspective. Volume 2 is primarily concerned with the religious aspects of cultural identity. Addressing this neglected topic are Patrick McNamara, Edwin Hernández, Caleb Rosado, Ada Maria Isasi-Díaz, Anneris Goris, David Abalos, the late Joseph P. Fitzpatrick, S.J., (to whom the book is dedicated), and the editors.

Volume 3 addresses the complicated topic of religious syncretism. Gustavo Benavides, Otto Maduro, David Carrasco, Mercedes Cros Sandoval, Migene González-Wippler, Orlando do Campo, and the editors expand horizons beyond the scope of Christianity in order to demonstrate its syncretistic character. Stevens-Arroyo's opening words, "Perhaps no other segment of the United States population has such frequent contact with healers, mediums, and sorcerers, with herb cures, hexes, and spells as the Latino people who live in the barrios of the United States," demonstrates the relevance of this topic for understanding the religion of Latinos. The indices makes both volumes user-friendly.

The editors, especially Stevens-Arroyo, who worked on all four volumes, are to be commended, along with the contributors, for demonstrating the religious plurality found within Latino culture.

*Eduardo Fernández, S.J.*

*Discovering Latino Religion: A Comprehensive Social Science Bibliography.* Anthony M. Stevens-Arroyo and Segundo Pantoja, eds. Vol. 4 of the PARAL series. pp. 142.

This fourth volume consists of four comprehensive bibliographies on the announced subject, two essays by sociologist Robert Wuthnow and series editor Stevens-Arroyo, a helpful "Note to the User" by editor Pantoja, and a "Postscript to Librarians and Researchers" by Kenneth Davis. Pantoja is the actual gatherer of the four bibliographies. While it delivers on its promise, most of the items included in the bibliographies are *not* from the social sciences. The four bibliographies are: From social sciences (pp. 45–75), from theology and religious studies (pp. 77–106), from other reports, papers, documents, and bibliographies (pp. 107–124), and from dissertations and theses (pp. 125–135). Quite thorough, they were mostly gathered through computerized indexes and catalogues. This allowed for a very broad and comprehensive search, but it also limited the results to what the data bases included. As Davis points out, there often are glaring omissions and mistakes (in reference to Latinos and religion) in computerized data bases. Consequently, titles are missing from each of the four bibliographies.

This is a welcome and solid contribution. For the first time a significant body of literature is alphabetically listed in manageable book form. The editors should be complimented for this service to the academic (and pastoral) community.

*Orlando O. Espín*

*This article originally appeared in Review for Religious Vol. 55 (1996) under the title, "U.S. Hispanic Catholics: Trends and Works 1995."*

# 1996 IN REVIEW

## Migrants and Immigrants

T he Church appears to support the rights of "people on the move" more consistently than ever. The opposite is the case with our government. An example of the latter is the beating of at least two Mexican immigrants by police officers of Riverside, California. United States bishops were quick to condemn the outrage (*National Catholic Reporter* [NCR], 19 April). The Catholic press also covered related stories: Twenty three Mexicans on death row (El Visitante Dominical [VD], 11 February) and the continuing overall positive impact immigration has on the country (La Voz Católica [VC], 19 January).

Nonetheless, a rash of legislation prejudicial to immigrants passed: Greater penalties for aiding the undocumented, denial of most public benefits formerly available to legal immigrants, political asylum more difficult to obtain, pilot projects to verify immigrant status. The *New York Times* (NYT, 28 August) reports that California has used these projects to obtain the desired effect of the notorious Proposition 187, which still languishes in court. The 1992 North American Free Trade Agreement—virtually the only government sponsored border crossing (of goods, not people)—exacerbates economic and social problems in the countries," quotes *Hispanic Link* (HL, 1 April). Consequently, the Region Eleven Commission of the Spanish Speaking (RECOSS) has adopted an "aggressive political stance" (NCR, 24 May). Many dioceses actively supported the 12 October March for Justice at the Nation's Capitol. These initiatives point out the suffering that will result from changes in welfare regulations (NCR, 11 October).

United States bishops have questioned the justice of this legislation and have noted that the reputation of the United States as a refuge of the oppressed is declining and that, when a group is denied basic medical attention, public health is threatened (*El Pregonero*, 4 January; *El Heraldo Católico* [HC], 18 January; *Crux of the News*, 19 February and 11 April; NCR, 5 April; VD, 21 January and 18 February). Individual bishops and other members of the clergy spoke out to protect the undocumented (HC, 19 May; VD, 6–2); the spring meeting of the National Conference of Catholic Bishops unanimously denounced this legislation (VD, 28 July). The local clergy supported a strike by farm workers in Florida (NCR, 19 April). Similar activity levered a contract between the United Farm Workers and Red Coach lettuce. Lay people, too, have organized to protest anti-immigrant laws (VD, 8 October).

## General Church News

The best and the worst is that the Hispanic Catholic most in the media was Sister Diana Ortiz. It is good news because her cause may finally receive the government attention it deserves; bad because the reason she had recourse to the government is the torture she endured in Guatemala, which may have direct United States links (NCR, 29 March, 12 and 19 April, 17 May; HL, 13 May; NYT, 1 April and 7 May). The Leadership Conference of Women Religious and the Conference of Major Superiors of Men support her cause (*Crux of the News*, 27 May). Her insistence and perseverance have led to breakthroughs for others interested in the United States role in Guatemala (NYT, 9 August), including Efraín Bamaca (NCR, 6 September).

A good many other Latinas have been in the news. Ada María Isasi-Díaz has a grant from the Louisville Institute for a project on empowering Latinas; she spoke at the Call to Action national conference. María Pilar Aquino was an invited speaker at over ten conferences, including two in Germany. Colombian singer Isadora spoke of her conversion experience (VC, 16 February). The death sentence of Guinievere García was commuted (VD 2–11 and 2–18). Ana María Díaz-Stevens won a grant from the Louisville Institute for research on the mission and vocation of Catholic women religious among Latinas. This included convoking, at Bayamon Central University, the first conference of Puerto Rican religious institutes for women; among the speakers were Mario Rodríguez, O.P., Dismas Soberal, Anthony Stevens-Arroyo, and Jaime Vidal.

The Missionary Catechists of Divine Providence celebrate the fiftieth anniversary of their foundation. Carmen María Cervantes and Paula González spoke at the twenty sixth biennial conference of the National Federation of Catholic Youth Ministry. Helen Alvaré was a featured speaker at the Signs of the Times conference held at George Washington University. Linda Chavez dialogued about assisted suicide in the July/August issue of Overheard. Dolores Huerta was featured in the August issue of Hispanic. Cecilia González was appointed director of Latino programming for Family Theater Productions. Martha Reyes sings a new video, "Shalom desde Israel." Ana María Pineda, R.S.M., received a second Lilly Endowment grant to continue her sabbatical; she also presented a workshop on congregational leadership funded by the Louisville Institute, on whose board she serves. Pineda was appointed to the evaluation commission of the Ecumenical Association of Third World Theologians, participated in a conference in Mexico sponsored by Maryknoll, and facilitated a Latin American-Caribbean conference of her community.

Yolanda Tarango was awarded an honorary doctorate by Incarnate Word University. Ann Francis Monedero, O.S.F., and Sylvia Chacon, A.S.C., collaborated with Eduardo Fernández, S.J., on the first course ever offered on Hispanic religious expressions at the University of Texas at El Paso. Rosa María Icaza, C.C.V.I., was awarded the Archbishop Flores Medal. Maruja Sedano attended the International Conference of Biblical Institutes. Sisters Anita de Luna and Gloria Loya taught at the Summer Hispanic Institute in Berkeley. Irma Corretjer Nolla was featured in the February issue of Maryknoll Magazine and was reappointed to the board of the Center for Applied Research in the Apostolate. Reverend Mother Mary Magdalen de la Garza, a nineteenth century Ursuline pioneer, the first United States Latina postulant of her community, was recognized for her extraordinary educational work.

Ernesto Cortes Jr. addressed the urban ministry conference in Milwaukee in October. Father Virgil Elizondo taught at the Collegeville Pastoral Institute and the Hispanic Summer Program. He spoke in Paris and Madrid and through television and a video series. As the new program development director of Catholic Television of San Antonio, he will continue to reach a large audience. With Father Juan Alfaro he also lectured at Incarnate Word University. The former produced a video series on Scripture, part of a growing trend of Hispanics in Catholic media. Alfaro's *Hope and Glory* tied for first place in the Scripture category of the Catholic Press Association book awards; Roberto S. Goizueta won honorable mention for *Caminemos con Jesús*. The editor of El Pregonero, Oscar Reyes, publicly recounted his conversion experience after his arrest and torture in Honduras (HC, 24 March). Nicaraguan Augusto César Suárez fled persecution and now serves Miami's Radio Paz (VC, 26 April). He helped organize the first international radio festival in Miami (VC, 23 August). Working with Suárez is Father José Luis Hernando, who began the station twenty five years ago (VC, 22 March).

Moises Sandoval and Demetria Martinez increased their contributions to NCR. Domingo Rodriguez was elected to the board of the

Conference of Major Superiors of Men. Gary Riebe-Estrella, S.V.D., newly elected dean of the Catholic Theological Union, addressed the National Catholic Education Association and the National Religious Vocation Conference. Eduardo Fernández, S.J., participated in a semester-long border spirituality seminar sponsored by the Tepeyac Institute and lectured at the Loyola Institute for Ministry in New Orleans along with Dr. Jeannette Rodriguez; Rodriguez also taught at the summer session of Santa Clara University. German Martinez taught the summer at Maryknoll, and Jaime Vidal organized the Midwest Conference of Seminarians, where Father Arturo Pérez and Mrs. Olga Villa Parra spoke.

Dr. Alejandro García-Rivera began penning pastoral reflections for Nuestra Parroquia. Father Juan Sosa spoke at several liturgical meetings and at the Great Lakes Pastoral Ministry Gathering in March. Jean-Pierre Ruíz gave a keynote address at the Society of Biblical Literature's recruitment conference. He and Fernando Segovia are minority mentors. Dr. Roberto Goizueta joined Maria Luisa Gaston, Domingo Rodríguez, S.T., and Dr. Carmen María Cervantes for a series of workshops sponsored by the Diocese of Houston–Galveston. The religious education conference at Anaheim, California, included Virgil Elizondo, Lorenzo Florian, Luz Lozano, and Armando Noguez. Timothy Matovina consulted with the CUSHWA Center and the Program for the Analysis of Religion among Latinos (PARAL), and received the Paul J. Foik and Summerfield G. Roberts awards for his book *Tejano Religion and Ethnicity*. Thirteen year old Richard Bautista won the Conference of United States Cardinals' Award given by Cardinal Roger Mahoney (*El Católico de Texas*, May).

Henry Cisneros, in his column in HL, 23 September, mentions the Virgin. Often in the news, he has not been the only Catholic Hispanic politician in the public eye: Raúl González, a justice of the Texas Supreme Court, testified to his Catholic faith in *Our Sunday Visitor*. The mayor of Hialeah, Florida, Raúl Martínez, seems to be winning his battle against accusations of corruption.

Four Florida Cubans died when their plane was shot down by aircraft from the island. They were members of the organization Brothers to the Rescue; all but one were Catholic. Bishop Agustin Román preached at their funeral.

Poet, archivist, and premier historian of New Mexico's Catholics, Fray Angélico Chavez died; he was the first native Hispanic of New Mexico ordained as a Franciscan. See Robert Wright's "In Memoriam" in *Catholic Southwest*.

Auxiliary Bishop Armando Ochoa was named ordinary of El Paso, Texas. The auxiliary of San Bernardino, California, Gerald Barnes, became ordinary of that diocese. He is also the new chair of the Bishops' Committee for Hispanic Affairs. Emilio Allué, S.D.B., was made auxiliary bishop of Boston. This brings to twenty two the number of Hispanic bishops; nine are ordinaries. Joining the Committee for Hispanic Affairs is Alejandro Aguillera-Titus. On 10 June in Corpus Christi, the committee held a meeting with all the regional directors of Hispanic ministry. The September issue of *En Marcha* carries a full report.

The Bishops' Committee for Hispanic Affairs published a document on small Christian communities, "Communion and Mission" (*Origins*, 25 January). The attorney general of Texas investigated Corpus Christi's Bishop Rene Gracida for misusing funds from the Kennedy Memorial Foundation. Later that diocese, which does not admit guilt, began to downsize in order to be less dependent on these moneys. San Antonio's Patricia Flores is involved in a new vocation outreach called Project Andrew, and in an endeavor to get gang members to freely exchange their guns for musical instruments. The late Cardinal Joseph Bernardin included concern for Hispanic Catholics as one of the urgent items in the Common Ground project.

This concern is well grounded. Parts of the Church's ministry to Hispanics atrophy. The Midwest Hispanic Catholic Commission closed. Among other things this meant canceling a Koch Foundation grant aimed at youth ministry—this when a recent study shows the need of programs aimed at the specific needs of Hispanic youth (VC, 20 September). Only four of the original eight regional offices of Hispanic ministry still function, and in some areas more than half of the diocesan offices for Hispanics have been closed.

Although the last twenty five years have seen a boom in the Hispanic population and a plethora of official position papers, "there is a gap between rhetoric and reality," says the *Christian Century* of 3 April. The NCR (29 March) reports some good news from Catholic schools. National Hispanic enrollment rose to 10.6 percent of the total (VC, 23 August). The University of St. Thomas in Miami, Florida, received $500,000 and recognition by Hispanic Outlook in Higher Education as notable for its service to Hispanics. Three schools have begun new Latino programs. The Oblate School of Theology (San Antonio) and Drew University offer doctor of ministry programs with a concentration in Hispanic ministry. And the Catholic University of America offers a new master of divinity degree with a similar emphasis.

## National Organizations

The Academy of Catholic Hispanic Theologians of the United States (ACHTUS) held its ninth annual colloquium in San Diego in June. Presenters included Allan Figueroa Deck, S.J., Milagros Peña, and María Pilar Aquino. Newly elected president Gary Riebe-Estrella, S.V.D., also spoke. The Virgilio Elizondo award went to Roberto Goizueta and the ACHTUS award to Lilly Endowment along with Olga Villa Parra.

In Houston, La Asociación Nacional de Diaconos Hispanos held its twelfth annual conference, called Diaconado Hispano Hacía el Tercer Milenio. The Asociación National de Sacerdotes Hispanos committed itself to ecumenism and the education of the laity in the Church's social-justice teaching (VD, 7 January). Its new president, José Gómez, led the seventh convention in Santa Rosa, California. Speakers included Allan F. Deck, S.J., and Bishop Placido Rodriguez. Information on its news-letter and other services is available via http://www.christus-rex.org/www1/NAHP/NAHP-index.html.

The Catholic Migrant Farm worker Network met in April to plan action steps based on its national consultation last year (VD, 14 January). The new president is María Marquez (NCR, 6 July) and the new executive director, Celine Caufield. Its new address is 1915 University Drive; Boise, Idaho 83706. Charis Missions held its twelfth annual charismatic conference in July. The fourteenth Encuentro Latino Internacional de Jovenes was celebrated 3–5 May in Los Angeles. Besides its annual evangelization school and conference for priests and religious, it puts out a newsletter that reaches over 25,000 people.

The Conference of Religious for Hispanic Ministry (CORHIM) publicized its 1997 seminar to be held 27 July–15 August in Sierra Madre, California. Information is available from the executive director, Clemente Barrón cp, at 700 Waverly; San Antonio, Texas 78201. Thirty representatives of CRECED (Comunidades de Reflexión Cubana en la Diáspora) met in Miami to analyze the current reality of Cubans and to plan an evangelization outreach for the year 2000. The Federación de Institutos Pastorales published a bilingual guide for pastoral institutes. For a copy, fax 305–279–0925.

The Hispanic Telecommunications Network announced new members of its governing board, among them Domingo Rodríguez, S.T., and Helen Mónica Vásquez. They cooperated with Maryknoll World Productions to produce English and Spanish programs, and with the Faith and Values channel to produce Our Family, a three part series on the human face of immigration. María de la Cruz Aymes is consulted on their catechetical programming.

LAS HERMANAS are already acting upon their desire to increase membership and fund raising. The archives at Our Lady of the Lake University in San Antonio, and their newsletter, provide invaluable historical and contemporary documentation of the contributions of Latinas. Instituto Fe y Vida held "Symposium: Sharing a Vision of Hope" in Moraga, California, June 30–July 7. Forty youth ministers gathered for training in small communities led by Dr. Richard Wood, Sister Dolores Díaz de Sollano, Dr. Carmen María Cervantes, and others.

The Instituto de Liturgia Hispana responded energetically to a loss of grant income. Among future activities are a cooperative colloquium with Catholic University and the publication of a book through the J.S. Paluch Company. The Mexican American Cultural Center (MACC) received grants for two new positions filled by Rudy Vela, S.M., and Irma Nolla. It also began fund raising for a new building. Anita de Luna, M.D.C.P., and Deacon Juan Barajas were among their summer faculty. MACC's Roberto Piña and Father Clarence Williams continue to successfully promote dialogue between African-American and Hispanic Catholics and now are extending that exchange to non-Catholic persons of color. In 1996 MACC initiated its silver jubilee, conducted a national survey on diocesan Hispanic ministry, and was chosen as a training location by the Center of Philanthropy.

The National Catholic Association of Diocesan Directors for Hispanic Ministry met 23–26 June 1996 in Denver. In meetings with the Bishops' Committee for Hispanic Affairs, they discussed how to continue to coordinate regional efforts in areas which no longer have regional offices. The National Catholic Council for Hispanic Ministry (NCCHM) convened the national congress, "Raices y Alas," in Chicago in August with 722 participants from the 56 national organizations. The keynote speaker, Marcelo Acevedo, S.J., set the tone for the nineteen leadership workshops. At the awards ceremony Cardinal Roger Mahoney and Mrs. Olga Villa Parra were honored for their faithful service to Latinos/as. A good summary (despite minor errors) is in Tim Unsworth's column (NCR, 6 September).

Thanks to a Lilly Endowment grant of $720,000, Adela Flores Gallegos will continue to direct the Leadership Development Initiative. A similar grant made possible the hiring of Armando Contreras as a development associate. Additionally, the NCCHM Congress invited youth and campus ministry leaders from around the country to consider founding a network of Catholic Latino/a youth and young adult ministry. They accepted, and NCCHM has provided funding for a future meeting to build upon this beginning.

PARAL continues a series of regional workshops and presented panels at the conferences of the Society for the Scientific Study of Religion and the Religious Research Association. PARAL has begun publishing a newsletter and occasional papers such as "Gender and the Politics of Location in Popular Religion" and, from *A Marginal Jew*, "Miracles and Modern Minds." *Hispanic Link* (15 January) featured its president, Anthony Stevens-Arroyo. The National Organization of Catechesis for Hispanics (NOCH) held its tenth annual conference in Detroit 25–27 February. The keynote speaker was Dolores Díaz de Sollano. NOCH was awarded the F. Sadlier Dinger award for its catechetical leadership. RECOSS met with Californian legislators as part of its move to act more assertively in the political sphere (HC, 24 March).

The Southeast Pastoral Institute hosted 160 young people on 10 February for its Pascua Juvenil. For the book *Sexualidad Humana* (and other publications), call 305–279–2333. It has also continued its outreach to migrants with a leadership formation workshop in St. Augustine, Florida.

## Resources

Oregon Catholic Press (OCP) published Jaime Cortez's *Spanish Litany of Saints* and his bilingual tape/CD *Rain Down*. He also collaborated with Bob Hurd to produce the bilingual *We Are the Body of Christ*. Each has instrumental accompaniment books. In Spanish, OCP offers a new tape/CD and accompaniment book by Tres Con Fe, and the Psalms set to guitar music by Armida Grajeda. Call 800–548–8749. Resource Publications offers a new bilingual parish handout, "Celebrating the Lectionary" (800–736–7600). New paraliturgical resources include *Emmanuel* magazine's *Way of the Cross* (216–449–2103).

The Public Broadcasting System released a series, now on video, of the Mexican American civil rights movement. Narrated by Henry Cisneros, it includes excerpts of César Chávez, 1965–1975. Also worthwhile is Public Radio's Latino USA. Sheed and Ward offers two new videos on Hispanic ministry and a multitude of print titles (800–333–7373). A video for training and spirituality in Spanish is available from the National Catholic Conference for Total Stewardship (800–572–2250).

*Catechetical Sunday* is an entire package of bilingual materials available through the United States Catholic Conference (800–235–8722). Also of interest are the age-appropriate lesson plans that explain the causes of immigration: *Reflections on Understanding and Welcoming Immigrants and Refugees*. En Marcha lists many other important new titles produced this year, including ones on domestic violence (*Cuando Pido Ayuda*) and *Small Church Communities* (#5–007), both available from 202–541–3212. Liguori (800–325–9521, ext. 522) offers two new booklets on sacraments in Spanish. Another good source for books and videos is Pauline Books and Media (800–876–4463).

*Valores para Jovenes* is a series of booklets published by the Diocese of Arlington, Virginia, and available through 703–524–2122. Other youth and children's resources include: Sadlier's bilingual books for First Communion and Reconciliation, 800–582–5437; small group material by the Diocese of Yakima, Washington, and available for $3 from Robert Fontan at 5301 B–Tieton Drive/Yakima, Washington 98908; Claretian Publications' bilingual, bicultural catechism program for children, Amigos de Jesus, 800–328–6515. Mexico's Fernández Publishing Company is breaking into the United States market using 800–814–8080; another newcomer is Prayer in the World Press, which does bilingual publishing for the domestic church and is at 619–582–9207; St. Mary's Press continues its unparalleled commitment to Hispanic youth ministry with *Dawn on the Horizon*. Published in English and Spanish, it seeks to foster small faith communities. Call 800–533–8095. The USCC Office for the Pastoral Care of Migrants and Refugees has a new publication about the Church's social teaching: *Who Are My Brothers and Sisters? A Catholic Educational Guide for Understanding and Welcoming Immigrants and Refugees*; call 800–235–8722.

The diverse information contained in Telemundo's newsletter *Hispanic Market Update* may interest scholars. While aimed at businesses, it provides much information on home ownership income and other often overlooked but important data. Also, Dean Hoge has embarked on a new study of United States young Catholic adults, including Latinas/os. A completed study of Catholic youth by the Center for Applied Research in the Apostolate (CARA) shows that Hispanics are more sensitive to cultural and moral issues than their Anglo counterparts. Contact CARA at Georgetown University for details.

New scholarship money is available from the Hispanic Theological Initiative. The Pew Charitable Trust granted the money in response to a study led by Edwin Hernández Ph.D. Information is available from Daisy Machado at 888–441–4785. A new edition of Lorayne Horka's *Los Hermanos Penitentes* is available from Horka Publications in Santa Monica, California. Several articles in the summer 1996 issue of United States Catholic Historian deal at least briefly with Latino/a issues.

## Significant Writings

Alvarez, Carmelo E. "Ecumenism in Transition? Hispanic Responses from the United States." *Journal of Hispanic/Latino Theology* (hereafter JHLT) 4, no. 2 (November, 1996): 60–74. The present moment in United States Hispanic theology constitutes a kairos for ecumenism because of concerns for the relationship between faith and justice.

Aquino, María Pilar. "The Collective 'Discovery' of Our Own Power: Latina American Feminist Theology." In *Hispanic/Latino Theology: Challenge and Promise*, eds. Ada María Isasi-Díaz and Fernando F. Segovia (hereafter *Hispanic/Latino Theology*, eds. Isasi-Díaz and Segovia), 240–258. Minneapolis: Fortress Press, 1996. Seeks "to examine briefly the sociocultural context of Latin American feminist theology . . . and to explore some characteristics of this theology."

_____. "Economic Violence in Latin American Perspective." In *Women Resisting Violence: Spirituality for Life*, eds. Mary John Mananzan, Mercy Amba Oduyoye, Elsa Tamez, J. Shannon Clarkson, Mary C. Grey, and Letty M. Russell, 100–108. Maryknoll: Orbis Books, 1996. Discusses "three major concerns: The violent nature of the current economic system; the framework of the free market economic model; and the sharing of a common theological agenda rooted in justice, integrity, and the well-being of all women."

Barrón, Clemente, C.P. "Racism and Religious Life." *Review for Religious* 55, no. 5 (September–October, 1996): 494–505. A personal reflection on racism in church and society calls for continued dialogue, solidarity, and the building of alliances to root out this institutionalized prejudice.

Cadena, Gilbert R. "The Social Location of Liberation Theology: From Latin America to the United States." In *Hispanic/Latino Theology*, eds. Isasi-Díaz and Segovia, 167–182. "Grounds the current theological discourse of liberation theology within a sociohistorical context . . . [comparing] Latin American and United States Latino theologies by briefly highlighting the social forces contributing to these theological movements."

Cadena, Gilbert R., and Lara Medina. "Liberation Theology and Social Change: Chicanas and Chicanos in the Catholic Church." *In Chicanas and Chicanos in Contemporary Society*, ed. Roberto M. deAnda, 99–111. Boston: Allyn and Bacon, 1996. "Discusses the changing demographics of Catholics, theories of religion and social change, liberation theology, and focus on a base community as an example of organizing within the socioreligious sphere." Good example of the continuing dialogue between social science and theology.

Castillo, Ana. *Goddess of the Americans: Writings on the Virgin of Guadalupe*. New York: Riverhead Books, 1996. Reprints of Richard Rodriguez, Jeannette Rodriguez, and others. Excellent example of supposedly secular authors engaging religious symbolism: "an unorthodox rosary . . . Many contributors, for all their renown, were very hesitant, even nervous about discussing their love of Our Mother. . . ."

Carrasco, David. "Those Who Go on a Sacred Journey: The Shapes and Diversity of Pilgrimages." *Concilium* 4 (1996): 13–24. Drawing on Victor Turner's thought, shows pilgrimage similarities among different cultures.

D'Antonio, William V., et al., eds. *Laity: American Catholics Transforming the Church*. Kansas City, Missouri: Sheed and Ward, 1996. Chapter Nine deals with Latinos and compares them with other Catholics. Although demographically distinct, on church issues Latinos are not very different. Good survey of studies to date.

Davis, Kenneth G. "Las Bodas de Plata de Una Lluvia de Oro," *Revista Latinoamericana de Teologia* 12, no. 37 (April, 1996): 79–91. An overview of the last quarter century of United States Hispanic Catholic theology.

Davis, Kenneth G., with Philip Lampe Ph.D. "The Attraction and Retention of Hispanics to Doctor of Ministry Programs," *Theological Education* (1996). Pagination not available at press time. Based on a Pew Endowment study headed by Edwin Hernández, this first publication on the results looks at Latinos in

D.Min. programs accredited by the Association of Theological Schools.

Deck, Allan Figueroa, S.J. "Hispanic Catholic Prayer and Worship." In *Alabadle! Hispanic Christian Worship*, ed. Justo L. González, 29–41. Nashville: Abingdon Press, 1996. Written from the perspective of Hispanic Catholics, this contribution to an important ecumenical effort highlights the importance of popular Catholicism. Honest and challenging in its criticism of both Catholic and Protestant pastoralists.

Díaz-Stevens, Ana María. "Aspects of Puerto Rican Religious Experience: A Sociohistorical Overview." In *Latinos in New York: Communities in Transition*, eds. Gabriel Haslip-Viera and Sherrie L. Baver, 159–164. Notre Dame: Notre Dame University Press, 1996. Excellent overview of the cutting edge of church history on the island. Outlines very pertinent pastoral ramifications.

_____. "In the Image and Likeness: Literature as Theological Reflection." In *Hispanic/Latino Theology*, eds. Isasi-Díaz and Segovia, 86–103. Has "recourse to Lukács's concepts of reification and Aufhebung as well as his understanding of the role of artists in society in order to cast light on religious reflections embodied in some samples of Hispanic literature."

Elizondo, Virgil P. "Sanación y Liberación Pentecostales: Respuesta de la Teología de la Liberación." In *Concilium* (June 1996): 481–487. Brief explanation of parallels and differences between these two movements, arguing that they both spring from and serve the poor through the action of the Holy Spirit.

_____. "Pastoral Opportunities of Pilgrimages." *Concilium* 4 (1996): 107–114. The coeditor of this issue presents some worthwhile practical points on pilgrimages' potential for spiritual growth.

Espín, Orlando O. "A Multi-cultural Church? Theological Reflections from Below." In *The Multi-cultural Church: A New Landscape in U.S. Theologies*, ed. William Cenkner (hereafter *Multi-cultural Church*, ed. Cenkner), 54–71. New York: Paulist Press, 1996. In the words of the book's editor, Espín "dissuades us from using the term multi-cultural and equally cautions against the reification of culture and experience, especially when outsiders define such terms."

_____. "Popular Catholicism: Alienation or Hope?" In *Hispanic/Latino Theology*, eds. Isasi-Díaz and Segovia, 307–324. Sees alienation because current cultural hegemony can maintain Latino subaltern status in society. But also finds hope because popular Catholicism offers "some of the most powerful and culturally authentic arguments and motives for social protagonism."

Fernández, Eduardo C., S.J. "La realidad latina en los EEUU: Sombras y luces." In *Reflexiones Catequéticas: Encuentro de San Antonio, Texas, Julio, 1995*, ed. Roberto Viola, S.J., 175–179. Bogota, 1996. Delivered in July 1995 at an international gathering of catechetical experts from both Latin America and the United States, this essay is a personal reflection on the "shadows and lights" of the United States Latino reality.

García-Rivera, Alejandro Roberto. "Border Crossings." *Momentum* 27, no. 2 (April/May, 1996): 42–44. Suggests a theology of "creature-liness," with the life of St. Martin de Porres as a model for embracing diverse ethnicities, races, and religions.

_____. "Creator of the Visible and the Invisible: Liberation Theology, Postmodernism, and the Spiritual." *JHLT* 3, no. 4 (May, 1996): 35–56. Proposes biblical wisdom literature and the use of an aesthetic semiotic stemming from some forgotten thinkers of early Iberian philosophy as resources for engaging these different philosophical and theological elements.

_____. "The 'Pilgrim Church' of Vatican II: A Tale of Two Altars." *Concilium* 4 (1996): 92–103. Excellent use of images to present pre- and post-Vatican II views. Goes beyond a caricature.

Goizueta, Roberto S. "In Defense of Reason." *JHLT* 3, no. 3 (February, 1996): 16–26. Continues the dialogue between United States Hispanic theology and both modern and postmodern philosophical thought. Concerned that Latinos are either stereotyped as being simply emotional (and therefore "irrational") or simplistically romanticized. Concludes that new Latino theologies must seize the challenge of articulating the rationality present in Hispanic culture and religion.

_____. "Bartolomé de Las Casas, Modern Critic of Modernity: An Analysis of a Conversion." *JHLT* 3, no. 4 (May, 1996): 6–19. Draws on Las Casas as seen by O'Gorman, Dussel, and Gutiérrez. The introduction states its major argument: "Unless we couple our understanding of Las Casas to rational universalism with his conversion and, most importantly, his praxis of solidarity, we fail to see the ways in which his conversion to the other is a 'conversion to the other in our world' and not some 'abstract' Other."

_____. "Response to Peter C. Phan." In *Multi-cultural Church*, ed. Cenkner, 131–139. Concludes, "In what we have come to call our post-modern world, we can no longer look exclusively to western social science and theology. That is both the challenge and the promise of our task. It is a challenge presented not only to United States Hispanic theology but to so-called contextual theologies as a whole."

_____. "U.S. Hispanic Popular Catholicism as Theopoetics." In *Hispanic/Latino Theology*, ed. Isasi-Díaz and Segovia, 261–288. Explores "the relationship between praxis, *theopoesis*, theology, and ethics as it manifests itself in United States Hispanic popular religiosity and, specifically, popular Catholicism.

Gómez, Raúl. "Professing Unity in Faith and Love: Hispano-Mozarabic Diptychs." *Liturgy* 13, no. 1 (1996): 60–63. Describes the recent revival (1992) of this ancient rite after nine centuries of suppression.

Gomez-Kelly, Sally. "Pointers for Pastoral Care: Ministering with the Hispanic Community." *AIM: Liturgy Resources* 14, no. 1 (Spring, 1996): 6–8. Summarizes some critical points which non-Hispanics should particularly be sensitive to when "ministering with and among the Hispanic community" in contrast to "ministering to the Hispanic community."

González, Rev. Robert A. "The Mariology of the *Nican Mopohua*." *Josephinum Journal of Theology* 3, no. 1 (Winter/Spring, 1996): 42–55. Mentions some anthropological aspects found in Aztec religion and culture which help explain the relation between traditional Mariology and the Guadalupan apparitions in sixteenth century Mexico. Disappointing in that it does not even mention the large amount of recent controversial material presented by such persons as Jacques Lafaye and Stafford Poole, which raises some serious doubts about his conclusions.

Gros, Jeffrey, F.S.C. "An Agenda for the Unity of the Church in the Western Hemisphere: Encounter with the Living Christ: The Way to Conversion, Communion, and Solidarity in America." *JHLT* 4, no. 2 (November, 1996): 6–33. Outlines recent initiatives between United States and Latin American Bishops' Conferences, as well as ecumenical priorities and accomplishments, in preparation for the Special Assembly for America of the Synod of Bishops in the year 2000. A well documented overview.

Herrera, Marina. "Response to M. Shawn Copeland." In *Multi-cultural Church*, ed. Cenkner, 24–34. Not only describes an important part of Herrera's theological journey, but also poses some challenging issues for the United States Church. As the first Latina to begin publishing (1974), her words are worth noting.

Isasi-Díaz, Ada María. *Mujerista Theology: A Theology for the Twenty First Century*. Maryknoll: Orbis Books, 1996. A collection of her essays published within the last decade, many of which she revised for this volume. Chapter Four, a new composition, is a summary of what she means by *mujerista theology*. Her introduction is a good road map to her work.

_____. "*Un poquito de justicia*—A Little Bit of Justice." In *Hispanic/Latino Theology*, ed. Isasi-Díaz and Segovia, 325–339. Describes *mujerista* theology, which takes as its starting point the cries against injustice of grass roots Latinas and proceeds to describe five modes of oppression. Moves to a *mujerista* account of justice.

_____. "Afterwords: Strangers No Longer." In *Hispanic/Latino Theology*, eds. Isasi-Díaz and Segovia, 367–374. Concludes the collection of essays on United States Hispanic/Latino Theology with the following observation: "Reading through these essays one can arrive at three conclusions about our young theology: It is a discourse that has attained a surprising maturity in a very short period of time; it is an ecumenical enterprise; it as a participatory theology, a theology of and by the community."

_____. "The Present-Future of EATWOT: A Mujerista Perspective." *Voices from the Third World* 19, no. 1 (June, 1996): 86–103. While appreciating this ecumenical group, the author begins with the criticism that it has not yet fully incorporated women into the group's theological dialogue. Offers three priorities for remedying this situation. See the response by J.B. Banawiratma.

_____. "Economic Violence against Minority Women in the USA." In *Women Resisting Violence: Spirituality for Life*, eds. Mary John Mananzan, Mercy Amba Oduyoye, Elsa Tamez, J. Shannon Clarkson, Mary C. Grey, and Letty M. Russell, 89–99. Maryknoll: Orbis Books, 1996. Argues convincingly that "most of the strategies of exploitation and domination that the USA uses in third world countries are first 'practiced' on us, the minority groups in the USA." Having given a good general description of minority women in the country, ends with some theo-ethical considerations.

López, José. "The Liturgical Year and Hispanic Customs." *AIM: Liturgy Resources* 14, no. 2 (Summer, 1996): 6–10. Good brief overview of various Hispanic customs and their relation to the liturgical year. Tries to get the pastoral agent to be sensitive to the stories behind these peoples or celebrations and to keep in mind the diversity that exists among various Hispanic communities.

Maduro, Otto. "Notes toward a Sociology of Latina/o Religious Empowerment." In *Hispanic/Latino Theology*, eds. Isasi-Díaz and Segovia, 151–166. Shares "some concepts, hypotheses, and modes of thought taken from the sociology of religions that . . . may prove stimulating, fertile, and thought-provoking in attempting to answer" questions about the relationship between one's religion and one's socioeconomic position in society.

Matovina, Timothy M. "Marriage Celebrations in Mexican American Communities." *Liturgical Ministry* 5 (Winter, 1996): 22–26. An excellent overview of Mexican American marriage celebrations. Valuable in that it relates the official to the popular, the current practice to the historical origins, and the theoretical to the practical.

_____. "Guadalupan Devotion in a Borderlands Community." *JHLT* 4, no. 1 (August, 1996): 6–26. Using the cathedral of San Fernando in San Antonio, Texas, "demonstrates that faith expressions can function both as a symbol of group cohesion and as a symbol of ethnic legitimation, and of resistance to the diminishment of a people's religious and cultural heritage." Uses incredible historical detail to illustrate the former.

_____. "Between Two Worlds." In *Delano Journey, 1770–1850*, ed. Gerald E. Poyo, 73–87. Austin: University of Texas Press, 1996. Although only a small section of this chapter is devoted to the role of religion during the time of the transformation of Texas from a

Hispanic entity into a United States one, argues convincingly that native San Antonio Tejanos underwent a process of accommodation and at the same time resistance to the Anglo-American invasion. Crucial to this resistance and therefore to the survival of Mexican culture were the popular religious celebrations, especially those around the feast of Our Lady of Guadalupe.

McNally, Michael. "Presence and Persistence: Catholicism among Latins in Tampa's Ybor City, 1885–1985." *U.S. Catholic Historian* 14, no. 2 (Spring, 1996): 73–91. "Explores the perceived 'problematic' character of the Latins of Ybor City [a cigar making town] and the changing relationship of Ybor City's Hispanics to their religious tradition, Catholicism, and its local expression, the parish, over a hundred year period." One of the best recent examples of the different types of operative Catholicism.

Mendieta, Eduardo. "From Christendom to Polycentric Oikonumé: Modernity, Postmodernity, and Liberation Theology." *JHLT* 3, no. 4 (May, 1996): 57–76. Reflects on the links as well as on the differences between the Judeo-Christian tradition and postmodernism; then looks at the relevance of liberation theology.

Mordey, Aurora. "Spanish Language Instruction at St. John's Seminary." *Seminary Journal* 2, no. 2 (Fall, 1996): 42–47. Describes a concrete learning program being used in this large seminary outside of Los Angeles to teach not only language skills, but also the wider Latino culture. One of the major pluses of the program is that it is tailored to pastoral needs.

Pineda, Ana María. "The Colloquies and Theological Discourse: Culture as a Locus for Theology." *JHLT* 3, no. 3 (February, 1996): 27–42. Opens with the 1524 theological colloquies between twelve Franciscan friars and indigenous Aztec sages, demonstrating why it was so difficult for each side to understand the other. Good summary of how the relationship between faith and culture operates in United States Hispanic theology.

_____. "In the Image and Likeness: Literature as Theological Reflection." In *Hispanic/Latino Theology*, eds. Isasi-Díaz and Segovia, 104–116. "Examine[s] the dynamics of the oral tradition of the Mesoamerican world in order to suggest ways in which the oral tradition continues to play a vital role in the forging of the United States Hispanic/Latino identity."

Riebe-Estrella, Gary. "American Cultural Shifts: Formation for Which Candidates? For Which Church?" In *Seminary Journal* 2, no. 2 (Fall, 1996): 27–33. "Given our concrete context today, might we not do better to see seminary formation as the business of forming pastors, rather than as the business of forming priests?" Calls for a sustained conversation between the seminarian, his seminary community, the Christian tradition, and the current cultural context of contemporary American society. A superb application of what a more contextual theology might look like in a seminary environment.

_____. "Movement from Monocultural to Multi-cultural Congregations." *Review for Religious* 55, no. 5 (September–October, 1996): 507–520. Challenges the simplistic notion that United States culture is moving from being mono-cultural to multi-cultural. Argues that, "historically, what appears to be a tolerance for cultural difference has often masked an attitude of cultural imposition." Good clear examples of existing racism; advocates a move beyond multiculturalism, which often does not bridge communities, to a more gospel centered paradigm.

_____. "Sangre llama a sangre: Cultural Memory as a Source of Theological Insight." In *Hispanic/Latino Theology*, eds. Isasi-Díaz and Segovia, 117–133. Pursues the concept of "cultural memory, of blood calling out to blood, by focusing on the image of Our Lady of Guadalupe as a salient example of this *something* that allows one access to the affective level, that surges up without rational trappings, that bears its own truth."

Rubio, José A. "El Cristo Latinoamericano." *Living Light* 33, no. 1 (Fall, 1996): 30–34. A reflection on the realistic suffering Christ of Hispanic art, which "represents [the] oppressed status [of] a conquered people."

Ruiz, Jean-Pierre. "Naming the Other: U.S. Hispanic Catholics, the So-Called 'Sects,' and the 'New Evangelization.'" *JHLT* 4, no. 2 (November, 1996): 34–59. "Examines several ways in which the New Evangelization has been understood [theologically] and implemented [pastorally] with regard to the United States Hispanic context." Demonstrates how even the terms we use when speaking about others can unsettle unity and evangelization. Definitely moves the ecumenical discussion a step forward.

San Pedro, Bishop Enrique, S.J. "The Pastor and the Theologian." In
*Multi-cultural Church*, ed. Cenkner, 140–151. The late bishop of
Brownsville, in attempting to describe the normative relationship
between the two entities involved, tackles two questions: What is
Catholic? and What is Catholic theology? His perspective,
substantiated solidly in official Church teaching, needs, however, to
be complemented, according to responder Edward Branch, by "a
perspective from below," that is, one which takes into account
"grass roots imperatives occasioned by our social and spiritual
history."

Segovia, Fernando F. "Aliens in the Promised Land: The Manifest
Destiny of U.S. Hispanic American Theology." In *Hispanic/Latino
Theology*, eds. Isasi-Díaz and Segovia, 15–42. One of the first
theologians to begin to describe the movement known as United
States Hispanic theology. Further develops ideas presented in 1991
article, maintaining that the movement will only continue.

_____. "In the World but Not of It: Exile as a Locus for a Theology of
the Diaspora." In *Hispanic/Latino Theology*, ed. Isasi-Díaz and
Segovia, 195–217. Begins formulating a variation of United States
Hispanic theology: "a theological tradition or accent that grows out
of, reflects, and engages my social location within the United States
Hispanic American reality and experience . . . a theology of the
diaspora, a theology born and forged in exile."

Sosa, Juan J. "Hispanic Weddings: A Family Affair." *Liturgy y Canción*
7, no. 3 (1996): 5–13. Defends the current practice of adapting the
Roman rite to the Hispanic reality by giving examples of the historic
diversity of the marriage rite. Written in both Spanish and English,
ends with some helpful recommendations for those involved in
marriage planning.

Stevens-Arroyo, Anthony M. "Juan Mateo Guaticabanú: The First to Be
Baptized in America." *Apuntes* 16, no. 3 (Fall, 1996): 67–77.
Relates a little known historical fact: That the first American convert
and martyr was this Taino Indian from the island of La Española.
Using substantial historical records to describe the political climate
of the time, presents a nuanced picture of the early evangelization
in this part of the Americas.

_____. "Puerto Rican Struggles in the Catholic Church." In *Historical
Perspectives on Puerto Rican Survival in the United States*, eds.

Clara E. Rodríguez and Virginia Sánchez Korrol, 155–165. Princeton: Markus Wiener Publishers, 1996. Originally formed part of the collection known as The Puerto Rican Struggle, 1984. Encouraging to see that such an essential topic of religion was not overlooked in the focus areas chosen. As the introduction suggests, this work broke new ground and much has happened since then to further the study of Puerto Ricans and religion.

Stiefvater, Robert X. "Que Viva Cristo Rey! Long Live Christ the King." *Liturgy* 13, no. 2 (1996): 28–33. A brief summary of the history of the "Cristero" Rebellion, illustrates why the Feast of Christ the King is so important in Mexico today. "Given this context the feast's liturgical prayers reflect the uniquely Hispanic sensitivity to the role of suffering in life and its ultimate vindication through heavenly justice."

Torres, Luis. *Voices from the San Antonio Missions*. Lubbock: Texas Tech Press, 1996. Published but not available at press time.

Tweed, Thomas A. "Identity and Authority at a Cuban Shrine in Miami: Santería, Catholicism, and Struggles for Religious Identity." *JHLT* 4, no. 1 (August, 1996): 27–48. Studies devotion at the shrine of Our Lady of Charity in Miami. "Argues for a view of cultural/ national and religious identity that is the ever changing product of contest and negotiation among competing understandings of what it means (in this case) to be Cuban American, and/or Catholic." A fascinating introduction to some aspects of Santería within a Catholic context. Understandably controversial.

United States Catholic Conference, Department of Education. *The Hispanic Experience in the United States: Pastoral Reflections Using the Catechism of the Catholic Church,* 1996. A bilingual pamphlet with bibliography. A brief introduction to the reality of United States Hispanics followed by a general introduction of the *Catechism*. Closes with a suggested format for adapting the latter to the former.

Vidal, Jaime R. "Pilgrimage in the Christian Tradition." *Concilium* 4 (1996): 35–47. Having provided a good historical background, including some facts not commonly known, examines some of the tensions that have existed around this tradition.

## New Books

This year's books related to United States Hispanic Catholics are quite varied. Most are not specifically theological, yet they offer an opportunity for theology to dialogue with the social sciences. That is, they address in some form the theology or religion of Latinos from the perspective of their own disciplines, for example, history, anthropology, and psychology. Of course, these disciplines overlap; nonetheless, the fact that they all somehow treat the role of religion is significant, for it means that the conversation between theology and other disciplines is constantly expanding.

Both *The Multi-cultural Church: A New Landscape in U.S. Theologies* (Paulist Press, $14.95), ed. William Cenkner, and *Hispanic-Latino Theology: Challenge and Promise* (Fortress, $25), eds. Ada María Isasi-Díaz and Fernando F. Segovia, stem from recent theological symposiums. More detailed summaries of the writings of United States Latinos/as included appear in this article's annotated bibliography. Jeannette Rodriguez's *Stories We Live: Cuentos Que Vivimos* (Paulist Press, $5.95) contains a selection from over one hundred stories gathered from Latinas. Having contextualized the role of experience in our theologizing, she integrates theory and practice. For the most part, the stories are quite good, as they reveal significant values such as hospitality, family, trust in God and Mary. The vibrant testimonies reveal an image of a God who saves us from isolation.

A more local history, *The New History of Florida*, ed. Michael Gannon (University Press of Florida, $34.95), is the first comprehensive history of the state written in a quarter century. The various authors not only present political, economic, military, and religious information, but also include social history and personal experiences. Particularly relevant to Catholicism are "First European Contacts" by the editor and "The Missions of Spanish Florida" by John H. Hann. The illustrations and bibliography help make it a valuable resource.

Also locally focused are the entries concerning Texan Catholics, many of whom are Latinos, found in the six volumes of *The New Handbook of Texas* (Texas State Historical Association). This completely revised major encyclopedic reference on Texas history contains more than 300 articles specifically dedicated to Catholic institutions, agencies, and persons. Father Robert Wright, of the Oblate School of Theology, contributed eleven articles, including the overview essays on the Catholic Church in Texas, the Spanish missions in Texas, and the Catholic diocesan church of Spanish and Mexican Texas. The editors' effort to include more on Hispanic and women's topics has led to other informative Catholic items. Additional articles on Mexican Catholic topics (all by Teresa Palomo Acosta) are Home Altars, Mexican-American Folk Arts and Crafts, Nuestra Senora de Guadalupe, Sociedades Guadalupanas, and the Bishops' Committee for Hispanic Affairs.

Largely responsible for the present theological revival in popular religion, anthropologists continue to produce studies that have Latino religious practices as their focus. Eugenio Matibag's *Afro-Cuban Religious Experience: Cultural Reflections in Narrative* (University Press of Florida, $49.95), using printed literature, explores various blends of Catholicism and African religions.

In *The Matachines Dance* (University of New Mexico Press, $25), Sylvia Rodríguez explores a folk dance that derives from a genre of medieval European folk dramas symbolizing conflict between Christians and Moors. It was brought to the Americas as a vehicle for Christianizing the Indians. Rodríguez, an anthropologist of northern New Mexico, explores how the dance, performed in many pueblos even today, reveals much more than the obvious. Her meticulous descriptions, together with many photographs, lead to an excellent final chapter in which one sees history, self-identity, economics, religion, and politics woven together. The work reveals the complex role that religion, especially in its popular manifestations, can play in a society. Also highlighted are the roles of humor, dance as worship, and the process of *mestizaje* (blending of races or cultures).

The *María Paradox: How Latinas Can Merge Old World Traditions with New World Self-Esteem* (G.P. Putnam's Sons, $22.95) by Rosa María Gil D.S.W. and Carmen Inoa Vázquez Ph.D. can be well classified as a psychological self-help work for the Latina in the United States. Its main question is simple: Can a Hispanic woman learn to skillfully steer a course through North American society without sacrificing the Latin tradition she treasures? The authors, drawing from endless examples of specific Latinas, answer a resounding yes. Among the book's positive qualities are its fine bibliography, its readability, and its practical methods for self-questioning and improvement. It should be applauded for tackling a very complex topic, cross-cultural sex roles, one which desperately needs to be addressed. It is a very valuable tool for pastoral agents, particularly non-Hispanics, because there is much in the culture that is not *said*, especially regarding sexuality. Both of the authors are immigrants, so they have experienced firsthand what they are talking about.

Problematic, however, are some definitions. *Marianismo* is said to characterize the attitude that comes from viewing the Virgin Mary as submissive and so forth. It seems that the authors never entertained the thought that Mary could also stand for empowerment, a basic tenet in the research of Jeannette Rodríguez. It would be interesting to hear more about the role religion plays in the sexual mores discussed, especially since much of Latino/a religious experience seems to be centered on women.

*This article originally appeared in Review for Religious Vol. 56 (1997) under the title, "U.S. Hispanic Catholics: Trends and Works 1996."*

# 1997 IN REVIEW

The most important events of 1997 may be the founding of the National Catholic Network de la Pastoral Juvenil Hispana (Hispanic youth ministry) and the United States bishops' call for a fourth *encuentro* (encounter or meeting). For the continuing authors of this article, the year's blessing was the collaboration of Verónica Méndez, R.C.D.

## Migrants and Immigrants

The face of immigration and the destination of migrants continues to change. Mayans from Guatemala work outside Phoenix, according to *El Visitante Dominical* (VD, 26 January, 1997). The *New York Times* (NYT, 29 February) reports that Dominicans are entering the United States at accelerating rates. On 4 February it said, "The dispersion of Mexicans into virtually all fifty states has increased since 1986 [and has] accelerated since the 1994 peso crisis." On 6 April it reported the increase of Central Americans in Miami's Little Havana. For instance, St. John Bosco Church, founded in 1963 for Cuban exiles, is now 68 percent Nicaraguan. This has caused some friction among Hispanic groups and also between Hispanics and native Blacks (NYT, 17 February). A good guide to Hispanic immigration is the magazine *Migrantes* (fax: 619–682–6358).

The Catholic Church is perhaps more publicly supportive of migrants and immigrants than ever before. On 30 March Cardinal Hickey of Washington, DC, directed that a letter denouncing the new federal immigration law be read from every pulpit. Other bishops did the same. The Migration and Refugee Services of the United States Catholic Bishops participated with others in an attempt to derail this legislation (VD, 19 March). The same paper documented the work of religious and diocesan personnel helping the undocumented in New York (23 February and 30 March). Other Catholic groups in Brooklyn (El Heraldo Católico, 23 February), Washington, DC (America, 19 April), and Texas (America, May 3) were similarly engaged (*National Catholic Reporter* [NCR], 17 January). Nevertheless, the most recent study by Michael

Foley reports that only twenty percent of Hispanic immigrants are touched by Catholic parishes.

Migrants most in the news were strawberry workers. The United Farm Workers, supported by many bishops such as Sylvester Ryan of Monterey, California, organized the 20,000 workers of this $550 million industry (NCR, 25 April). They also enjoyed the public support of the National Catholic Rural Life Conference. While Hispanics as a whole are the "poorest of the poor in the U.S." (NYT, 30 January), farm workers are particularly destitute. For 20 years their wages have not even kept pace with inflation (NYT, 31 March). For information from a pastoral perspective, listen to *Overheard* for January–February, 1997. Its July and September issues also included Latinos and Latinas.

## General Church News

Pedro Medina was first in the news because postponement of his execution came after pleas by the pope and Florida's bishops (NCR, 14 February). Later he made headlines when his face was incinerated during his electrocution (11 April). Texas executed Tristan Montoya. Better news came for Ricardo Aldape: He was freed after fifteen year old charges were dropped (VD, 4 May). Crime was also in the news when Father Rafael Marín León recounted the shootout in North Hollywood (VD, 20 April) and when Father Armando Martínez was murdered in New Mexico. Marines patrolling the United States-Mexican border shot and killed Ezequiel Hernández. The case is under investigation.

Natural death claimed Coca Cola CEO Roberto Goizueta, Sr.; San Antonio's representative in the United States Congress Frank M. Tejeda; Christian Brother James Bonilla; and Jorge Mas Canosa, the leader of the Cuban American National Foundation. Felix Varela, a Cuban priest who died in New York in 1853, and early missionary Junipero Serra were honored by United States postage stamps.

Henry Cisneros departed from the Clinton cabinet for the presidency of Univisión, but was later indicted for lying to the F.B.I. Federico Peña moved from the Department of Transportation to the Energy Department.

Good news for Catholic schools: Derek Neal's study of urban Catholic students says 91 percent of Hispanics graduated; 27 percent go on to college (*Crux*, 7 April). However, only 10 percent of Catholic school students are Hispanic, says La Voz Católica (VC, 22 August). All the more important, then, is the opening of a new Jesuit high school in

Chicago, Cristo Rey. Revista Maryknoll reported a new Montessori school opening in San Francisco parish of East Los Angeles.

Upon the retirement of Bishop Rene Gracida of Corpus Christi, Roberto González succeeded as ordinary. He was also elected chair of the bishops' committee on the Church in Latin America. He, Archbishop Patricio Flores (San Antonio), Ricardo Ramírez (Las Cruces, New Mexico), and Raymundo Peña (El Paso) were delegates to the Synod for America. Flores was also in the news for promoting Hispanic priestly vocations and addressing the international convention of Worldwide Marriage Encounter. Bishop Carlos Sevilla became the ordinary of Yakima, Washington. Gilberto Fernández was named auxiliary of the archdiocese of Miami. Ricardo García was named auxiliary bishop of Sacramento. Bishop Alvaro Corrada del Rio was named apostolic administrator of Caguas, Puerto Rico. The late Bishop Alphonse Gallegos was immortalized in a statue erected in his honor in Sacramento, California. And the archdiocese of Louisville, Kentucky, began an Hispanic apostolate.

Miami's auxiliary Bishop Augustin Roman is among many who refused to go along with a controversial plan to have Floridians participating in the pope's January 1998 visit to Cuba go there by chartered cruise ship. The plan was canceled, but others arranged to go by other means, considering their presence a way to support Cuba's Roman Catholic Church. Still others opposed any visits to Cuba at this time by any means of transportation whatever, thinking that such visits could only help Castro remain in power.

The November meeting of the country's bishops unanimously endorsed a fourth *encuentro* (national meeting) of Hispanic Catholics for the year 2000. They also elected El Paso's Bishop Armando Ochoa to head the Catholic legal immigration network. Later they approved a Spanish language sacramentary.

Other Hispanic Catholics in the news included: (1) Rosa María Sánchez, appointed the second executive director of the National Catholic Council for Hispanic Ministry; (2) Sisters Frances Felice Mojica and Rosa María Icaza and lay women Paulina Espinoza and Mary Frances Reza spoke at the Southwest Liturgical Conference; (3) Network's "Women of Justice" included Sister Petra Chávez and Ms. Delia Gómez; (4) Puerto Rican historian and political mentor Pilar Barbosa died; (5) Ada María Isasi-Díaz was among some thirty women who staged a walkout in favor of more discussion of gender issues by the Ecumenical Association of Third World Theologians, was appointed to the selection committee of the Grawemeyer Award, and spoke at

Lexington Theological Seminary; (6) Ana María Díaz-Stevens was awarded two grants by the Louisville Institute to study Catholic religious women in Puerto Rico; (7) María Pilar Aquino is now published in Portuguese and German, and she addressed the diocese of Fresno, California, the University of San Diego, St. Catherine's College, and the Catholic Theological Society of America; (8) Virgil Elizondo was awarded Notre Dame's Laetare Medal and the Quasten Medal of the Catholic University of America; (9) Ricardo Olvera was named editor of El Heraldo Católico. (10) Rudy Vela, Arturo Pérez Rodriguez, and Jaime Cortez spoke at the Southwest Liturgical Conference; (11) Anthony Stevens-Arroyo was named to the Board of the Pew Nexus project, delivered the Furfey lecture at the annual meeting of the Association for the Sociology of Religion, was twice featured in *Hispanic Link*, was named (with Ana María Díaz-Stevens) associate editor of the Macmillan Encyclopedia of Contemporary Religion, delivered a paper on Puerto Rican theology at a conference at the Universidad de Puerto Rico, and was recognized as a distinguished faculty member of the City University of New York; (12) Lara Medina and Segundo Pantoja were granted doctoral dissertation fellowships by the Louisville Institute; (13) the author of the 1964 *Misa Jibara*, William Loperena Soto, died in Bayamon, Puerto Rico; (14) Jaime Vidal, appointed professor of Catholic studies at Iowa State University, is the first Catholic Hispanic awarded an endowed chair at a public university in this country; (15) newly retired José Dimas Sobernal addressed the Centro de Estudios de los Dominicos del Caribe, the Congreso Historia y Sociologia de la Religión en Puerto Rico, the Simposio Cristologia en la Religiosidad Popular Puertorriqueña, and began a research project for the Episcopal Conference of Puerto Rico; (16) Jean-Pierre Ruiz was appointed chair of the department of theology of St. John's University, received the Society of Biblical Literature Regional Scholar Award, was elected associate editor of the Catholic Biblical Quarterly, and serves the Society of Biblical Literature and the Hispanic Theological Initiative. (17) Father Roden-Lucero of El Paso was featured (NYT, 27 October) for his leadership in community organization in El Paso; (18) Rosendo Urrabazo was elected general consultant of the Claretians; (19) Allan Figueroa Deck was appointed director of the Loyola Institute for Spirituality in Orange, California; (20) Arturo Pérez Rodríguez hosted several symposia featuring his new publications; (21) Ronaldo Cruz was named an expert to the Synod for America; (22) Eduardo Fernández received a grant from the Hispanic Theological Initiative and was appointed an adjunct professor at the Jesuit School of Theology at

Berkeley; (23) Nylda Aldarondo was instrumental in writing the Pastoral Plan for Hispanic Ministry in the diocese of Orlando; (24) Alejandro García-Rivera gave the keynote presentation to the Environmental Justice Conference of the National Conference of Catholic Bishops and the plenary presentation to the College Theological Society; (25) Carmen María Cervantes was recognized as a Distinguished Lasallian Educator at the twenty fifth Huether Annual Conference.

Scholars gathered at the University of San Francisco for the October conference on the cultural location of Hispanics. Others visited Harlem's Museo del Barrio for their exhibit on *santos* (images of saints). The winter 1997 CARA Report included information on a study of "small Christian communities." The Hispanic groups were three times more likely to be female than other groups, met more often than other groups and more often in home settings, were the least formally educated, were the youngest, and participated almost exclusively in Hispanic majority groups. They emphasized Scripture and had an almost 30 percent chance of meeting for six years or more. Another CARA study concluded: "Youth who seriously consider vocations are much more likely to be Hispanic/Latino . . . some 21 percent." Andrew Greeley (America, 27 September) repeated his previous assertion that "defection among Hispanics [from Catholicism] is the worst . . . in . . . history."

Forthcoming research includes a team effort headed by Dean Hoge on the spiritual needs, values, religious training, sense of identity, and Catholic character among young Anglo and Hispanic Catholics. Also, Michael W. Foley is surveying Church programs and ministries for eight immigrant and ethnic groups in nine dioceses.

## Organizations

The colloquium of the Academy of Catholic Hispanic Theologians of the United States (ACHTUS) convened 8–11 June in Seattle. Keynoters were Adelaida Del Castillo, Gail Perez, and Carlos Maldonado. Respondents included Gary Riebe-Estrella, and Jean-Pierre Ruiz. The ACHTUS award was presented to the National Catholic Council for Hispanic Ministry.

The Asociación Nacional de Sacerdotes Hispanos (ANSH) held its eighth conference in Corpus Christi 13–16 October. One hundred priests and six bishops gathered. The keynote, "Jesucristo, Cabeza y Pastor de la Iglesia y el Sacerdote Hispano," was delivered by Bishop Godínez-Flores of Mexico. The next convention is set for Chicago.

The Apostolado para la Cosagración de la Familia began an annual "Catholic Family Land" experience in preparation for the jubilee year. The first gathering was held 14–17 August in Ohio.

For information on the Catholic Migrant Farmworker Network, try their new website: www.cmfn.org.

Charismissions held their fourteenth conference for couples, the thirteenth congress for lay leaders, a spiritual mission for priests and religious, their eighteenth international charismatic encounter in Spanish, and their fifteenth international youth days. Speakers included retired Bishop Juan Arzube, priests Pedro Nunez, Eugenio Cardenas, Ricardo Castellanos, Andres Davila, Carlos Martínez, and lay women Esther Garzon and Marilyn Krammar.

The Conference of Religious in Hispanic Ministry canceled its 1997 seminar scheduled for Sierra Madre, California. Coordinators were to be Clemente Barrón, Cathy García, Benita Herta, Verónica Méndez, Bernadine Reyes, and Gary Riebe-Estrella. Lack of registrants led to the cancellation.

Comunidades de Reflexión Eclesial en la Diáspora (CRECED) held their second international meeting 31 July–3 August in Saint Augustine, Florida. Four bishops joined more than one hundred thirty others to discuss relations between those in Cuba and those in exile. They also considered the 1998 papal visit to the island.

LAS HERMANAS held their biannual assembly 25–27 July in New York and explored spirituality for Latinas of the twenty first century. After considering the lives of exemplary women from the past 25 years, they elected new board members and a national coordinator.

Instituto Fe y Vida held its third national symposium in Texas. It was an intensive week preparing people to use their Prophets of Hope model for evangelization and faith formation. They also offered training for advisors and leaders of small Christian communities of youth. Eduardo Arnoil represented the Instituto at a Latin American conference on youth and young adult ministry. With members of the United States Catholic Conference, the Instituto also participated in the meeting of Latin American National Directors of Youth Ministry sponsored by the Episcopal Conference of Latin America.

The new president of the Instituto de Liturgia Hispana is Heliodoro Lucatero. In cooperation with the Catholic University of America (ably represented by Peter Casarella) they sponsored a conference titled, "The Hispanic Presence in the United States Catholic Church." Virgil Elizondo was the keynoter. Plenaries were given by Roberto Goizueta, Ana María Díaz-Stevens, and Juan Sosa. Among the workshop speakers were Marina Herrera, Ana María Pineda, and Eduardo Fernández. They also offer a new marriage preparation booklet titled *Don y Promesa.*

The Louisville Institute sponsored an ecumenical gathering of African American and Hispanic scholars in January. The gathering supported networking between young scholars and the exploration of critical issues. This dialogue will continue. They also granted Timothy Matovina a Summer stipend to investigate Guadalupan devotion along the Mexican border.

The Mexican American Cultural Center (MACC) spent 1997 celebrating their Silver Anniversary. Events included the June Founders Week and the October workshop, "Hispanic Bishops Speak with their People" transcribed by Eduardo Fernández. MACC has completed a national survey of diocesan Hispanic ministry, and seeks certification through the United States Catholic Conference. They have also formed new mobile teams to visit interested dioceses nationwide.

In June the National Conference of Agents and Diocesan Directors of Hispanic Ministry (NCADDHM) met in Denver. They looked at Hispanic Ministry from the Tercer Encuentro to the year 2000.

The National Conference of Hispanic Deacons held their July meeting in Florida. Speakers included Bishops Agustín Román of Miami and René Valero of Brooklyn. The National Organization of Catechists for Hispanics held its eleventh national gathering in Florida. Speakers at the April conference were Irma Nolla and Ronaldo Cruz.

Armando Contreras was appointed development associate for the National Catholic Council for Hispanic Ministry (NCCHM). After elections, the board includes Kenneth Davis and José Gomez. Work to facilitate a federation of Hispanic youth was brought to fruition and this group was part of the national meeting in San Antonio on 4 December. The Program for the Analysis of Religion among Latinos (PARAL) has launched in March 1997 a scholarly exchange with Cuba. At the November 1997 of the Society for the Scientific Study of Religion and the Religious Research Associates PARAL sponsored roundtable discussions, and panels on "Latinas and Religious Agency," "Crossing the Borders in Latino/a Religious Healing," and "The PARAL Commission Report on Religion in Cuba Today." Anthony M. Stevens-Arroyo has been awarded $569,699 by Lilly Foundation to conduct a national survey of Latino parishes and congregations. To be conducted in three segments, with additional funding comparable to this grant, the survey will be the most comprehensive to date on Latinos in the U.S.A. and on their neighborhoods and churches. Stevens-Arroyo will direct a team of eight researchers from PARAL.

Region XI of the Hispanic Commission (RECOSS) is preparing policy initiatives opposing propositions 187 and 209.

The Southeast Pastoral Institute (SEPI) plans to complete twenty five double occupancy rooms in its newly designed headquarters. It continues to set an example for both good ministry and fine stewardship. The Knights of Columbus are making concerted efforts to lure Latinos. The national coordinator, José Moreno, reports that there are forty five Spanish speaking councils. He was hired to increase that number.

After two years of planning sponsored by the National Catholic Council for Hispanic Ministry with the support of the Secretariat for Hispanic Affairs, a new organization has been born. Welcome the National Catholic Network of Pastoral Juvenil Hispana. Its constitutive assembly was held in San Antonio 3–5 October. The first board of directors includes Rudy Vargas IV, Damian Hinojosa, Elvia Torres, José María Matty, and Mario Vizcaino.

*Editor's note. The Midwest Conference of Seminarians for Hispanic Ministry was hosted by Mundelein Seminary in Mundelein, Il.*

## Resources

Oregon Catholic Press (800–548–8749) offers new music by Eleazar Cortés, Jaime Cortez, and Al Valverde. A new charismatic cassette by Lori Juárez, *Abrásame Señor*, is available from 818–930–5623. GIA offers new bilingual Christmas carols by Bruce Trinkley (800–421–7250). The Federation of Diocesan Liturgical Commissions' six Spanish titles are sold with rights to reproduce them. Dial 202–635–6990. World Library Publications (800–566–6150) offers a new Spanish hymnal, cassettes, and liturgical music. Liturgy Training Publications (800–933–1800) published Cardinal Roger Mahony's pastoral letter. For other liturgical information consult "Embracing Diversity," Catechumenate (March), pages 28–34, or "Five Rules for Celebrating Bilingual Masses," Modern Liturgy (August), pages 6–7. A new catalog of religious art, *Our Saints among Us*, is available from 505–344–9382. Demetria Martínez has published a new book of poems, *Breathing between the Lines*; contact the University of Arizona Press (800–426–3797).

Sadlier has expanded its Spanish language line. Call 800–221–5175 for *Sembrando la Palabra: Manual para Catequistas* or the bilingual *Catholic Prayers and Devotions*. Other Spanish prayer books are offered by Our Sunday Visitor (800–348–2440), Oblate Missions (210–736–1685), and Ecos Cristoferos (12 East 48th Street; New York,

NY 10017). Liguori has similar works and new educational books such as *La Familia de Dios* (800–325–9521). For RCL's new Spanish catechetical literature, dial 800–527–5030, ext. 6454. Saint Mary's Press published the newest book of the Agents of Hope series, *Dawn on the Horizon: Creating Small Communities.*

Dialogue between Latinos and African Americans is the theme of the USCC's new *Reconciled through Christ* (800–235–8722). They also offer videotapes, especially for migrants and immigrants, the annual *Domingo Catequético*, and a trilingual CD-ROM of the new Catechism. A new peace and justice kit is available by calling 314–533–4445.

Novalis Publishing, a Canadian firm, enters the market with cooperation from several Mexican publishers. For their catalogue write: Novalis Mexico; Insurgentes Sur 1650—505; Colonia Florida; 01030 México, D.F.

A new ecumenical journal of Puerto Rican theology, Casabe, is available by calling 787–787–7274.

## New Books

The three broadest categories are theological, liturgical, and historical. First are *Guadalupe: Mother of the New Creation* ($14) by Virgil Elizondo and *The Faith of the People: Theological Reflections on Popular Catholicism* ($17), a collection of key articles by Orlando Espín. Elizondo's work, which incorporates the research of several recent Guadalupan scholars, writes from a theological rather than a scientific or historical perspective. His exposition centers on the *Nican Mopua*, the oldest Aztec account of the apparitions of Our Lady of Guadalupe, and argues for a greater appreciation of the *sensus fidelium* of these apparitions as a model of inculturation. His missiological arguments challenge the Roman Church to be more inclusive and conscious of the poor. (See p. 208 for a complete review.)

(Incidentally, another book on Guadalupe, albeit a small one, is Richard D. Fisher–San Juan's *The Virgin of Guadalupe: Artistic Expressions of Love and Beauty on the U.S.-Mexico Frontier* (Sunracer Publications, $9.95). This bilingual, illustrated, thirty two page collection of photographs, essays, stories, poems, prayers, and songs dedicated to the Virgin has a wonderful "people-feel" to it. The money raised from its sale goes to a Tarahumara Indian Famine Relief Fund.)

Espín's articles, which were published from 1991 to 1995, provide not only easy access to critical developments in his thought on popular religion, but also the advantage of a perceptive foreword by Roberto S.

Goizueta. He describes Espín's distinctive contribution to United States Hispanic theology, and consequently, to the wider Church. Largely because of Espín's own self-reflective comments found in the introduction, words which reveal a man aware of his own growing edges, the book provides the necessary context for entering into the current theological conversation about Hispanic popular religion. Espín skillfully gives us his "take" on where he has been and where he sees himself moving.

The second category comprises books connected with worship in a Hispanic context. All three represent a dialogue between the larger Church and the Latino way or ways of worship. They are designed as resources for liturgists, educators, and pastoral agents. The essays, edited by Kenneth Davis, show how Hispanic pastoral studies are now developing around specific liturgical topics. His collection, *Misa, Mesa, y Musa: Liturgy in the U.S. Hispanic Church* (World Library Publications, $6.50), covers inculturation, the roots and substance of popular religion, the liturgical year, leadership, music, and the quinceñera. Its writers are accomplished liturgists who have formed the Instituto de Liturgia Hispana, the main center for Hispanic liturgical resources. The book's readability on important topics makes it a must for any course or workshop on Hispanic liturgy.

In light of the growing need for Hispanic liturgical resources, two books published by Liturgy Training Publications are destined to be staples: *Primero Dios: Hispanic Liturgical Resource* ($18), by Arturo J. Pérez Rodríguez and Mark R. Francis; and *Los Documentos Litúrgicos: Un Recurso Pastoral* ($15). *Primero Dios* brings together United States Catholic culture and Hispanic/Latino culture as it is lived in the United States. Written in an appealing style, it provides catechetical and pastoral notes and an excellent bibliography for each of the Hispanic celebrations surrounding life cycle moments such as birth, adolescence, marriage, sickness, and death. Its examples or actual models of rituals, reflecting the reality that sacraments are about life, are quite respective of Hispanic people's living traditions. This resource reveals that popular and official worship need not be opposed to each other. *Los Documentos Litúrgicos* is, at one level, the Spanish edition of *The Liturgy Documents: A Parish Resource* put out by the same publisher. However, it is much more because its contents have been adapted to the reality of Hispanics in the United States. Pérez Rodríguez and Francis collaborated also on this project, together with other veterans of Hispanic ministry preparation: Raul Gómez, Juan Alfaro, Rosa María Icaza, Sally Gómez-Kelly, Juan S. Sosa, and Jaime Lara. Each of the documents is preceded by a general view which notes its origins, importance, and strengths. It attempts to bridge the gap between what is said and what is done liturgically.

The year's historical works include Thomas Steele's *New Mexican Spanish Religious Oratory: 1800–1900* (University of New Mexico Press, $65), a collection of sermons preached in nineteenth century New Mexico. Steele brings the texts to life, introducing the twelve Catholic and Protestant preachers, among them Spaniards, New Mexicans, Italians, Frenchmen, and North Americans, and then providing excellent annotations. With all the present concern today of the need for a contextual theology, Steele's work is a fine example of how these men sought to inculturate the gospel message in their time and place.

A work which spans the evolution of a syncretic form of a religion whose origins are Catholic and African is George Brandon's *Santeria from Africa to the New World: The Dead Sell Memories* (Indiana University Press, cloth, $31.50). Although this history, which examines the Yoruba religion's trans Atlantic route from Africa to Cuba to New York City, first came out in 1993, it became available in paperback just this year.

A social history of evangelical Protestantism in Puerto Rico is *Protestantismo y Política en Puerto Rico, 1898–1930: Hacia una Historia del Protestantismo Evangélico en Puerto Rico* (Editorial de la Universidad de Puerto Rico). Beginning with the United States invasion of 1898, it examines the cultural and political impact of Protestantism on the Hispanic and Catholic society of the time.

Related books are *In Quest of a Vision: Sister Isolina's Own Story of Gospel Servanthood among Puerto Ricans* (Paulist Press, $7.95) by Sister María Isolina Ferré and *The Stranger Is Our Own: Reflection on the Journey of Puerto Rican Migrants* (Sheed and Ward, $15.95) by the late Joseph P. Fitzpatrick, S.J. Both are incredible stories of two people who were not afraid to take risks in service of the poor. Sister Isolina, the recipient of sixteen honorary doctorates, describes her journey in founding and directing one of the most successful prógrams of community revitalization and youth development in the United States. Fitzpatrick's book consists of his personal reflections as well as the articles, papers, lectures, and talks that he made in defense of Puerto Ricans from 1961 to 1983.

Too late for review was the December release of Ana María Díaz-Stevens and Anthony Stevens-Arroyo's *Recognizing the Latino Resurgence in U.S. Religion: The Emmaus Paradigm* (Boulder: Westview Press). Stevens-Arroyo was also published in *Anales del Caribe* and *The City and the World* (New York: Council on Foreign Relations Press).

## Other Significant Writings

Audinet, Jacques. "Beyond Multi-culturalism: A European Perspective." *Listening* 32, no. 3 (Fall, 1997): 161–173. Speaks about the meaning of "culture," how it became a part of MACC's name, and the meaning of *mestizaje*.

Azevedo, Marcello. "Hispanic Leaders: Faith and Culture in the New Millennium." *Chicago Studies* 36, no. 3 (December, 1997): 224–242. Abbreviated version of his keynote address to the Chicago gathering "Roots and Wings."

Barber, Janet, I.H.M. "The Guadalupan Image: An Inculturation of the Good News." *Josephinum Journal of Theology* 4 (Supplement 1997): 65–81. Concentrates on the miraculous nature of the image itself and explains why the *tilma* may be seen as a "double inculturation" of the gospel.

Becker, Sister Jean, O.S.F. "Hispanic Associates: Gift and Challenge." *Sisters Today* 69, no. 6 (November, 1997): 454–455. Speaks of the special gifts and challenges that having Hispanic associates brings to an American religious community.

Borran, George. "Hispanic Catholic Youth in the United States." *Chicago Studies* 36, no. 3 (December, 1997): 243–254. Drawing on experiences in Latin America and the United States, this offers worthy insights and helpful suggestions.

Clark, Kevin. "Snapshots from the Edge: A Report from the U.S./ Mexican Border." *Salt of the Earth* (May/June, 1997): 12–18. A description of one of the border cities (Nogales) and the tremendous contrasts north and south of the border.

Corona, Ignacio. "Guadalupanism: Popular Religion and Cultural Identity." *Josephinum Journal of Theology* 4 (Supplement 1997): 6–22. Traces the ideological evolution of Guadalupanismo as a cultural force in Mexican national consciousness and examines some reasons why the Virgin of Guadalupe continues to be a symbol of cultural identity.

Davis, Kenneth G. "A New Catholic Reformation." *Chicago Studies* 36, no. 3 (December, 1997): 216–223. Argues that the Church needs to integrate its leadership if it is to respond to the massive defection of Hispanics. Issue coedited by Davis and Allan F. Deck, S.J.

_____. "Challenges to the Pastoral Care of Central Americans in the United States." *Apuntes* 17, no. 2 (Summer, 1997): 45–56. Contends that little has been done on the topic, provides some historical background, and raises issues specific to each Central American community.

_____. "A Survey of Contemporary U.S. Hispanic Catholic Theology." *Theology Digest* 44, no. 3 (Fall, 1997): 203–211. Covering 1968 to the present, this concise summary highlights major developments, mentioning also the work that remains to be done.

_____. "A Silver Anniversary and a Rain of Gold." *Listening* 32 no. 3 (Fall, 1997): 147–151. As guest editor with Virgil Elizondo, the author introduces the writers of the articles which all honor the Mexican American Cultural Center's twenty fifth anniversary. Also speaks of the importance of culture in ministry.

Deck, Allan, F., S.J. "Latino Religion and the Struggle for Justice: Evangelization as Conversion." *Journal of Hispanic/Latino Theology* (hereafter *JHLT*) 4, no. 3 (February, 1997): 28–41. Explores how contemporary views about conversion engage the reality of Latinos, especially in areas of life in which religion plays a profound but often unconscious and unanalyzed role.

Engh, Michael E., S.J.. "Companion of the Immigrants: Devotion to Our Lady of Guadalupe among Mexicans in the Los Angeles Area, 1900–1940." *JHLT* 5, no. 1 (August, 1997): 37–47. Explores Guadalupan devotion among Mexican immigrants in the Los Angeles area early in the twentieth century.

Elizondo, Virgilio. "Guadalupe: An Endless Source of Reflection." *JHLT* 5, no. 1 (August, 1997): 61–65. Examines the theological implications of the other essays in this issue. He and Timothy Matovina coedited this issue.

_____. "The Mexican American Cultural Center Story." *Listening* 32, no. 3 (Fall, 1997): 152–160. Tells the story of how MACC came to be.

Fernández, Eduardo. "Seven Tips on the Pastoral Care of U.S. Catholics of Mexican Descent." *Chicago Studies* 36, no. 3 (December, 1997). Deals with Chicanos through personal experience and interviews with Mexican American ministers.

Folliard, Dorothy, O.P. "MACC as Graced Whirlpool: Some Reflections from a Non-Hispanic." *Listening* 32, no. 3 (Fall, 1997): 179–187. By using the whirlpool as a metaphor, the author speaks of the strengths at the center of MACC and the energies that flow from it.

Galles, Duane, L.C.M. "The Hispanic Musical Presence in the New Evangelization in the United States!" *Sacred Music* 124, no. 2 (Summer, 1997): 6–11. The hope is expressed that the music which was so instrumental in the first evangelization may be allowed to play an important role in this new evangelization.

García-Rivera, Dr. Alejandro. "A Matter of Presence." *JHLT* 5, no. 2 (November, 1997): 22–53. A parochial, liturgical, and cultural clash provides an opportunity to do an analysis from the perspective of a semiotics of culture.

Goizueta, Roberto. "Catholic Theological Education and U.S. Hispanics." In *Theological Education in the Catholic Tradition: Contemporary Challenges,* eds. Patrick W. Carey and Earl C. Muller, S.J. New York: Crossroad Publishing Company. pp. 340–350. Addresses three (of many) anthropological and epistemological dichotomies that militate against the full participation of United States Hispanics in Catholic seminaries and theological departments.

_____. "The Back Roads: Alternative Catholic Intellectual Traditions." In *American Catholic Traditions, Resources for Renewal,* eds. Sandra Yocum Mize and William Portier. *College Theology Society Annual* 42, 1996. pp. 24–28. In response to Professor Mize's presentation, the author teases out some exciting questions and possibilities.

_____. "San Fernando Cathedral: Incarnating the Theology Born of the Mexican American Cultural Center." *Listening* 32, no. 3 (Fall, 1997): 190–202. A concise yet thorough discussion of how Virgilio Elizondo and his successors have incarnated at San Fernando Cathedral the pastoral consequences of doing theology in the MACC style.

Gómez, Raúl. "The Day of the Dead: Celebrating the Continuity of Life and Death." *Liturgy* 14, no. 1 (Spring, 1997): 28–40. A substantial background to the Hispanic manner of celebrating All Souls Day as well as an example of a novena and prayers for the dead.

Guerrero, Father José Luis. "El Nican Mopohua: Magistral Ejemplo de Inculturación." *Josephinum Journal of Theology* 4 (Supplement 1997): 23–49. Addresses some of the salient theological features of the Nican Mopohua, explaining how it united the Spanish and Aztec cultures and how important it is. A summary English translation is provided.

Gutierrez, Gustavo. "Discovering a People." *Listening* 32, no. 3 (Fall, 1997): 174–178. The author shares how he came to realize the Mexican Americans were a people with an identity distinct from Latin Americans and therefore needed a theological reflection properly their own.

Hall, Suzanne. "Welcoming the Stranger." *Momentum* 18, no. 3 (August–September, 1997): 19–22. A path through some of the best of the church's documents on a Christian's proper response to immigrants and immigration.

Isasi-Díaz, Ada María. "Round Table Discussion: Nondiscrimination and Diversity." *Journal of Feminist Studies* in Religion 13, no. 2 (Fall, 1997): 87–89. Speaks about the call to embrace differences as a call to justice.

Jensen, Carol. "Roman Catholicism in Modern New Mexico: A Commitment to Survive." In *Religion in Modern New Mexico*, eds. Ferenc M. Szasz and Richard W. Etulain. Albuquerque: University of New Mexico Press, 1997. pp. 1–26. Good summary of recent events and their challenges. Not simplistic, realizes that Native Americans and Hispanics have had different agendas than liberal Anglo-Catholics. Especially good about mentioning the important role women have played.

Jordan, Brian. "Immigration: Public Policy, Pastoral Practice." *Church* 13, no. 2 (Summer, 1997): 20–23. Clarifies some pertinent questions in the ever confusing reality of immigration law.

LaSalle, Don. Proceedings of the North American Academy of Liturgy. Annual Meeting, Chicago (January, 1997): 69–70. Short report on the presentation made by Mark Francis and Arturo Pérez on their book *Primero Dios* (Liturgy Training Publications, 1997).

Matovina, Timothy. "New Frontiers of Guadalupanismo." *JHLT* 5, no.1 (August, 1997): 20–36. Traces the eighteenth and nineteenth century development of Guadalupan devotion in San Antonio, Texas; coedited this issue.

_____. "Sacred Place and Collective Memory: San Fernando Cathedral, San Antonio, Texas." *U.S. Catholic Historian* 15, no. 1 (Winter, 1997): 33–50. Based on research from the San Fernando Cathedral Project, the article covers a part of the history of the cathedral, from the oral memories of the parishioners.

Pérez Rodríguez, Arturo. "Mestizo Liturgy: A *Mestizaje* of the Roman and Hispanic Rites of Worship." *Liturgical Ministry* 6 (Summer, 1997): 141–147. Addresses the discipline and discernment necessary to develop liturgies appropriate for local communities. Includes a suggested rite. The entire issue is devoted to cross-cultural liturgy.

Pineda, Ana María. "Hospitality." In *Practicing Our Faith: A Way of Life for a Searching People*, ed. Dorothy C. Bass. San Francisco: Jossey-Bass, 1997. pp. 29–42. The customs of *posadas* or the Portuguese practice of hospitality at Pentecost are ways of renewing the Christian practice of hospitality.

Riebe-Estrella, Gary, SVD. "Latinos and Theological Education." *JHLT* 4, no. 3 (February, 1997): 5–12. A sketch of the dimensions of theological education as reenvisioned by Hispanic Catholic theologians—a vision that is both Hispanic in terms of its attention to the primacy of praxis, context, and method and Catholic in terms of its attention to the great Tradition.

Robeck, Cecil M., Jr. "Evangelization or Proselytism of Hispanics? A Pentecostal Perspective." *JHTL* 4, no. 4 (May, 1997): 42–64. Underlines the need for sustained dialogue in arriving at a common understanding and working that promotes authentic witness to the gospel.

Rodríguez, Edmundo, S.J. "Jesus, Power and the ONE." *Review for Religious* 56, no. 1 (January–February, 1997): 87–94. An application of Jesus' insistence on *one* Father, Teacher, Owner, One who is good) to social justice and the consequences that would flow from this.

Rodriguez, Jeannette. "Contemporary Encounters with Guadalupe." *JHLT* 5, no. 1 (August, 1997): 48–60. Offers a reflection on contemporary non-Hispanic followers of Guadalupe.

Romero, Gilbert C. "Amos 5:21–24: Religion, Politics, and the Latino Experience." *JHLT* 4, no. 4 (May, 1997): 21–41. Suggests insights into ways in which connections between religion and politics in the Book of Amos might help one understand the links between religion and politics for Latinos.

Ruiz, Jean-Pierre. "Revelation 4:8–11, 5:9–14: Heavenly Hymns of Creation and Redemption." In *Prayer from Alevader to Constantine*, ed. M. Kiley. London: Routledge, 1997. pp. 244–249. Shows how Rv 4–5 was intended to be read within the early Christians' liturgy to reinforce their commitment to Jesus.

_____. "The Politics of Praise: A Reading of Revelation 19:1–10." In *Society of Biblical Literature: 1997 Seminar Papers*. Atlanta: Scholars Press. pp. 374–393. Represents a further step in the development of an approach to the Apocalypse that Ruiz had first suggested in a former essay.

Schelkshorn, Dr. Hans. "Discourse and Liberation: Toward a Critical Coordination of Discourse Ethics and Enrique Dussel's Ethics of Liberation." *JHLT* 5, no. 2 (November, 1997): 54–74. Seeks to familiarize readers with the dialogue between German philosopher Karl Otto Apel and Argentinian philosopher and historian Enrique Dussel.

Tabares, Fanny. "Pastoral Care of Catholic South Americans Living in the United States." *Chicago Studies* 36, no. 3 (December, 1997): 269–281. Excellent introduction of a topic not treated elsewhere. Provides census data and helpful suggestions.

Trasloheros H., Jorge E. "The Construction of the First Shrine and Sanctuary of Our Lady of Guadalupe in San Luis Potosí, 1654–1664." *JHLT* 5, no. 1 (August, 1997): 7–19. Documents the construction of the first Guadalupan shrine after the original sanctuary in Tepeyac.

*This article originally appeared in Review for Religious Vol. 57 (1998) under the title, "U.S. Hispanic Catholics: Trends and Works 1997."*

# 1998 IN REVIEW

## Migrants and Immigrants

F
ormer president Jimmy Carter and Bishop John J. Nevins of Venice, Florida, were among those who supported a hunger strike in Florida by tomato harvesters. After thirty days the growers agreed to raise wages, which had stagnated for twenty years (*Visitante Dominical* [VD], 22 February). The *National Catholic Reporter* (NCR, 17 July) reported on the church's ministry to those detained by Immigration and Naturalization Services and on Raleigh's Bishop F. Joseph Grossman's support for organizing cucumber pickers. The *Catholic Herald* (CH, 4 April) reported that the California Catholic Conference supports that state's strawberry workers. CH also highlighted the work of Sister María Padilla and Estella Guajardo for their years of service to migrants. And Bishop John W. Yanta of Amarillo, Texas, who chairs the bishops' committee on migration, has traveled the country in support of that ministry.

Less visible aid to migrants has long been provided. Bishop Ricardo Ramírez told the Catholic Extension Society that without their annual $200,000 and other monies from the American Board of Catholic Missions, he could never sustain the salaries or building maintenance needed by the Diocese of Las Cruces, New Mexico. Ramírez has been active in community organization. Extension gave the Puerto Rican Church over $500,000. The National Center for Farm Worker Health published a glowing article about the Catholic Migrant Farm Worker Network.

A 15 March article in the Chicago Tribune notes how churches in the suburbs are trying to serve new immigrants. Whether directly from their home countries or from urban centers of the United States, Latinos follow job opportunities to Prospect Heights, Illinois; Gainesville, Georgia; Dodge City, Kansas; and other towns not traditionally associated with them. The San Antonio Express News reported on a Mass offered for persons who died attempting to cross the United States–Mexican border.

NCR on 3 April noted how the sanctuary movement has been revitalized as a result of new anti-immigrant legislation. This included Central Americans who fasted to underscore their plight. They were joined on 23 April by Archbishop Oscar Rodríguez Maradiaga of Tegucigalpa, Honduras (NCR, 8 May). And on 29 July Latinolink News Service reported that several northeastern dioceses issued a joint statement in favor of a blanket amnesty for all undocumented immigrants.

A temporary reverse migration greeted Pope John Paul II during his visit to Cuba. *La Voz Católica* (VC) dedicated most of its January issue to the initially controversial but ultimately successful visit. National news was full of La Virgen de la Caridad, the 1960s Operation Peter Pan, and contemporary human rights. This was followed by over five hundred tons of medical supplies and foodstuffs the Archdiocese of Miami and the ecumenical group "Pastores por La Paz" sent to Cuba. This kind of ecumenical effort by the clergy was also successful in mediating the strike by Puerto Rico's telephone workers, reported *Hispanic Link* (HL, 13 July).

The 17 July VC reported a study that confirmed that immigrants actually help the United States economy. *Migrantes* is an excellent resource for this pastoral work; write P.O. Box 430387, San Diego, California 92143. See also the Autumn, 1998 issue of *Glenmary Challenge*. The Holy Father requested that all nations grant amnesty to the undocumented within their borders as a just and peaceful way to celebrate the new millennium (VC, 16 October). After Hurricane Mitch devastated several countries of Central America, the United States government granted their citizens limited legal status in this country. The United States also hopes to stem future immigration from the ravaged isthmus through aid to the region. Such foreign aid is being administered by the churches, but will almost certainly be too little if not too late.

## General Church News

Good news for the Spanish Catholic press. Over three thousand people attended the Catholic Communications Expo in Miami along with singers Tony Melendez and Anna María. For more information about retailers and suppliers to United States Hispanic and Latin American markets, call Rafael de los Reyes Jr. at 305–445–6583 or visit the website at www.paxcc.org. Los Angeles's *Vida Nueva* won seventeen print awards from the National Association of Hispanic Publications, including "Outstanding Spanish Language Weekly." Family Theater Productions won two Gabriel awards from Unda-USA for best national religious program and best national news and information program—the first time this award was won by a Spanish-language program. The Dioceses of San Francisco, Oakland, and Sacramento will publish a regional monthly called *El Heraldo.*

NCR (4 December) noted a controversy in Dallas over the sale of a predominantly Mexican-descent parish. The Smithsonian Institution and the University of Texas sponsored the May conference "Image of Devotion, Icon of Identity: The Virgin Mary in the Americas." María Herrera Sobek, Virgil Elizondo, Sandra Cisneros, Yolanda Tarango, and Miguel Bretos all participated. Elizondo's project in collaboration with Timothy Matovina on San Fernando Cathedral has been at the North American Academy of Religion and the American Society of Church History. History noted two anniversaries: The centennial of the United States invasion of Puerto Rico and the fourth centenary of the evangelization of New Mexico.

The four most well-known Hispanic Catholics in the news were Dolores Huerta, named Woman of the Year by Ms. magazine; Federico Peña, who resigned from the United States Department of Energy; actor James Olmos, who returned to the church; and Chicago Cubs batter Sammy Sosa, named Outstanding Player of professional baseball's National League. Sosa also distinguished himself with his generosity.

Others include María Pilar Aquino, receiving academic tenure, appointed to the board of Concilium, lecturing in San José, El Paso, San Bernardino, and also internationally, and serving as a panelist at the American Academy of Religion; Rosa Flores, receiving a Catholic women's award from the Archdiocese of St. Louis; María Elena González, teaching at Maryknoll's summer workshop, speaking to the National Association of Church Personnel Administrators, and giving the keynote address at the 1998 Parish Ministry Conference; Ada María Isasi-Díaz, spending the summer at River College, teaching in the Philippines and Cuba, and keynoting the Semper Reformanda meeting of the Presbyterian Church; Carmen and José Rivera, featured on the cover of *Catholic Digest*; María Angélica Moreno, addressing the Midwestern Conference for Seminarians in Hispanic Ministry held at St. Meinrad School of Theology; Jeanette Rodriguez-Holguin, doing widespread consultant work, completing her presidency of ACHTUS, being awarded an Andrew W. Mellon Fellowship, and speaking at the national conference of Call to Action and at the "Jesus in the 21st Century" seminar; Maruja Sedano, the first Hispanic ever elected president of the

National Catholic Conference of Catechetical Leaders; Yolanda Tarango and Gary Riebe-Estrella, appointed to the advisory board of the Center for the Study of Religious Life; Dolores Vazquez, featured in the 15 May issue of NCR; Diana Ortiz, speaking before the United States Congress's human rights caucus; Lorenzo Albacete, delivering a workshop at the Mile-Hi Congress in February; death of Medal of Honor recipient Roy Benavidez; Miguel Díaz, teaching Hispanic theology at the University of Dayton; Allan F. Deck, speaking at the Collegeville Pastoral Institute; he and Kenneth Davis, editing an issue of *Chicago Studies* that won a third place award from the Catholic Press Association; Virgil Elizondo, teaching at the summer program of the Catholic Theological Union and speaking at the conference of the National Catholic Education Association; Orlando Espín, presenting papers at the University of Florida and the University of Dayton; Eduardo C. Fernández, a keynoter at the National Association of Catholic Family Life Ministries and a presenter at the Hispanic Theological Initiative, the Cultural Orientation Program for International Priests, and the Oblate School of Theology; the death by Marine gunfire last year of eighteen year old Ezequiel Hernández, about which the United States Congress will hold hearings; Anthony Stevens-Arroyo, publishing thrice in HL; Francisco Tapia, appointed director of the Hispanic Formation Institute in Sacramento; Rufino Zaragoza, bringing out a CD commemorating the bicentennial of modern Mission San Luis Rey; Ezequiel Sanchez, named director of Hispanic Ministry in the Archdiocese of Chicago; Lorenzo Florian, chosen director of the Center for Latino Studies at Northpark College; Jaime Lara, appointed professor at the Institute of Sacred Music and Art at Yale University; Puerto Rican Carlos M. Rodriguez Santiago, declared venerable by the Vatican; Rudy Vargas, speaking at the 1998 Parish Ministry Conference; Miguel Díaz, Eduardo Fernández, and Ana María Pineda, all participating in the Louisville Institute's consultation of young Hispanic and African American scholars; Eduardo Fernández and James Empereur, recipients of a $40,000 grant from the Louisville Institute for a project titled "Celebrating Sacraments in a Hispanic Context." These are some of today's leading newspersons.

A report by the Center for Applied Research in the Apostolate (CARA) holds good news for tomorrow. Fifteen percent of women and 16 percent of men in initial religious formation are Hispanic. Only 2 percent of professed female and 4 percent of professed male religious are Hispanic. Fourteen percent of graduate Catholic seminarians are Latino, up from 11 percent in 1993. Eighteen percent of college seminarians are Hispanic, and there are approximately twelve Hispanic minor seminarians. Thirteen percent of men in diaconate formation are Latino, but 32 percent of people in lay ministry and 40 percent of new members of United States secular institutes are Hispanic. Some of tomorrow's leaders gathered in Lawrence, Massachusetts, for the Third International Latino Youth Congress hosted by Jovenes en Acción and the Paulist Hispanic Evangelization and Leadership Program. A study by Dean Hoge confirmed the religiosity and orthodoxy of Hispanic young adults (VC, 20 November). Unfortunately, there is still bad news. A parish on Long Island was accused of refusing to admit twelve Hispanic children to first communion because they took required classes in Spanish (*La Prensa Grafica*, 7 July).

Also planning for the future is the Encuentro 2000 National Steering Committee chaired by Bishop Gabino Zavala of Los Angeles assisted by Bishops Emilio Allué of Boston and Agustin Román of Miami. Also serving are María Elena González, Mary Lou Barba, Noemi Castillo, Heliodoro Lucatero, María Cepeda, Ana María Pineda, Gonzalo Saldaña, Rosa María Sánchez, Rodolfo Vargas, Luis Velásquez, Mario Vizcaino, and Celine Caufield. The Life Cycle Institute of Catholic University has been contracted to make a national study of Hispanic Catholics before the Encuentro that will be held 13–16 July in Los Angeles.

Other bishops making the news: Colombian Gabriel Montalvo was named papal nuncio. Francis George of Chicago encouraged implementation of his archdiocese's Pastoral Plan for Hispanic Ministry; he also met with the five state representatives of the Midwest Catholic Association for Hispanic Ministry. Gilbert Chávez of San Diego, California, Richard Garcia of Sacramento, California, Placido Rodriguez of Lubbock, Texas, Gabino Zavala of Los Angeles, and Juan Arzube (retired) all signed a letter with 294 other religious leaders which asked Presidents Clinton and Zedillo to stop the violence in Chiapas, Mexico. Anthony J. Bevilacqua of Philadelphia joined an ecumenical walk for peace. Bishop Roberto González of Corpus Christi spoke at the Confederación Interamericana de Educación Católica; education of Hispanics, especially the laity, may be aided by the million dollar Lilly Endowment grant to the Washington Theological Union. Gerald Barnes of San Bernardino, California, announced five goals for his diocesan planning process and represented the Bishops' Committee for Hispanic Affairs at the first meeting of North and South American bishops concerning catechesis.

## Organizations

The Academy of Hispanic Theologians of the United States (ACHTUS) held a colloquium titled "Towards a Christian Cosmology." Besides a major presentation by Alejandro García-Rivera, Peter Casarella, Jean-Pierre Ruiz, and Nancy Pineda delivered papers. Fernando Segovia was awarded the Virgilio Elizondo award for distinguished contributions to theology. The Hispanic Theological Initiative was given the ACHTUS award for promoting higher theological education. La Asociación de Diáconos Hispanos held its fifteenth conference in Lorain, Ohio. Deacon Nestor Chávez and his family were featured in *Revista Maryknoll* (October) for their jail ministry.

La Asociación de Sacerdotes Hispanos convened in Mundelein, Illinois, to consider "Life and Ministry of the Hispanic Priest in the Holy Spirit." Juan Sosa, José Malagreca, Arturo Perez-Rodriguez, Verónica Méndez, and Fernando Gil presented workshops. The Catholic Migrant Farm Worker Network met with Archbishop Patrick Flores for a 12–17 February course on pastoral care. Twenty four persons from ten states and thirteen dioceses attended. The Koch Foundation funded this class taught by Rosa María Icaza, Irma Nolla, Toby Lardie, and Roberto Piña. Their June newsletter highlights the Encuentro 2000. In November they sponsored the National Day of Fasting and Prayer in Solidarity with America's Farm Workers.

The Conference of Religious for Hispanic Ministry is discerning its future. It sent a survey to the membership in July to ascertain how best to meet its goals with new methodologies. On Easter, Family Theater Productions interrupted its regularly scheduled program "La Historia de Quien Soy/Conversando" to air a one hour Spanish language presentation of Christ's passion and resurrection. Featured were Roberto Gutiérrez, Hugo Isaac, Daniel Novoa, Eduardo López Rojas, Fernando Escandón, Melba Tirado-Novoa, and Beatriz Mandy. It and other cassettes and CD's are available from 1–888–AMIGO–11.

El Instituto de Liturgia Hispana held its eighth biennial conference at the University of Seattle. Featured speakers were Bishops Ricardo Ramírez and Emilio Allué, and George Salazar, Rosa María Icaza, and Juan Sosa. With the Oblate School of Theology, they also presented the San Antonio conference on "Predicando la Enseñanza: Liturgia y Justicia Social." Its president, Heliodoro Lucatero, was featured in the November issue of *Revista Maryknoll*.

Instituto Fe y Vida held a symposium and a seminar at Loyola University in Chicago. The director, Carmen María Cervantes, has published her fifth book, *Covenant with God*, which is available in English or Spanish from Saint Mary's Press. The institute also offered its first annual seminar on Hispanic youth ministry, and, with a grant from the Koch Foundation, is implementing its "Prophets of Hope" model in four dioceses. Eduardo Arnouil represented them at the CELAM Congress on Youth Ministry. Youth work is increasingly important. In June, Emerging Trends reported that 93 percent of Hispanics polled expressed a religious preference and that the major determining factor for that preference was their age.

The Mexican American Cultural Center (MACC) cosponsored the first National Orientation Program for Diocesan Directors of Hispanic Ministry. The 19–20 February event was presented with the Secretariat for Hispanic Affairs. Its many workshops included Rudy Vela's "Spirituality for a Multi-cultural World" and Rosa María Icaza, C.C.V.I., and Roberto Piña's "History of Hispanics in the United States Church." The center has broken ground for its new building and has received accreditation from the United States Catholic Conference. See the new website: www.maccsa.org.

Bishop Emilio Allué will serve as episcopal moderator of the National Catholic Network de Pastoral Juvenil Hispana (La Red). More than fifteen dioceses were represented at the first annual membership meeting. Joe Ocampo and Ivannia Vega represented the network at the continental youth and young adult gathering in Chile.

Rosa María Sánchez, the executive director of the National Catholic Council for Hispanic Ministry, was featured in VD on 22 March. At the October membership meeting in Houston, José Gomez was elected treasurer and Carmen Aguinaco secretary. While cooperating with Encuentro 2000, the council is planning its third national congress for 2002.

La Oficina Regional del Sureste para el Ministerio Hispano (SEPI) reports that the number of Hispanics in its region jumped by one million between 1994 and 1996 and continues to explode. In addition to its valuable workshops, mobile teams, and degree program, this year SEPI inaugurated its first retreat rooms and a pilgrimage to Rome and the Holy Land. The 17th issue of Pascua Juvenil is available from the SEPI bookstore (305–279–2333).

La Organización Nacional de Catequistas para Hispanos (NOCH) held its annual conference in Milwaukee, Wisconsin. Saturnino Lajo was the major presenter. Workshops were given by Nuria Checkouras and José Sánchez Herrero.

The Program for the Analysis of Religion Among Latinos (PARAL) received grants totaling $1.5 million to train postdoctoral fellows who will conduct a national survey into "how religious institutions affect Latino culture, community organizations, and local activism . . . various denominations and alternative religions will be included." More information from 718–951–3121.

The Louisville Institute is funding another study on Hispanic ministry directed by Dean Hoge of the Catholic University of America and Ronaldo Cruz of the Bishops' Secretariat for Hispanic Affairs. Consultants include Raúl Gómez and Manuel Vasquez.

## Resources

Cultural resources include the video *Soul of the City/Alma del Pueblo* from JM Communications in Houston (713–524–1382). Great Events Publishing (888–433–8368) features César Chávez. *Nuestra Identidad Católica* is a booklet published by Resources for Christian Living (800–822–6701). QvMagazine (818–766–0023) published an issue on religion among gay Latinos.

Family resources in Spanish are burgeoning at Catholic Familyland (800–FORMARY). These include new conferences, books, and radio and television programs. The Liturgical Press (800–858–5450) just released Oracional Bilingue para Niños. See also Pedro Núñez's *Conozca Primero Su Fe Católica* available from Liguori Publications (800–464–2555). *Notas de Ayuda* are pamphlets that offer advice on issues such as the death of a spouse or parent: Order from 800–328–6515. The North American Forum for Small Christian Communities is seeking Hispanic members; call 860–243–9642. Sadlier (800–221–5175) launched new bilingual religious education products.

Liturgists will be interested in the new magazine *Gracias!* from Liturgy Training Publications (LTP, 800–933–4213). LTP's *Liturgy 90* offered two articles on Hispanic liturgy written for "gringos." It offers a new video guide in Spanish for Communion ministers, and tapes based on the book *Primero Dios*. It also offers a resource for inculturation: *Mestizo Worship: A Pastoral Approach to Liturgical Ministry* (a collection of previously published articles: 800–858–5450). Oregon Catholic Press (800–548–8749) includes Jaime Cortez's *Qué Alegría/ Rejoice* for the Easter season, new additions to the *Cantar Alabanzas* series, *Danzas* by Mariano Fuertes, and over twenty other new cassettes and videos. A new bilingual missalette and *Misa de Santa María del Lago* by Steven R. Jenco is available from World Library Publications (800–566–6150). Preachers consult Ana María Pineda's "Death: A Call to Live," in

Living Pulpit (July–September issue). The United States Bishops approved a revised Spanish funeral rite and new lectionary readings. Both decisions await Vatican confirmation.

For resources about the millennium, see *Acompañamiento Espiritual* and new titles from Angela Erevia MCDP available from the Mexican American Bookstore (210–732–2156). See also the National Catholic Conference's *Preparando el Jubileo: Guía de Feligreses* and the newsletter *En Marcha*. Nine other new Spanish titles are also available from the USCC (800–235–8722).

Youth ministers will be interested in George Boran's new book, *El Futuro Tiene Nombre: Juventud* from Librerías Paulinas (800–872–5852 or PaulinasFL@aol.com). See also Michele Salcedo's *Quinceañera! The Essential Guide to Planning the Perfect Sweet Fifteen Celebration.* For Catholic vocational material, contact the National Coalition for Vocations in the Church at 800–671–NCCV.

## New Books

The bulk of this year's books are historical. The most noteworthy in terms of coverage is *The Encyclopedia of American Catholic History* edited by Michael Glazier and Thomas J. Shelley (Collegeville: Liturgical Press, $79.95). Twenty two entries deal specifically with the history of Hispanics in the United States. The work highlights the early presence of Hispanics and features figures such as Christopher Columbus, José Antonio Martínez, Felix Varela, Joseph Fitzpatrick, and César Chávez. Competent scholars present the latest research from various angles. Jaime Vidal writes an impressive, sizable essay on "Hispanic Catholics in America." Floyd McCoy has a substantial essay on the Catholic Church in Puerto Rico. Other significant contributions are Stafford Poole's "Missions in Colonial America" and Carl F. Starkloff's "Native Americans and the Catholic Church," which includes the Spanish mission era. In terms of the United States period, the role of courageous religious and lay women who established and ran a phenomenal network of parochial schools, orphanages, and hospitals for the immigrant church is acknowledged in various entries that trace the history of these communities.

Two biographies are Lynn Bridgers's *Death's Deceiver: The Life of Joseph P. Machebeuf* (Albuquerque: University of New Mexico Press, $21.95) and Charles Polzer's *Kino: A Legacy* (Tucson: Jesuit Fathers of Southern Arizona). Bridgers's story about the man who became the first bishop of Denver reveals a Frenchman who possessed a broad understanding and love of Hispanic culture. Regina Siegfried

ASC (Review for Religious, March –April 1998, p. 220) calls Bridgers's historical rendition "captivating reading." Similarly, Polzer chronicles the life of an earlier missionary pioneer of the Southwest and northern Mexico, the Jesuit priest Eusebio Kino. The book's fluid prose, well illustrated with maps and photographs of Kino's missions and the surrounding terrain, makes for enjoyable reading. Polzer describes many of the reasons behind the Italian missionary's success. A key contribution is the inclusion of his collaborators, Jesuit and lay. A companion book, *Kino: His Missions, His Monuments,* by the same author and publisher, serves as an excellent travel and research guide. A new edition of essays about early Catholic history in Texas, originally published between 1929 and 1931, has just been reissued by editor Jesús F. de la Teja: *Preparing the Way: Preliminary Studies of the Texas Catholic Historical Society.* (Austin: Texas Catholic Historical Society, $17.95). Among the essays are a narration of the earliest Catholic activities in Texas, two eighteenth century exploration diaries, and a description of education in Mexico City during the sixteenth century by the famed Mexican historian Joaquín García Icazbalceta. Various maps and a bibliography of more recent scholarship enhance the book.

*Seeds of Struggle, Harvest of Faith* is a collection of the papers presented at the Santa Fe Archdiocese's Cuatro Centennial Conference on the History of the Catholic Church in New Mexico (Albuquerque: LPD Press, $49.95). The event commemorates the 400th anniversary of both Spanish influence and Catholic faith in the state and surrounding territory. An informative essay by the present Archbishop Michael Sheehan acknowledges that the "seeds of the gospel" were already present in the Pueblo Indians at the time of the Spaniards' arrival. The twenty three essays not only are filled with valuable bibliographic material, but also draw from family histories, interviews, diaries, parish registers, lyrics of popular hymns, and photos. We are introduced to missionaries, educators, and pastors in the broader sense, that is, those women and men who kept public religious practices alive in their little towns. The editors and contributors are to be commended for their work. What is lacking in the volume, however, is at least one essay from the perspective of Native American Catholics, in this case, Pueblo Indians. While attempts were made here and there to address historical tensions between them and the conquering Spaniards, this omission is baffling.

Another somewhat historical book, but actually one which draws extensively from other disciplines such as anthropology, sociology, theology, and political science, is *Recognizing the Latino Resurgence in U.S. Religion: The Emmaus Paradigm* (Boulder, Colorado: Westview

Press, $24) by Ana María Díaz-Stevens and Anthony M. Stevens-Arroyo. In many ways, the book tells the story (especially the socio-political story) of the emergence of Hispanic ministry in the United States in light of the "signs of the times." Aside from helping to balance a history that has often been overly represented by the Southwest, the Puerto Rican authors convey an element of personal witness to what they are writing about. "We were there!" Among the book's other contributions are a treatment of the many ways in which Hispanics managed to change the United States Catholic Church, an acknowledgment of the countless unsung heroines and heroes who were behind the Latino resurgence, and an honest treatment of the tensions that surfaced among the various Latino groups. While the writing style is at times a bit strained, the documentation of those turbulent yet creative years, together with current sociological data and its relation to the church's continuing prophetic role in the light of the poor, ensures the permanent value of this labor of love.

Peter Casarella and Raúl Gómez ably edited *El Cuerpo de Cristo: The Hispanic Presence in the U.S. Catholic Church* (New York: Crossroad Publishing Company, $19.95). The book was compiled from a national conference and is composed of three sections: "Theology, Liturgy, and Spirituality," "Church, Family, Ecumenism," and "Faith Generates a Culture." Besides fine essays by well-known authors in the field, the work includes chapters by Jeffrey Gros on ecumenism, Gelasia Márquez Marinas on family life ministry, Mario García on Catholic social doctrine, and Marcos Martínez on the sacred in Chicano theater. These essays are particularly significant as there are so few published works on these themes in relation to Hispanics. The book is illustrated and has copious notes.

*Our Saints among Us: 400 Years of New Mexican Devotional Art* (Albuquerque: LPD Press, $44.95) by Barbe Awalt and Paul Rhetts presents a commendable example of how art can be viewed as an extension of the devotion of Hispanic people. Unlike other works, which focus just on the art or on the people, the essays by Thomas J. Steele, whose work on the area's santos is becoming a classic, and Charles Carrillo, a santero artist himself, provide a helpful background for novice and expert alike in regard to this popular devotional art. The book's engaging illustrations and overall arrangement are very attractive.

A similar work is *Vírgenes, Magos, y Escapularios: Imaginería, Etnicidad, y Religiosidad en Puerto Rico* edited by Ángel G. Quintero Rivera. Covering the fourteenth to twentieth centuries, it is a magisterial treatment of the values, history, and aesthetics of religion on the island. It also presents a cinematographic treatment of material religion among Puerto Ricans. Scholars, artists, and anyone interested in "lo Boricva" will appreciate this book.

As devotion to Our Lady of Guadalupe grows, so do the number of books dedicated to her. This year Virgilio Elizondo and Friends penned *A Retreat with Our Lady of Guadalupe and Juan Diego: Heeding the Call* (Cincinnati: St. Anthony Messenger Press, $7.95). Part of the publisher's retreat series, it consists of seven sessions which readers may adapt to their own schedule or the needs of a group. Along with picking up Elizondo's obvious devotion to Guadalupe, the reader/retreatant is invited to see her and Juan Diego through the eyes of such Hispanics as Jeanette Rodríguez, Rosendo Urrabazo, Gloria Loya, Alex García-Rivera, and Anita de Luna. The work is quite anecdotal. Juan Diego's story unfolds throughout as the authors provide glimpses of their own families, often their own mothers. Besides a good use of Scripture, this little book provides bibliographic and visual resources for further growth and exploration.

Elizondo and Timothy Matovina, in consultation with experts in congregational studies, pastoral ministers, theologians, and social-science and media professionals, have also written a book in which the history and the stories of San Fernando (patron of the San Antonio, Texas, cathedral parish) come alive through stunning photographs and their reflections (*San Fernando Cathedral: Soul of the City*, Maryknoll: Orbis Books, $16). The treatment of parishioners by name and the vivid descriptions of vivacious liturgies and age old faith practices of popular piety make the reader feel invited into the congregation's faith life. As a companion to Adan Medrano's exquisite video Soul of the City, this work is a creative example of the type of theology that results when the *sensus fidelium,* the living reality of faith in the life of the people, is taken seriously.

## Other Significant Writings

Aquino, María Pilar. "Latin American Feminist Theology." *Journal of Feminist Studies* 14, no. 1 (Spring, 1998): 89–107. Presents five topics that address the methodology and main characteristics of Latin American feminist theologians.

———. "Construyendo la Misión Evangelizadora de la Iglesia: Inculturación y Violencia Hacia las Mujeres." In *Entre La Indignación y La Esperanza*, ed. Ana María Tepedino and María Pilar Aquino, pp. 63–91. Bogotá: Indo-American Press Service, 1998. Examines the conceptual presuppositions in the evangelizing mission of the church and proposes a new approach towards the relationship between faith and culture in order to promote new socioecclesial relationships more compatible with the gospel.

Aquino, María Pilar, and Roberto S. Goizueta, eds. *Theology: Expanding the Borders.* The Annual Publication of the College Theology Society. Mystic, Connecticut: Twenty Third Publications, 1998.

Burgaleta, Claudio M., S.J. "The Theology of José de Acosta (1540 –1600): Challenge and Inspiration for Bridging the Gap between the Academy, Society, and the Church." *Theology Today* 54, no. 4 (January 1998): 470–479. Reintroduces a theologian from Latin America's colonial past who challenges us to do a theology that is academically rigorous, socially responsible, and pastorally relevant. This issue was edited by Kenneth G. Davis and Justo González.

Casarella, Peter. "The Painted Word." *Journal of Hispanic/Latino Theology* 4, no. 2 (November, 1998): 18–42. Sees the Latino/a faithful as icons of "God's hope-filled love for humanity." Significant for its use of South American religiosity.

Cervantes, Fernando. "'The Defender of the Indians': Bartolomé de las Casas in Context." *Way* 38, no. 3 (July 1998): 271–281. A brief summary of Las Casas's world and experiences that puts his call, conversion, and actions into context.

Cunningham, Hilary. "Sanctuary and Sovereignty: Church and State along the U.S.-Mexican Border." *Journal of Church and State* 40, no.2 (Spring, 1998): 371–386. Explores the United States-Mexico border as a contested zone of power that has relevance for scholars of church-state relations in the United States.

Díaz-Stevens, Ana María. "Syncretism, Popular Religiosity, and Communitarian Spirituality among Puerto Ricans and Hispanics in the United States." *Listening* 33, no. 3 (Fall, 1998): 162–174. An analysis of all these terms with relation to the author's own term "communitarian spirituality."

Doyle, Dennis M. "Communion Ecclesiology on the Borders: Elizabeth Johnson and Roberto S. Goizueta." In *Theology: Expanding the Borders*, eds. María Pilar Aquino and Roberto S. Goizueta, pp. 200

–218. By bringing the works of von Balthasar, Johnson, and Goizueta into dialogue with each other, proposes a communion ecclesiology that promotes authentic unity in diversity.

Elizondo, Virgilio P. "Transformation of Borders: Border Separation or New Identity." *In Theology: Expanding the Borders,* eds. María Pilar Aquino and Roberto S. Goizueta, pp. 22–39. An update of his ideas on *mestizaje,* addresses the ambiguous.

Empereur, James L., S.J. "Popular Religion and the Liturgy: The State of the Question." *Liturgical Ministry* 7 (Summer, 1998): 105–120. Speaks of the integration of popular religion and the liturgy as the task of the third millennium and a necessary component of postmodern liturgy.

Fernández, Eduardo C. "The Contributions of the Jesuit Order in the New Mexico-Colorado-West Texas Area as the Rocky Mountain Mission, 1867–1919." In *Seeds of Struggle, Harvest of Faith,* eds. Thomas J. Steele, S.J. Paul Rhetts, and Barbe Awalt, pp. 135–148. Albuquerque: LPD Press, 1998. Recognizes the progress these Italian Jesuits and their collaborators made in evangelization, church leadership, education, social services, and historical documentation.

Francis, Mark. "The Challenge of Worship in a Multi-cultural Assembly." *Liturgy* 14, no. 4: 3–9. Deals with specifically liturgical issues in a multi-cultural parish.

———. "The Hispanic Liturgical Year: The People's Calendar." *Liturgical Ministry* 7 (Summer, 1998): 129–135. Addresses how the liturgical year received from the Roman tradition is experienced and interpreted by Hispanics.

Isasi-Díaz, Ada María. "Doing Theology as Mission." *Apuntes* 18, no.4 (Winter, 1998): 99–111. Develops a saying of Augustine to provide a tripartite guide to Hispanic, specifically Latina, theology.

Levitt, Peggy. "Local-level Global Religion: The Case of U.S.-Dominican Migration." *Journal for the Scientific Study of Religion* 37, no. 1 (1998): 74–89. Contributes to a more systematic understanding of local-level religious globalization by exploring Catholic Church ties that span Boston and the Dominican Republic.

Loya, Gloria Inés. "Considering the Source / Fuentes for a Hispanic Feminist Theology." *Theology Today* 54, no. 4 (January, 1998): 491 –498. Explores some methodological aspects and key expressions of Hispanic faith and culture as a source for constructing a Hispanic feminist theology.

Matovina, Tim. "San Fernando Cathedral and the Alamo: Sacred Place, Public Ritual, and Construction of Meaning." In *Proceedings of the North American Academy of Liturgy,* 1998. Examines the contested interpretations of San Antonio history as embodied in the sacred space and public ritual at these sites.

————. "Hispanic Faith and Theology." *Theology Today* 54, no. 4 (January, 1998): 507–511. Through an accounting of a Christmas levantada, Matovina mentions five commonalities found in Latino/a theology.

McClure, John S. *Best Advice for Preaching.* Minneapolis: Fortress Press, 1998. Virgilio Elizondo is quoted throughout this book. Mendieta, Eduardo. "From Christendom to Polycentric Oikonumé: Modernity, Postmodernity, and Liberation Theology." In *Liberation Theologies, Postmodernity, and the Americas*, eds. David Batstone et al., pp. 253–272. New York: Rutledge, 1998. Addresses the links and differences between the Judeo-Christian tradition and post-modernism.

Perez y Mena, Andrés I. "Cuban Santería, Haitian Vodun, Puerto Rican Spiritualism: A Multi-culturalist Inquiry into Syncretism." *Journal for the Scientific Study of Religion* 37, no. 1 (1998): 15–27. In an analysis of the above mentioned beliefs, the author holds that the syncretism was a deterministic tool of the slaves and not an unconscious act.

Pineda, Ana María. "Liberation Theology: Practice of a People Hungering for Human Dignity." *Way* 38, no. 3 (July, 1998): 231–238. Shows how liberation theology is a process that is rooted in the poor.

Riebe-Estrella, Gary, S.V.D. "Latino Religiosity or Latino Catholicism?" *Theology Today* 54, no. 4 (January, 1998): 512–515. Argues that what is viewed by Northern Hemisphere Catholicism as popular religiosity is, in truth, Latino Catholicism.

Rodriguez, Jeanette. "U.S. Hispanic/Latino Theology: Context and Challenge." *Journal of Hispanic/Latino Theology* 5, no. 3 (February, 1998): 6–15. This presidential address of ACHTUS traces the background against which the challenges of Latino/a theologies arise, highlights some key concerns raised by United States Latino/a theologians, and examines implications for the trajectory of their work.

Rubio, José Antonio. "Checklist for Multi-cultural and Multi-lingual Worship." *Liturgy* 14, no. 4: 23–26. A quick reference on what to do and not to do in planning multi-lingual liturgies.

Ruiz, Jean-Pierre. "U.S. Hispanic/Latino Theology: 'The Boom' and Beyond." *Catholic Issues* 09/20/98 01:06. Reviews some of the Hispanic theological works published since 1992.

———. "Four Faces of Theology." In *Teaching the Bible*, eds. Fernando F. Segovia and Mary Ann Tolbert. New York: Orbis Books, 1998. Speaks of four biblical figures who model the challenge of theology for the author.

Segovia, Fernando. "Pedagocial Discourse and Practices in Cultural Studies: Toward a Contextual Biblical Pedagogy." In *Teaching the Bible* (see just above), pp. 137–168. Pursues the question of pedagogical discourse and practices within the context of the cultural studies paradigm. Segovia also wrote the introduction.

Sevilla, Bishop Carlos, S.J. "The Ethics of Immigration Reform." *Origins* 27, no. 43 (April, 1998): 728–732. Discusses migration as a global phenomenon and principles of Catholic social teaching that address migration's global and transnational dimensions.

Sosa, Juan J. "Textos Litúrgicos para los Católicos Hispanos en los Estados Unidos (Liturgical Texts for Spanish-speaking Catholics of the United States)." *Liturgia y Canción* 9, no. 3 (Tiempo Ordinario 1, 1998): 12–21. Attempts to answer questions that have been asked for decades about Spanish texts for Catholic assemblies.

Stevens-Arroyo, Anthony. "Latino Barrio Religion." *Catholic Issues* 09/20/98 23:16:08. Speaks of the differences between Latino religion in Latin America and the United States and points out how this is enfleshed in the barrio churches and their importance for our society.

————. "The Latino Religious Resurgence." *Annals of the American Academy of Political and Social Science* 558 (July, 1998): 163–177. Views religion among Latinos as part of a more general social history of the United States. Current population trends are described, and three areas for further research are profiled.

————. "The Evolution of Marian Devotionalism within Christianity and the Ibero-Mediterranean Polity." *Journal for the Scientific Study of Religion* 37, no. 1 (1998): 50–73. A sociohistorical description of the evolution of Marian devotion after the 16th century rift in Christianity that generated today's Catholicism and Protestantism.

Tepedino, Ana María, and María Pilar Aquino, eds. Introduction to *Entre la Indignación y la Esperanza*, pp.7–10. Bogotá: Indo-American Press Service, 1998. The editors state their hope to explore the perspectives that have evolved in Latin American feminist theology since the first meeting of Latin American women theologians in 1985.

Valdéz, Jorge Luis. "U.S. Hispanics between the Borders of Catholicism and Protestantism." In *Theology: Expanding the Borders*, eds. María Pilar Aquino and Roberto S. Goizueta, pp. 219–239. Using a Johannine understanding of unity to interpret the border between United States Hispanic Protestants and United States Hispanic Catholics, examines the issue of unity in diversity within the United States Hispanic community.

Vera, Alexandrina D. "Guitars in Hispanic Liturgy Today." *Pastoral Music* (January, 1998): 32–35. Directed to pastoral musicians who are concerned about authenticity and fidelity to tradition in working with music in Hispanic and multi-cultural communities.

Wright, Robert E. "Popular Religiosity: Review of Literature." *Liturgical Ministry* 7 (Summer, 1998): 141–146. This essay considers representative theoretical approaches and contemporary Catholic Hispanic popular worship and includes a representative bibliography.

*This article originally appeared in Review for Religious Vol. 58 (1999) under the title, "U.S. Hispanic Catholics: Trends and Works 1998."*

# 1999 IN REVIEW

T his is the last in this series documenting and celebrating the annual accomplishments of the Hispanic Catholic community in the United States. Those successes now are so numerous that not even a committee of three can adequately report on them in a single article. We thank our readers, contributors, proofreaders, and especially David Fleming, S.J., and the staff of *Review for Religious* for their commitment to "la causa."

## Migrants and Immigrants

Dolores Huerta, vice president of the United Farm Workers' Union, bemoaned the effect of California's harsh winter on migrant laborers. Hurricanes on the United States east coast had a similar effect. César Chávez, the union's founder, was inducted into the Labor Hall of Fame. Denver offers good news. Its Catholic charities opened a $3.9 million affordable housing complex which includes a community center, a plaza, and childcare facilities (*Catholic Herald* [CH], 9 October).

Bishops continue to advocate for immigrants. The *National Catholic Reporter* (NCR, 1 October) mentions their lobbying Congress for funds to reduce the backlog of 1.8 million naturalization applications. The same issue reports on the conference for immigrant rights sponsored by the church in Tucson. In Mexico City the bishop of Dallas, Charles Graham, challenged United States immigration policy and recounted what the United States church is doing for immigrants (*Hispanic-Vista.com*, 20 October). *Our Sunday Visitor* (OSV, 17 October) reports on the Catholic Legal Immigration Network's three million dollar project in fifty four dioceses to help 40,500 disabled, elderly, and poor immigrants complete forms for naturalization. Finally, many dioceses are aware that the hurricane in Central America will increase immigration from those countries.

## General Church News

Surveys of note include Bernard Lee's findings that some twenty percent of small Christian communities are Hispanic and that they are virtually the only ones to include children. Eighty seven percent of Hispanic participants (mostly immigrants and Mexican) see these small communities as their primary spiritual sustenance. The Life Cycle Institution showed that ten percent of United States seminarians are Latino, with many coming from outside the country. Another study by the same group concluded that Hispanic young adults are "traditional [in] doctrinal beliefs, [have] a stronger overall loyalty to things Catholic, [and have] frequent personal devotional practices." NCR (29 October) says that Latinos make up just thirteen percent of the United States church, figures that contradict others, such as the *Boston Globe* saying (26 September) that forty percent of the church is Hispanic although large numbers continue to become disaffected. The Center for Applied Research in the Apostolate (CARA) reported on data from the Archdiocese of Los Angeles. Finally, the research office for Religion in Society and Culture at Brooklyn College is conducting a major survey of Latino parishes and congregations. The director of this study, Anthony Stevens-Arroyo, also appeared in the 11 January and 13 September issues of *Hispanic Link*.

All this research will be invaluable for Encuentro 2000, scheduled for Los Angeles 6–9 July, 2000. Bishop Gerald Barnes of San Bernardino commented: "The Encuentro, unlike previous ones, celebrates the many cultures in our church. As such, it is the perfect follow-up to *Ecclesia in America*." Since the entire National Conference of Catholic Bishops (NCCB) is behind this project, more than nineteen thousand parishes have received mailings. New participants of the planning subcommittee include African American Bishop Curtis Guillory (auxiliary of Galveston-Houston) and Native American Archbishop Chaput of Denver. More information is in NCR (27 August) or at http://www.nccbuscc.org/hispanicaffairs/encuentro.htm. The St. Louis Sisters of Mercy, American Church, and the Oregon Catholic Press donated $330,000 to the Encuentro.

Good news about media. The third Catholic Communications Exposition was held in August in Miami. That Archdiocese's Pax Catholic Communications now broadcasts twenty four hours in Spanish (OSV, 28 February), and its diocesan paper, *La Voz Católica*, won the Catholic Press Association's first prize for general excellence among Spanish-language publications. Other media coverage included the Odyssey cable program on Hispanics in the Church (11, 18, 25 October) and the *Los Angeles Times* (LAT) report on yard shrines (16 October).

Top news among bishops is the appointment of Roberto O. González, O.F.M., as archbishop of San Juan, Puerto Rico. He and fellow Puerto Rican bishop Alvaro Carrada wrote a pastoral letter supporting protestors on the Puerto Rican island of Vieques who oppose the United States Navy's use of the island for live fire training. Arturo Tafoya, bishop of Pueblo, Colorado, was elected chair of the USCC's committee on Hispanic affairs. Auxiliary Bishop Richard J. Garcia of Sacramento was appointed to the bishops' committee on migration. He was also asked to visit the schools of his diocese. Gabino Zavala of Los Angeles addressed the full body of bishops in November on plans for Encuentro 2000. Bishop Nicholas DeMarzo, Newark auxiliary and chair of the USCC committee on migration, testified before Congress against deporting permanent residents who have completed prison sentences. He also joined those who urged the government to include Salvadorans and Guatemalans in temporary protection status, which shields them from immediate deportation (NCR, 23 April).

Others in the news include: • Sisters Aurora González and Ana Rosa Aceves for their dedication to education; • Ana María Díaz Stevens, first Latina/o tenured by Union Theological Seminary; • theologian Jeanette Rodríguez-Holguin, featured in the January, 1999 Revista Maryknoll, who also spoke at the Jubilee 2000 celebration in Albuquerque; • María Elena González, speaker at the National Catholic Gathering for Jubilee Justice; • Gloria Soto, joining the Sacramento diocese's office of family life; • Lucas Bents, winner of the Catholic Campaign for Human Development's first Cardinal Bernardin prize for leadership in social justice; • Raquel Guzman-Vargas and her husband, Jorge, featured in the *National Catholic Register* in August for their work with Natural Family Planning; • Father Alberto Cutié, hosting a new talk show for Telemundo; • Ronaldo Cruz, featured in the 27 August NCR; • Virgil Elizondo, teaching during the summer session at Santa Clara University; • Primitivo Romero, former director of Hispanic ministry in Phoenix, died; • Germán Toro, appointed director of the Hispanic apostolate for the diocese of Sacramento; • Jaime Vidal, appointed director of the Franciscan Press at Quincy University; • Joe Gutiérrez, highlighted by NCR 7 May for his commitment to the poor; • prison inmate Richard Hernández, in NCR 2 July; • Roberto Goizueta, speaker at the College Theology Society; • Sacramento mayor Joe Serna died; • Yolanda Tarango and Gary Riebe-Estrella, offering, through the Center for the Study of Religious Life, conferences titled "What Mission Confronts Religious Life Today in the United States?" • María Pilar Aquino, receiving a sabbatical grant from the Louisville Institute and speaking at the University of San Francisco, the Catholic Theological Society, the Ecumenical Institute for Theological Studies, the Catholic Educators'

Conference, Seattle University, and the International Panel of Feminist Theologians. She now also sits on the advisory board of the Women's Alliance for Theology, Ethics, and Ritual.

Other schools were in the news. The University of Notre Dame held a 10–12 October hemispheric consultation which brought together many well-known Hispanics of both Americas. They also appointed Gilberto Cardenas the founding director of the new Institute for Latino Studies. Fordham University's graduate school of social service became the first in the nation with a research center dedicated to the mental health of Hispanics (NCR, 3 September). Florida's Barry University received almost four hundred thousand dollars from Housing and Urban Development to assist Hispanic communities. St. Thomas University was recognized as one of the best by the Hispanic Association of Colleges and Universities. The eleventh Instituto Hispano at the Jesuit School of Theology in Berkeley featured Agustín Escalante, Eduardo Fernández, Alejandro García-Rivera, Gloria Loya, and Javier Saravia. The Academy of American Franciscan History will offer two $10,000 fellowships for projects on Franciscan history in Latin America or the United States borderlands. E-mail: acadafh@aol.com.

Young people in the news include Sandy Caldera, a gospel singer from Tijuana, who credits her parish priest with inspiring her career (LAT, 2 August). The *Catholic Herald* reports on the Oblates of St. Joseph beginning a youth retreat center (23 October) and on Angel Calderon helping young people avoid illegal drugs (25 September). Yolanda Tarango published an article in *Vision: The Annual Religious Vocation Discernment Guide*, available through the National Religious Vocation Conference and Claretian Publications.

## Organizations

The 1999 Academy of Catholic Hispanic Theologians of the United States (ACHTUS) award went to St. Vincent de Paul Regional Seminary. Their Virgilio Elizondo award was given to Gustavo Gutiérrez, who was unfortunately too ill to accept in person.

The Asociación Nacional de Diáconos Hispanos held their seventeenth conference in Austin, Texas, in July. They continue their Holy Land pilgrimages.

The Asociación Nacional de Sacerdotes Hispanos (ANSH) held their tenth annual conference 27–30 October in San Diego. Speakers included Bishop Ricardo Ramírez (Las Cruces, New Mexico), Allan Figueroa Deck, John Yzaguirre, and Ron Cruz. ANSH's director of communications, Miguel Angel Soloranzo, published "A North American College in Mexico" (NCR, 10 December). The National Association of Priests' Councils devoted their convention to the multi-cultural church and invited Roberto Piña.

The twenty first national assembly of LAS HERMANAS 1–3 October in Denver reflected on the new millennium. Speakers included Alicia Cuaron, Paula Gonzáles, and Rosa Guerrero. They have a national coordinating team of three people: Rosanna Padilla, Dolores Florez, and Linda Chavez, S.C.

Instituto Fe y Vida offered its fifth symposium and two seminars at Denver's Regis University 12–19 June. With St. Mary's Press, the institute now offers a new CD, *Cantemos como Profetas de Esperanza* (call 800–533–8095). This institute was also the host of the fifth Encuentro of Latin American Institutes for the formation of leaders and advisors of youth and young adult ministry.

The National Catholic Network de Pastoral Juvenil Hispano (La Res Católica) held their second membership meeting in Chicago 4–7 November. New officers include Rey Malavé, president; Jaime Castillo vice president; and Juan José Rodríguez, secretary. They collaborated with the National Conference of Catholic Bishops in sending a delegation to the Second Latin American Youth and Young Adult Conference held in Chile.

The Instituto de Liturgia Hispana met in Mexico City from 31 October to 2 November. Speakers were Juan Sosa and Alberto Aranda. Mention was made of the change of Our Lady of Guadalupe to a liturgical feast for all the Americas, the confirmation of the Spanish language funeral rite, and the bilingual edition of *Pastoral Care of the Sick*. Institute member Mary Frances Reza helped organize the 10–13 June Hispanic Conference for Pastoral Musicians in Albuquerque. The institute has also had success with their new mobile teams.

The twentieth anniversary of the Jesuit Hispanic ministry in San Antonio, Texas, 24–27 January, 1999 enthusiastically received reports on the new Cristo Rey High School in Chicago, where students help earn tuition through work study programs; on the increasing number of middle schools in poor areas on the "Nativity" model; on ministry among Immigration and Naturalization Service detainees in the Los Angeles area; on a new mobile team for the formation of lay ministry in the Great Lakes region; and on various creative attempts at giving the Spiritual Exercises to Hispanics (such as the Loyola Institute of Spirituality in Orange, California). Hispanic ministry veteran Pablo Sedillo was given the Joseph Fitzpatrick, S.J. Award.

The Mexican American Cultural Center (MACC) has begun its new five million dollar complex of offices, living quarters, classrooms, library, and meeting rooms. The center has received a Pew grant to do a collaborative study of Latino/a religion and civic involvement. Also, the staff has become much more active internationally.

The National Catholic Council for Hispanic Ministry elected Msgr. Jaime Soto president during its 18–21 November membership meeting in Washington, DC. After a reception for the United States bishops, there were training sessions on stewardship and on lobbying governments in social-justice issues. NCCHM completed a study of lay ministry formation through a grant from the Pew Charitable Trust.

The National Organization of Catechists for Hispanics announces new officers: Fanny Pedraza as president, Charlotte F. Seubert FSPA as vice president, Rosa María Montenegro as secretary, and Alicia Restrepo as treasurer. Also at this thirteenth conference, a public document was issued concerning recent violence in public schools.

The Program for the Analysis of Religion Among Latinos (PARAL) entered the second phase of the ground breaking National Survey of Leadership in Latino Parishes and Congregations (NSLLPC). This will be the largest survey ever conducted among Latinos and Latinas, in addition to being the first of its kind on religious topics. This survey is funded by Lilly Endowment and the Ford Foundation, among others. A report in 2001 will provide computerized data that can be correlated with other important congregational studies of American religion and with the United States census.

In January 1999 PARAL held a workshop at Princeton University for the fifteen persons selected for fellowships in a national competition. Directed by Anthony M. Stevens-Arroyo, the faculty for the training included: Milagros Peña, Ana María Díaz-Stevens, María Pérez y González, Andrés Pérez y Mena, Richard Flores, Lara Medina, Gilbert Cadena, Segundo Pantoja, and the associate director of research, Anneris Goris. In June the fellows met again in Orlando, Florida, for a week-long training in field research. Additional members of the faculty were Luis León, Felipe Martínez, and Hector López Sierra from the Interamerican University in Puerto Rico.

In November PARAL sponsored two panels at the annual meeting of the Society for the Scientific Study of Religion and the Religious Research Association held in Boston, Massachusetts. Both panels addressed theoretic issues concerned with the relationships between theology and culture, especially those focused on the agency of women. The Las Casas Lecture at Brooklyn College was delivered in April by

Professor Elpidio Laguna Díaz of Rutgers University. The Olga Scarpetta Award for 1999 was won by Susan Eichenberger of the University of Florida with a paper titled "We Are Called to Love One Another: Priests and Administrators' Perceptions of Discrimination of Latinos/as in the Catholic Church." Gilbert Cadena will serve the next two years as president of PARAL.

PARAL members achieved some personal distinctions. Ana María Díaz-Stevens, presently the council senator for PARAL, was excerpted in NCR (26 February). She is now a member of the steering committee of the Common Ground Initiative, spoke on the Latina experience at the Wethersfield Institute in Manhattan, and delivered the keynote address at the meeting of the International Society for the Sociology of Religion at the Catholic University of Leuven, in Belgium. She was awarded a sabbatical year grant by the Cushwa Center at Notre Dame to conduct research on women religious who served as missionaries to Puerto Rico. Another Cushwa award went to Lara Medina for field research in Mexico on Día de los Muertos. Milagros Peña published findings from a survey of Latinas in the Journal for the Scientific Study of Religion. Gustavo Benavides was elected vice president for the North American Association for the Study of Religion. Anneris Goris, Andrés Pérez y Mena, and Luis León presented a panel on Latino religious experiences in Mexico City at the Latin American Association for the Study of Religion. Anthony M. Stevens-Arroyo was named director of a new research facility at Brooklyn College, Religion In Society and Culture (RISC). Along with Ana María Díaz-Stevens, he was coeditor of the two volume *Encyclopedia for Contemporary Religion* to be published by the Macmillan Reference Library. Many PARAL scholars contributed noteworthy articles to this prestigious publication. The editors' previous work, *Recognizing the Latino Resurgence in U.S. Religion,* was recognized as an outstanding academic book for 1999 by *Choice* magazine. Stevens-Arroyo delivered a paper at the ISSR meeting in Belgium on the Cuban devotion to Our Lady of Charity; it will be published in French in a forthcoming issue of the journal for l'Ecole de Haute Etudes in Paris. In May, 1999 Stevens-Arroyo was named Distinguished Scholar of CUNY by that institution's chancellor.

The Southeast Regional Office for Hispanic Ministry celebrated its twentieth anniversary in part by extending itself. The region will now include the dioceses of Kentucky. Its school of ministry has also extended to other dioceses, and now their regional gatherings are multi-cultural.

## Resources

Latinos are avid radio listeners. An evangelization resource, "Tu Compañero Católico," a weekly half hour radio magazine in the Spanish language, is produced by the Redemptorists of the Denver Province. The program is provided free to dioceses and Hispanic-language radio stations to sponsor locally. It is especially designed for the newly arrived to help them navigate living in the United States Segments include interviews with Hispanic ecclesial personalities, spiritual counseling, religion, health, legal and cultural advice, and selected Latino music. For more information and for samples, contact Rev. Gary Ziuraitis, C.S.S.R., project director, at 314–436–4449 or at 1118 N. Grand Boulevard; St. Louis, Missouri 63106.

"De Palabras a Obras: Continuación de la Reflexión sobre el Papel de la Mujer en la Iglesia" is a pastoral reflection of 32 pages available from the USCC at 800–235–8722.

The Task Force on Central America and Mexico offers a package of materials concerning human rights and the liturgy. Call 202–529–0041. The National Farm Worker Ministry offers "Farm Worker Sabbath" as a way for parishes to help migrant workers.

"Notas de Ayuda" is a series of brochures from Abbey Press's One Caring Place division, 800–325–2511, (also available in English as Help Notes) that deal with themes such as grieving, loss, and illness. They are also available from Claretian Publications: 800–328–6515. Claretian's Hispanic Resource editor Carmen Aguinaco published a review of Latina literature in the November issue of United States Catholic.

"Gozando la Vida" is an audio CD intended to help parents and teens talk about vocations. Call 800–671–NCCV.

The September issue (vol. 67, no. 3) of the Journal of the American Academy of Religion published several articles concerning Hispanic Pentecostals.

For youth, see Saint Mary's Press's *Followers of Jesus: The Catholic Youth Bible* and MACC's *Quinceañera: Celebration of Life*.

## New Books

This year's books, although covering a vast array of topics, all make the same plea: Pay attention to context! In the area of pastoral theology, a failure to do so will only end up in disaster. *Bridging Boundaries: The Pastoral Care of U.S. Hispanics* (University of Scranton Press), edited by Kenneth Davis and Yolanda Tarango, brings together ten published articles that reflect the diversity found in the Latino communities in the

United States It also provides concrete pastoral suggestions for bridging gaps involving age, country of origin, denomination, gender, and level of assimilation. Particularly helpful are the historical backgrounds and current cultural and religious challenges present in ministering to several Latin American groups: South Americans (Fanny Tabares), Dominicans (Anneris Goris), Cuban Marielitos (Adele J. González), Puerto Rican women (Irma C. Nolla), and Mexican Americans (Eduardo C. Fernández). George Boran, responding to an immense dearth in the literature, writes on Hispanic youth. Kenneth Davis's articles sprinkled throughout reveal a Hispanic's struggle to provide tools for all who wish to respond to the ministry's incredible challenges. The preface by Ada María Isasi-Díaz, and the conclusion by Yolanda Tarango as well, highlight the fact that these reflections come from a committed praxis, contribute greatly to the building up of the greater church, and present a challenge for this church to actually become universal by responding to individual cultural contexts. The supplementary bibliography is icing on the cake, in many cases listing articles with much anthropological content. This book could easily become a primer for those interested in committing themselves to the diversity found in Hispanic ministry.

Another work of significant pastoral application, one also well rooted in a specific context, is Juan J. Sosa's *Sectas, Cultos, y Sincretismos* (Miami: Ediciones Universal). Designed specifically to address pastoral issues arising around various forms of popular religiosity and syncretic forms of religion, it includes several ecclesial statements in its appendices.

In the area of systematic theology, the two most noteworthy works of the year are *From the Heart of Our People: Latino/a Explorations in Catholic Systematic Theology* (Orbis) edited by Orlando O. Espín and Miguel H. Díaz, and *The Community of the Beautiful: A Theological Aesthetics* (Liturgical Press) by Alejandro García-Rivera. *From the Heart of Our People,* a collection of twelve original essays, is the fruit of extensive collaboration among Latina/o scholars who met periodically. Contained within are glimpses of their personal journeys along with theological insights of theirs from contexts very different from mainstream theological discourse: "The faith of the people" or popular religion is a major primary source. The book asks: "What would Catholic systematics look like if it were done from a Latino/a perspective?" The contributors, most of them well known in the field, tackle different relevant topics: María Pilar Aquino (method), Virgilio Elizondo (role of theologians), Alejandro García-Rivera (metaphysics as cosmology), Roberto S. Goizueta (fiesta), Jean-Pierre Ruiz (Bible), Orlando O. Espín (sin and grace), Miguel H. Díaz (Our Lady of Charity), Gary Riebe-Estrella (pueblo and church), Jeanette Rodríguez-Holguín (la tierra, the earth), and Ruy G. Suárez Rivero (United States Latino/a theology). Justo L. González comments from a Protestant perspective, and Arturo J. Bañuelas provides a selective bibliography. The book's collaborative methodology, index, and glossary, together with each writer's substantial footnotes, help make this work a wonderful representation of the progress being made in the writing of Latino/a theology.

García-Rivera's work is, in the words of Virgilio Elizondo, "a beautiful contribution toward a truly Pan-American theology of the next millennium." His writing, a perceptive dialogue with various streams of thought from American pragmatist philosophy and Latin American history and philosophy, embodies the new *mestizaje* (mixture). Autobiographical at times, it is quite interdisciplinary as insights from art history, the physical sciences, literature, philosophy, and theology skillfully contribute to a theological aesthetics of "lifting up the lowly." This incisive, poetic work is a fine example of what can happen when both Hispanic American and Euro-American theologies are placed in dialogue.

*Mapas para la Fiesta* (Atlanta: AETH, 1998) by Otto Maduro, a Venezuelan sociologist and philosopher of religion now at Drew University, is an exposé of how one's experience or one's world view shapes the individual or societal understanding of "reality" or "truth." One walks away with a better understanding of why people in a Latin American context understand "reality" so differently from people in a North American or European context, where economic and political "progress" seem to be more prevalent. The work has a very "desde la base" (basic, grass roots) feel as it incorporates everyday experience of Latin Americans.

An historical piece that not only reveals a specific context, but also tells the story of a Jesuit missionary who understood much of its complexity, is *José de Acosta, S.J. (1540–1600): His Life and Thought* (Chicago: Loyola Press) by Claudio M. Burgaleta, S.J. Chronicling the life of Acosta—missionary, theologian, orator, playwright, economist, jurist, administrator, and diplomat at the court of Philip II—Burgaleta introduces him to the English-speaking world. The book incorporates both primary and secondary archival sources found in various countries. Throughout, the author emphasizes Acosta's principle "that the Amerindians can indeed be evangelized and saved." A key missiological concept that surfaces is that of "Jesuit theological humanism." At a time when Latino theology is struggling to understand the circumstances surrounding the conquest and early evangelization, Burgaleta's meticulously researched book presents significant historical evidence to debunk the myth of a monolithic 16th century church. The work, complete with glossary, maps, appendices, and index, is very "user friendly."

Another historical work about a Mexican American historian is Felix D. Almaraz's *Knight without Armor: Carlos Eduardo Castañeda, 1896–1958* (Texas A & M University Press). Castañeda taught at the University of Texas at Austin and compiled an impressive multi-volume history of the church in Texas. Almaraz's book was not available at press time and so cannot be reviewed. Likewise we regret the unavailability of the promising new book by Lilya Wagner and Allan Figueroa Deck, S.J., *Hispanic Philanthropy: Exploring the Factors That Influence Giving and Asking* (San Francisco: Jossey-Bass, 1999).

Jesús F. de la Teja edited *Wilderness Mission: Preliminary Studies of the Texas Catholic Historical Society* (Austin, 1999), our final historical work. This collection includes primary documents from the colonial period (each with helpful notes) as well as contributions by contemporary scholars. The bibliography includes both manuscript and secondary citations. Placing all of this in one volume, in context, and in English is a great contribution to the field.

Some African American theologians have looked to gospel hymns and current novels and biographies as a reflection of the faith of their communities, especially under difficult circumstances. Ellen Mc Cracken's *New Latina Narrative: The Feminine Space of Postmodern Ethnicity* (University of Arizona Press) provides a much needed background for doing the same with recent Latina literature. Focusing on the dynamic writing published in the 1980s and 1990s by Mexican American, Puerto Rican, Cuban American, and Dominican American women, the book shows these writers redefining the concepts of multiculturalism and diversity in American society. Of particular importance with regard to the influence of religion is Chapter Four: "Remapping Religious Space: Orthodox and Non-Orthodox Religious Culture." McCracken has done her homework. Her ease in presenting the religious background behind many of these narratives provides an important entry into how one might reflect theologically on this often overlooked manifestation of the "faith of the people."

A community quite intent on paying attention to its theological context, especially as manifested in its folklore and popular religiosity, is the Nuevomexicanos. As the following books demonstrate, religion has played and continues to play a key role in shaping these culturally distinct peoples' worldview. A new book on Our Lady of Guadalupe, one which summarizes current controversies around its historicity but does more than that, is *Guadalupe: Our Lady of New Mexico* (Santa Fe: Museum of New Mexico Press) by Jacqueline Orsini Dunnington. Among the unique contributions of what at first seems like "yet another book on Guadalupe" is that she does not engage in apparition polemics. At the same time, she does not ignore its extensive literature. Her key contribution is to provide visual, oral, and written histories that, in the context of the devotion of the faithful, furnish a greater appreciation of the *sensus fidelium*. The book is replete with local New Mexican examples of art, fiestas, shrines, dances, drama, and literature that all reveal the love of a people for their Mother. The photographs, some in color, and an impressive up to date Guadalupan bibliography are indispensable.

The apparitions of Our Lady of Guadalupe also appear in *Six Nuevomexicano Folk Dramas for Advent Season* (University of New Mexico Press), a collection translated and illustrated by Larry Torres. This bilingual edition of these classic folk dramas is produced both for those acting in the plays and for students of the literature. The plays, products of late medieval Spain modified over the past four hundred years in New Mexico, mix didactic morality, miracle stories, and folk inspiration. The six works presented in the book make up an Advent and Christmas cycle: The Four Apparitions of Our Lady of Guadalupe; Las Posadas; Los Pastores; Los Moros y los Cristianos; Los Matachines Desenmascarados; and Los Tres Reyes Magos. Torres provides historical notes and production suggestions as well as abundant illustrations to help directors and actors visualize scenes and block characters. Typical of the context of New World *mestizaje*, the works not only reveal Jewish, Christian, Moorish, and Amerindian blends, but also an array of artistry as religion, history, dance, music, and visual arts are integrated in the conveyance of a living tradition. Torres's painstaking efforts make accessible in written form the religious folk literature and oral traditions of this part of the world, a treasure for pastoralists and theologians alike.

Few things speak of context as clearly as visual art. In *Cuando Hablan los Santos: Contemporary Santero Traditions from Northern New Mexico* (University of New Mexico Press), the work of thirteen outstanding New Mexico folk artists and their families is highlighted in a bilingual volume compiled by Mari Lyn C. Salvador. Composed of bounteous illustrations and essays by six scholars on various aspects of the history, iconography, and marketing of these increasingly popular woodcarvings and paintings, this cross generational exposé is a wonderful example of "ethnoaesthetic research." Its approach is described as "interest not only in the artwork per se but in the perspective of the artists and their views regarding their work and the development of its style." Much of the spirituality of the artists and the community comes through as the reader is introduced to the prayer life and devotional use from their point of view. What results in the stories behind this folk art, often in the words of the artists themselves, is a realization that ritual, spirituality, history, and art are intimately connected.

Not to be overlooked in examining context, especially in regard to popular religiosity, is the role of physical space. *Pilgrimage to Chimayó: Contemporary Portrait of a Living Tradition* (Santa Fe: Museum of New Mexico Press) by Sam Howarth and Enrique R. Lamadrid, a small book of photographs and essays, does precisely that. Chimayó, the site of a small adobe chapel in northern New Mexico, is one of the most important spiritual sites in the Southwest and the center of the largest religious pilgrimage in the United States Four photographers and two oral historians document the annual pilgrimage held around Holy Week. The book's two essays put the event into historical and cultural context, while testimonials by the participants, many of whom walk to the sacred site, reveal the spirituality behind this ancient practice. One of the pilgrims, Raymond Jones, says: "This is my favorite time of the year because everything that has to do with our redemption becomes focused. I think that's the way we have to do it. Move through it in prayer, and just stay close to Jesus."

## Other Significant Writings

Awalt, Barbe, and Paul Rhetts. "The Images of Nuestra Senora in New Mexican Devotional Art: Traditional and Contemporary." *Marian Studies* 49 (1998): 19–40. Speaks of the predominance of Marian images in the New Mexican tradition of making santos.

Davis, Kenneth, O.F.M.Conv. *"Sensus Fidelium:* Vehículo para la Inculturación en Culturas Concretas." In *Abrir Caminos a la Vida,* ed. Rosemarie Kamke. Rome: Institución Teresiana, 1999, pp. 120–127. Gives a brief history of this doctrine and how it relates to Hispanic popular Catholicism.

———. "When a Bilingual Preacher Is Made, Not Born." *AIM Liturgy Resources* (Winter, 1999): 18–19. Demonstrates why mastering Spanish is necessary but insufficient for preaching cross-culturally.

———. "Cursillo de Cristiandad: Gift of the Hispanic Church." *Chicago Studies* 38, no. 3 (Fall–Winter, 1999): 318–328. History of this movement with emphasis on its impact on United States de Luna, Sister Anita. "One and Many: Cultivating Cultural Diversity." *Church* (Summer, 1999): 23–27. Shows why pastoral ministers must provide opportunities that enable the church to be receptive to diversity.

Deck, Allan F., S.J., and Christopher Tirres. "Latino Popular Religion and the Struggle for Justice." In *Religion, Race, and Justice in a Changing America,* eds. Gary Orfield and Holly Lebowitz Rossi. New York: A Century Foundation Book, 1999, pp. 139–210. Explores how Latino popular religion continues to be both a symbolic resource of meaning and a potential agent for change in concrete social and political concerns. Based on an address given by Allan Deck at the Harvard University School of Law. Christopher Tirres is a second year doctoral student at Harvard Divinity School.

Elizondo, Virgilio. "Transformation of Borders: Border Separation or New Identity." In *Theology: Expanding the Borders,* eds. María Pilar Aquino and Roberto Goizueta. Mystic, Conn.:Twenty Third Publications, pp. 22–39. A reflection on how Christians negotiate borders by becoming intercultural. Other chapters include important reflections by non-Hispanics on Latino/as and others by Protestant Hispanics.

Fandel, Cecilia, O.S.M. "The Border and Immigration: An Invitation to Posada." *New Theology Review* 2, no. 1 (February, 1999): 32–42. Shows how the spirit of posada (shelter), not the walls we have built at the border, is the proper Christian response to immigrants.

Garcia, Sixto. "Hispanic Theologians as Actors, Poets, and Prophets of Their Communities." *Journal of Hispanic/Latino Theology* 6, no. 4 (May, 1999): 5–18. Speaks of the theologian as the protagonist and prophet of God's people.

Lassalle-Klein, Robert. "The Potential Contribution of C.S. Peirce to Interpretation Theory in United States Hispanic/Latino and Other Culturally Contextualized Theologies." *Journal of Hispanic/Latino Theology* 6, no. 3 (February, 1999): 5–34. Uses semiotic theory to explore the insights of Roberto Goizueta and Virgil Elizondo concerning popular Catholicism.

Lovrien, Peggy. "Inculturation and Multi-culturalism." *Ministry and Liturgy* 26, no. 7 (September, 1999): 12–14. Addresses the importance of having a sense of why both inculturation and multi-culturalism are important when serving multi-cultural communities.

Maldonado, Pérez, Zaida. "Death and the 'Hour of Triumph': Subversion within the Visions of Saturus and Polycarp." In *Theology: Expanding the Borders,* eds. María Pilar Aquino and Roberto Goizueta. Mystic, Conn.: Twenty Third Publications, pp. 121–144. Argues that the visions of the early martyrs reflect their contemporary grass roots theology, which sometimes challenged Greco-Roman church and society.

Martin, Shane, and Ernesto Colin. "The Novels of Graciela Limon: Narrative, Theology, and the Search for Mestiza/o Identity." *Journal of Hispanic/Latino Theology* 7, no. 1 (August, 1999): 6–25. Introduces readers to four novels, suggesting that this writing engages in a rich dialogue between literature and theology.

Matovina, Timothy M. "The National Parish and Americanization." *U.S. Catholic Historian* 17, no. 1 (Winter, 1999): 45–58. Argues for the greater effectiveness of the national or "personal" parish in efforts to evangelize our many different immigrants.

————. "Religion and Ethnicity in San Antonio: Germans and Tejanos in the Wake of United States Annexation." *Catholic Southwest: A Journal of History and Culture* 10 (1999): 29–49. Shows how German and Tejano religion and ethnicity were shaped by interactions with English-speaking United States citizens, who often presumed they represented the cultural norm for all San Antonians.

————. "Representation and the Reconstruction of Power: The Rise of Padres and Las Hermanas." In *What's Left? Liberal American Catholics,* ed. Mary Jo Weaver. Bloomington: Indiana University Press, 1999. History and critique of a Chicano priest and a Latina religious organization since 1969.

Mejido, Manuel Jesús. "Theoretical Prolegomenon to the Sociology of U.S. Hispanic Popular Religion." *Journal of Hispanic/Latino Theology* 7, no. 1 (August, 1999): 27–55. Suggests that sociologists of religion have much to learn from United States Latina/o theologians who insist that popular religion is a crucial locus for Hispanic theology.

Ostendorf, David L. "Exploiting Immigrant Workers," *Christian Century* (5 May, 1999): 492–493. Meat packing industries profitably and unjustly exploit the immigrant workers; pastoral responses to this.

Philibert, Paul, O.P., and John Reid. "Su Futuro, Nuestro Futuro." *Touchstone* 14, no. 3 (Spring, 1999): 10–11. Tells of the proceedings of the 1998 National Consultation on Hispanic Pastoral Concerns held at Notre Dame, Indiana.

Riebe-Estrella, Gary. "La Virgen: A Mexican Perspective." *New Theology Review* 12, no. 2 (May, 1999): 39–47. Shows how, in the Mexican context, La Virgen functions as an icon of God rather than as a special saint.

Rodriguez, Jesús, B.C.C., D.Min. "Chaplains' Communication with Latino Patients: Case Studies on Non-Verbal Communication." *The Journal of Pastoral Care* 53, no. 3 (Fall, 1999): 309–317. Introduces non-Latinos to aspects of nonverbal communication dynamics one may encounter with some Latino patients. Provides specific insights into the communication styles of some Latinos.

Sosa, Juan J. "Liturgy and Popular Piety: A Marriage Made on Earth." *Church* 15, no. 3 (Fall, 1999): 13–16. Addresses the relationship between official church liturgy and popular piety within the Catholic community.

Suarez Rivero, Ruy G. "Teologia en la Frontera: Limite y Encuentro de Dos Mundos." In *Theology: Expanding the Borders,* eds. Maria Pilar Aquino and Roberto Goizueta. Mystic, Conn.:Twenty Third Publications, pp.40–59. Examines the sociology and theology of Catholic popular religion along the Tijuana/San Diego border.

Toomey, Don. "'Bautismo de Jesús,' A Magnificent Bulto by *Santero* Filimón Agular." *Catholic Southwest* 10 (1999): 51–60. Illustrated survey of this artist's work.

Turek, Doris Mary, S.S.N.D. "La Tierra Prometida: A Mother's Sacrifice." *New Theology Review* 12, no. 1 (February, 1999): 70–74. Shows how the laws of the Immigration and Naturalization Service force immigrants to make unbearable sacrifices.

Wright, Robert. "Sacred Sites: Building Churches and Communities in 19th Century South Texas." *Heritage* 17, no. 1, pp. 16–20. Surveys worship spaces 1846–1899, especially those created by the Oblates of Mary Immaculate.

*This article originally appeared in Review for Religious Vol. 59 (2000) under the title, "U.S. Hispanic Catholics: Trends and Works 1999."*

# Appendix I: Expanded Bibliography

*The following are books and articles which were not included in the Review for Religious articles which appeared from 1990–2000. The major research index used to generated this list is that of the American Theological Library Association.*

## Journal Articles and Chapters

Albacete, Lorenzo, "The Hispanic Presence in the Church in the United States." *Origins* 25, (August, 1995): 157–161. His address to the Hispanic Convocation '95 on June 24th in San Antonio, Texas, in which he maintains that the Hispanic presence in the United States is not a problem but rather a blessing. His talk centers on the relation between faith and culture as relevant to the task of evangelization.

Bañuelas, Arturo, ed. "US Hispanic Roman Catholic Theology: A Bibliography." *Apuntes* 11, (Winter, 1991): 93–103. A listing of what was then the most comprehensive of bibliographies.

Barron, C.P., Clemente. "On My Mind: Hispanics, Racism and Vocations." *New Theology Review* 3 (November, 1990): 92–103. Addresses the loss of Hispanic Catholics, the Catholic response, and the lack of Hispanic vocations within a discussion of racism and the preferential option for the poor.

Christiano, Kevin J. "Religion Among Hispanics in the United States: Challenges to the Catholic Church." *Archives de Sciences Sociales des Religions* 38, (July–September, 1993): 53–65. Basically presents the state of the question, lamenting the need for more research on the incorporation of Hispanics into the Roman Catholic Church in the United States.

Copeland, M. Shawn. "Black, Hispanic/Latino, and Native American Theologies." In *The Modern Theologians: An Introduction to Christian Theology in the Twentieth Century*, ed. David F. Ford. Cambridge, Mass.: Blackwell Publishers, 1997, pp. 357–388. Surveys these emerging voices in the field of contextual theology, outlining individually the historical context of their emergence and development, surveying critical writers, and summarizing their achievements, assessments, and agendas.

Deck, Allan Figueroa. "Hispanic Theologians and the U.S. Catholic Church." *New Theology Review* 3 (November, 1990): 22–27. The text, adapted from his inaugural speech as president of the Academy of Hispanic Theologians (ACHTUS), summarizes the contributions these theologians have made and the challenges which remain.

Díaz-Stevens, Ana María. "Ministerio y Cambio Institucional." *Cristianismo y Sociedad* 31/4–32/1, (1993–1994): 29–42. Discusses the impact of Puerto Rican migration on the Archdiocese of New York in the twentieth century.

Erevia, Angela. "Happy to be Hispanic." *Religion Teacher's Journal* 25, (October, 1991): 35–37. Basing herself on the way Jesus related to people, the author presents some of the gifts which Hispanics bring to the wider Church. Contains some excellent suggestions for catechists.

Foley, John P. and Geoffrey R. Hammond. "We Do it Our Way." *Momentum* 29, (February – March, 1998): 27–28. Presents reasons behind the great success of Cristo Rey Jesuit High School, which opened in 1996 in an economically disadvantaged area of Chicago. The innovative school, predominantly Hispanic, combines serious academic preparation with off-site work (thus keeping it affordable), and all-school daily prayer.

Francis, Mark. "Hispanic Popular Piety and Liturgical Reform." *Modern Liturgy* 18 (1991): 14–17. Aside from outlining some important historical aspects behind the present relationship between popular piety and liturgical reform, says that "much of popular piety strikes political, social, cultural as well as religious cords among many Hispanics." Calls for a "cross-fertilization between popular religion and liturgy."

Francis, Mark. "Popular Piety and Liturgical Reform in a Hispanic Context." In *Dialogue Rejoined: Theology and Ministry in the United States Hispanic Reality*, eds. Pineda and Schreiter, pp. 162–177. Collegeville: The Liturgical Press, 1995. Presents historical reasons why non-Hispanics who minister in a Hispanic context or those who teach Hispanic students should not equate the devotionalism of their youth with expressions of Hispanic popular religiosity and presents grounds for future dialogue between popular piety and liturgical reform.

Ginoris, Esperanza. "We Can be Bridge-Builders." *Religion Teacher's Journal* 26, (November–December, 1992): 35. Calls for a greater sensitivity to Hispanic culture in catechetics.

Gonzalez, Adele J. "Companion on Pilgrimage: The Hispanic Experience." In *Common Journey, Different Paths*, eds. Susan Rakoczy, I.H.M., pp. 121–127. Maryknoll: Orbis Books, 1992. Basing herself on her experience of being spiritual director for Hispanics, summarizes key values and themes such as family, suffering, dignity, and living life to its fullest. Warns against the danger of Hispanic ministers neglecting the quality of their personal time with the Lord.

Herrera, Marina and Jaime Vidal. "Evangelization: Then And Now(?)" *New Theology Review* 3 (November, 1990): 6–21. Presents some of the ambivalence surrounding the 500th anniversary of the arrival of Europeans to the Americas. Presents a more positive interpretation of that period than is commonly perceived.

Huitrado-Rizo, M.C.C.J., Juan Jose. "Hispanic Popular Religiosity: The Expression of a People Coming to Life." *New Theology Review* 3 (November, 1990): 43–55. Introduces some of the reasons behind a new appreciation of this phenomenon in Latin America and among Hispanics in the United States.

Hunt, Larry L. "Hispanic Protestantism in the United States: Trends by the Decade and Generation." *Social Forces* vol. 77, no. 4, (June, 1999): 1601–1624. Renders the results of a study designed to explore the temporal and socio-demographic factors that predict differences between Catholic religious affiliation and other affiliations, especially Evangelical and Pentecostal forms of Protestant affiliation that are apparently increasing. Challenges the notion that fundamentalist Protestantism is gaining large numbers of converts from Catholicism.

Icaza, Rosa María. "Espiritualidad–Mística–Liturgia." In *Visión Profética: Reflexiones Pastorales sobre el Plan Pastoral Para el Ministerio Hispano*, eds. S. Galerón, R. Icaza, and R. Urrabazo, Kansas City: Sheed and Ward, 1992: 65–72. Using the Bishops' Pastoral Plan as a point of reference, describes the spirituality of Hispanics, demonstrating how the sacraments, home devotions, and familial relations are all intertwined. Concludes with a call for a greater inculturation of the liturgy.

Icaza, C.C.V.I., Rosa Mara. "Multi-culturalism in Catholic Education." *Today's Catholic Teacher* (March, 1996): 49–52. Offers reasons for and concrete suggestions for embracing multi-cultural sensitivity in the classroom. Goes beyond political correctness to demonstrate that Christian faith requires it.

Isasi-Díaz, Ada María. "On the Birthing Stool: Mujerista Liturgy." In *Women at Worship*, eds. Marjorie Procter-Smith and Janet R. Walton, pp. 191–210. Louisville: Westminister/John Knox Press, 1993. Describes in great detail a Mujerista Liturgy held at the 1989 National Conference of LAS HERMANAS. Included are preparation, environment and symbols, texts and hymns, sequence of the ritual, and a final analysis and critique.

Lampe, Philip E. and Flores, Patricio. "Up from the Cellar: Philip E. Lampe Interviews Patricio Flores." *Critic* 49, (Autumn, 1994): 55–69. In this interview with the Archbishop of San Antonio, the first Mexican American Bishop, once a high school dropout and migrant worker, discusses such an array of topics as race relations, the role of women in the Church, education, liturgy, ministry, the loss of members, and the need to be needed.

Loya, Goria Inés. "Hispanic Faith and Culture — and USA Religious." *Review for Religious* 53, (May – June, 1994): 460–66. Presents some thoughts and reflections of her life experience as a Mexican-American woman religious. Key components to fostering vocations to religious life from the Latino community include a long-range pastoral commitment to these peoples as well as a concern for community and spirituality.

Lyke, James P. "Give the Poor a Chance." *Momentum* 23, (April, 1992): 36–38. In his keynote address, the African-American Archbishop of Atlanta makes the case for keeping open Catholic schools, especially those serving poor communities whose populations often include Blacks and Hispanics.

Marín, Gerardo and Raymond J. Gamba. "The Role of Expectation in Religious Conversions: The Case of Hispanic Catholics." *Review of Religious Research* 34, (June, 1993): 357–371. Surveyed 269 Hispanics (Catholics and Non-Catholics) to study their expectations toward their church and the possible reasons for conversions away from Catholicism. In general, "Catholics expected more direct guidance and spiritual strength from their church while Non-Catholics emphasized salvation together with the sense of spiritual strength." Also contains some reasons given for choosing to leave the Catholic Church.

Martínez, O.P., Dolorita. "Basic Christian Communities: A New Model of Church Within the United States Hispanic Community." *New Theology Review* 3 (November, 1990): 35–42. Examines the theology behind a movement which began in Latin American and has spread to the United States.

Pérez, Arturo J. "Signs of the Times: Towards a Hispanic Rite, *Quizás.*" *New Theology Review* 3 (November, 1990): 80–88. Blends liturgy and spirituality in a Hispanic context. Concludes that there already exists a rite of Hispanic worship.

Pineda, R.S.M., Ana María. "Pastoral de Conjunto." *New Theology Review* 3 (November, 1990): 28–34. Explains the origin and method of this process of evangelization, especially as it relates to Hispanic Catholics in the United States.

Poole, Stafford. "The Roman Catholic Missionary Experience in Ibero-America" *Word and World* 12, (Spring, 1992): 138–145. By presenting a brief historical overview of centuries of evangelization, the author substantiates his reasons for saying that "Christianity in the Americas was based on a late medieval Iberian model and was filtered through the prism of various native American cultures and beliefs." He concludes that " . . .

the fusion is such that the old has dominated the new, and the result is neither Christian nor pre-Christian but a mixture of the two."

Ramírez, Ricardo, Bp. "500 Years of . . ." *Apuntes* 12, (Summer, 1992): 98–107. In an address given at the Perkins School of Theology at Southern Methodist University in Dallas, the Bishop of Las Cruces, New Mexico tackles the controversy around the celebration of the quincentennial, especially in light of the Indian-Spanish history in Latin American and the Southwest. He concludes by recognizing current challenges.

Riebe-Estrella, S.V.D., Gary. "'Underneath' Hispanic Vocations." *New Theology Review* 3 (November, 1990): 72–79. Comparing what the Church's general documents say about priesthood with those more specific to the Hispanic community, the author explores the issue of Hispanic vocations, concluding that there are two very different ecclesiologies at work.

Romero, C. Gilbert. "On Becoming 'Apiru: An Agenda for Latino Theology." *Apuntes* 16, (Summer, 1996): 59–61. Compares the 'Apiru, a marginated group in fifteenth century B.C.E. Middle East, to Latinos today. Says that, like them, Latinos, despite their marginalization, should draw from their religious traditions and practices, especially those found in popular religiosity, in order to remain in solidarity with other fellow outcasts.

Roof, Wade Clark and Christel Manning. "Cultural Conflicts and Identity: Second-Generation Hispanic Catholics in the United States." *Social Compass* 41, no. 1, (1994): 171–184. Explores the situation of second-generation Hispanics in the United States, giving various reasons for affirming that theirs is a very different experience from that of previous immigrant groups to the United States.

Rywalt, Lawrence. "El Arco Iris de María: Mary's Rainbow." *Modern Liturgy* vol. 18, no.10, (1992): 20–22. Addresses the difficulty of celebrating Marian feasts where the Hispanic communities come from diverse Latin American countries. Proposes a common feast day around August 15th, giving suggestions for a four part celebration which consists of vigil, procession, prayer service, and party.

Sandoval, Moisés. "The Church Among the Hispanics in the United States." In *The Church in Latin America: 1492–1992*, ed. Enrique Dussel, pp. 230–242. Maryknoll: Orbis Books, 1992. Traces the history of the Church from the sixteenth century to the twentieth. Author combines both conventional and more recent social history approaches.

Sedano, Maruja. "When Parents are Upset." *Religion Teacher's Journal* 26, (January, 1993): 17. Orients the reader as to how catechists can help Hispanic parents, often not accustomed to United States parochial practice, to retain their traditional values, yet benefit from a greater emphasis on preparation.

Sosa, Juan J. "Renewal and Inculturation." *Liturgy* 9, (Winter, 1990): 17–23. On the occasion of the tenth anniversary of the Instituto de Liturgia Hispana, the author recounts, not only some of the institutes' accomplishments, but also some of the challenges which remain, especially in light of the never ending task of inculturation.

Sosa, Juan J. "Reflections from the Hispanic Viewpoint." In *The Awakening Church: 25 Years of Liturgical Renewal*, ed. Lawrence Madden, S.J., pp. 121–124. Collegeville: The Liturgical Press, 1992. A condensed version of his 1990 article published in Liturgy.

Sosa, Juan J. "Hospitality for and by Musicians: Melody and Text." *Pastoral Music* 17, (February–March, 1993): 18–21. Having established the importance of providing music in Hispanic culture and its relation to Christ-like hospitality, the author presents various points which musicians should keep in mind when helping to create a welcoming environment at liturgies.

Suarez, Rivero, Ruy G. "Teologia en la Frontera: Limite y Encuentro de Dos Mundos." In *Theology: Expanding the Borders,* ed. Maria Pilar Aquino and Robert Goizueta. Mystic, Conn.: Twenty-Third Publications, pp. 40–59. Examines the sociology and theology of Catholic popular religion along the Tiajuana/San Diego border.

Toomey, Don. "'Bautismo de Jésus,' A Magnificent Bulto by Santero Filimón Agular." *Catholic Southwest* 10 (1999): 70–74. Shows how the laws of the Immigration and Naturalization Service force immigrants to make unbearable sacrifices.

Wright, Robert. "Sacred Sites: Building Churches and Communities in nineteenth century South Texas." *Heritage* 17, no. 1, pp. 16–20. Surveys worship spaces 1846–1899, especially those created by the Oblates of Mary Immaculate.

Tarango,C.C.V.I., Yolanda. "The Hispanic Woman and Her Role in the Church." *New Theology Review* 3 (November, 1990): 56–61. Drawing from her family's experience, explores the changing roles for Hispanic women in the church.

Viramontes-Gutiérrez, Theresa. "A Look at Confirmation Through 'Spanish' Eyes." In *Confirming the Faith of Adolescents*, ed. Arthur J. Kubick, pp. 96–106. Mahwah, New Jersey: Paulist Press, 1991. Drawing from her experience as DRE and consultant for the Los Angeles Archdiocese, the writer presents some practical ideas for confirmation programs with the Hispanic community.

Zapata, SH, Dominga. "Ministries Among Hispanics in the United States: Development and Challenges." *New Theology Review* 3 (November, 1990): 62–71. Reviews the leadership roles which various groups have assumed in the Hispanic community and the kinds of ministries that are still in need of attention.

## Book Reviews

*What follows are a brief presentation of books which, published during 1990–2000, were not included in the Review for Religious articles. Only one of them, a reprint by Timothy Matovina which appeared in The Living Light 31, no. 2 (Winter, 1994): p. 76, can be attributed to a person other than one of the three editors of this book. The books are in chronological order.*

### Religiosidad Popular: Las Imagenes de Jesucristo y la Virgen Maria en America Latina by the Instituto de Liturgia Hispana. San Antonio, 1990.

This small publication (42 pages), issued in Spanish on the 10th anniversary of the Instituto, reflects the organization's desire to study the spirituality of Hispanics in the United States so as to work towards a greater inculturation of the liturgy. The five contributors are Rosa María Icaza, C.C.V.I. (prologo), William Wrothos ("Arte Popular Cristiano"), Jaime Lara ("Las Imagenes de Jesucristo Populares en Latinoamérica"), and Bishop Agustín Román with Rogelio Zelada ("Las Imágenes de María en la Piedad Popular Latino-americana"). With the help of many illustrations, the authors present a brief historical background of the major devotions found in Latin America around Jesus and Mary, including a discussion of how they manifest themselves in popular religiosity.

### Primero Dios: Alcoholics Anonymous and the Hispanic Community by Kenneth Davis. Selinsgrove, PA.: Susquehanna University Press, 1994. Hardback. $29.95.

The author addresses the applicability of Alcoholics Anonymous (AA) for Mexican-descent Catholic males living in the United States. The book's primary purpose is to empower pastoral agents as mediators between Mexican American communities and the twelve step program of AA. An earlier companion volume based on this work's theoretical reflection, *Cuando el tomar ya no es gozar: Una respuesta católica al alcoholismo* (Franciscan Communications, 1993), offers a practical guide to teach pastoral agents the twelve steps.

Davis integrates the insights of an experienced pastor with an impressive command of the scholarly literature on Mexican American Catholicism and alcoholism. His succinct, readable account identifies three parallel themes in the spiritualities of Mexican-descent Catholics and AA: The importance of *respeto* (respect) and *verguenza* (shame), the experience of the world as divinely-ordained but not rigidly ordered, and the belief that suffering is redemptive and liberative. Mexican-descent Catholics mediate these themes in foundational faith expressions like those associated with death, Our Lady of Guadalupe, and other saints. AA's emphasis on mutuality, serenity, and "hitting bottom" as the first step to recovery also reflects these three respective themes. Conversion in the Mexican American community and in AA entails "a response to a contextualized crisis that reinforces (these three) existing values" (58).

These common core religious themes and notions of conversion suggest that AA can serve as an "indigenous folk therapy" for alcoholics in the Mexican-descent Catholic community. Davis tested the usefulness of the AA approach by offering an eleven week lay ministry training course on the twelve steps in an urban California diocese. The ten Mexican-descent Catholics who took the course improved their scores threefold on an alcoholism awareness instrument. More importantly, they expressed greater confidence in responding to the disease of alcoholism in their families and ministry.

As Davis himself admits, the description of conversions presented in this study needs further development. The claim that a crisis precipitates the process of conversion is not true in all cases. Furthermore, conversion can involve more than a return to the core values of Mexican Catholic faith expressions or AA. Another limitation of the study is the fieldwork, which encompassed a single course with ten students. However, the reception of *Cuando el tomar ya no se goza* in pastoral circles will further test the author's thesis for pastoral agents in Mexican American communities.

All in all, *Primero Dios* provides a fascinating comparison between two of the most potent spiritual forces in the United States today: Hispanic faith expressions and twelve step programs. This volume initiates a significant dialogue for theologians and pastoral ministers, twelve step practitioners, and anyone interested in contemporary spiritualities.

*Reviewed by Timothy M. Matovina*
*Mexican American Cultural Center*
*San Antonio, Texas*

*Perspectivas: Hispanic Ministry* edited by **Allan Figueroa Deck, Yolanda Tarango, and Timothy M. Matovina. Kansas City: Sheed & Ward, 1995. Paper. $12.95.**

The articles in this volume, all published during the previous ten years, appear as a single volume resource for pastoral agents. "Collectively they illustrate the diversity of issues and perspectives in Hispanic ministry, as well as the diversity among the Latino population in the United States." Some of the articles are excerpts of longer articles. The collection's appendices include pastoral resources (Kenneth Davis), information about the authors, and the original source of the articles. The twenty two essays are as follows: "Models" (Allan Figueroa Deck); "The Poor in a Middle-Class Church" (Joseph P. Fitzpatrick); "Caribbean Contribution" (Dominga Zapata); "Pluralism" (Ada María Isasi-Díaz); "Multi-culturalism as an Ideology"(Allan Figueroa Deck); "No Melting Pot in Sight"(Timothy M. Matovina); "Women"(Yolanda

Tarango); "Youth and Culture" (Alicia C. Marill); "Youth and Evangelization" (Carmen María Cervantes); "New Immigrants" (Joseph P. Fitzpatrick); "Empowering Leaders" (Timothy M. Matovina); "Formation in Religious Communities"(Verónica Mendez); "Catechesis"(Angela Erevia); "The Challenge of Proselytism"(J. Juan Díaz Vilar); "Preaching as a Second Language" (Kenneth G. Davis); "Religious Imagination"(Alex Garcia-Rivera); "Spirituality" (Arturo Perez Rodriguez); "Popular Religion"(Virgilio Elizondo); "Liturgy"(Timothy M. Matovina); "Pastoral de Conjunto" (Ana María Pineda); "Basic Christian Communities" (Dolorita Martínez); "Reasons for Our Hope"(Allan Figueroa Deck).

***The Regis Santos: Thirty Years of Collecting* by Thomas Steele, S.J., Barbe Awalt, and Paul Rhetts. Albuquerque: LPD Press, 1997. Hardback. $54.95.**

Documents three hundred pieces of Santero art found in the teaching collection assembled on a very limited budget by Thomas Steele. The tradition and images cover almost four hundred years of New Mexican history. As Awalt and Rhetts report in the foreword: "This was one of those times that a curator and teacher had an opportunity to tell the stories behind the collection. As this is a teaching collection, the reason the teacher chose individual pieces is in itself a lesson for students. The result is a very personal story of one person's love affair with one particular art form." Aside from the fine illustrations, the book contains a bibliography and other sources for future research.

***A Literary Reading of John 5: Text as Construction* by Francisco Lozada, Jr. New York: Peter Lang, 2000. Studies in Biblical Literature, Volume 20. Hardback. $40.95.**

A critical study of John 5 from a literary and ideological perspective which employs a *text-as-construction* reading strategy that examines both the role of the implied reader within the narrative context of John 5 and the impact of John 5 on the implied reader. It argues that John 5 can be read as a reconstructed coherent and meaningful text centered on the conflict of belief and unbelief, which through the device of a failed *anagnorisis* can lead to an ideology of superiority for the implied reader. In the book's final chapter, Lozada situates himself as a Hispanic reading the text, thus engaging in an ideological exercise of the theory he has put forth.

***Beyond Borders: Writings of Virgilio Elizondo and Friends* by Timothy Matovina. Maryknoll, New York: Orbis Books, 2000. Paper. $25.00.**

Published on the occasion of the famed theologian/pastoralist/catechist's 65th birthday. After a foreward by Gustavo Gutiérrez and an introduction by the book's editor, thirteen essays, most by well-known authors, appear in the work's five parts, together with certain previously published works by Elizondo which are pertinent to the topic: 1) "Religious Education as Pastoral Theology"(Gloria Inés Loya, Anita de Luna, Thomas H. Groome, R. Stephen

Warner); 2) "Popular Religion" (Orlando O. Espín, Jeanette Rodríguez); 3) "*Mestizaje* and a Galilean Christology" (Jacques Audinet, Roberto Goizueta); 4) "Sin, Forgiveness, and the Experience of God" (Carlos Mendoza-Alvarez, Justo L. González); and 5) "Beyond Borders" (John A. Coleman, Alejandro García-Rivera, Rosino Gibellini). A good index adds significantly to the organization and usability of a collection covering such breadth.

The collection not only provides a thorough introduction to the pioneer theologian's prolific work but also a commentary on much of it by several scholars with an international reputation. The work is speckled with gracious anecdotes, attesting to Elizondo's gift of bringing people together. In a way, these provide the "stories behind his essays." The result is also an indispensable contextualization of what was happening at the time and why the famed Mexican American's contribution continues to be so significant. Such significance quickly demonstrates why his work has gained such an international reputation and engaged other theologians throughout the world.

*La Cosecha: Harvesting Contemporary United States Hispanic Theology (1972–1998)* **by Eduardo C. Fernández, S.J. Collegeville: The Liturgical Press, 2000. Paper. $19.95.**

It is only as recently as the early 70s that Roman Catholic and Protestant scholars such as Elizondo, González, Isasi-Díaz, Deck, Aquino, Goizueta, Costas, Espín, and Villafañe began opening theologians' eyes to the Latino/Latina perspective. There has been such an explosion of material since 1972, however, that a guide or introduction to this theology is needed. This book provides this overview and contextualization of Hispanic theology.

By dialoguing with other disciplines such as history, anthropology, sociology, and economics, the work reveals an emerging theology in touch with the modern world. Chapter One begins with a description of the cultural context within which Hispanic theologians are writing. Chapter Two provides an overview of U.S. Latina/Latino theology, rendering highlights of what has been written over the last twenty five years or so by a group of fifteen authors. To provide an overall perspective, the author shifts in Chapter Three to a description of the general trend toward contextualization in the Church today.

Chapter Four combines the information in Chapter Two and Three by taking the various categories presented in the discussion models and applying them to eight Hispanic theologians. In this manner, the contribution to contextual theology *and* the distinctiveness of each author can then be assessed. The final chapter summarizes the results of these comparisons and makes overall observations regarding the current state of United States Hispanic theology and in what direction it needs to move in the future. Aside from containing a detailed index and the most up-to-date bibliography, it is so far the only book-length treatment of such a topic.

If the wider Church is to remain authentic to the call of the Gospel, it must take into account the Hispanic perspective. At a time when the words "inculturation," "local theology," and "contextualization" are becoming commonplace in theological discourse, the book exhibits the Hispanic Church's vast contribution to the wider, global community of believers.

*This article originally appeared in Review for Religious Vol. 59 (2000) under the title, "U.S. Hispanic Catholics: Trends and Works 1999."*

# Appendix II: Internet Resources

*This appendix provides an introduction to Internet sites that deal with the religious experience of United States Hispanics, especially Catholics. It is not comprehensive (for instance, diocesan outreaches are not listed), but representative. It does attempt to highlight the better sites, and to give a brief description of each.*

## AIDS

*http://clnet.ucr.edu/research/aids/binational/rs.html* **Religion and Spirituality** presents eight selections concerning AIDS and spirituality.

## BORDER (Mexican-United States)

*http://www2.utep.edu/~angomez/murales.htm* **Religion at the Border** is a wonderful place to begin. It is written clearly and accurately.

## CHRISTMAS CUSTOMS

*http://www.navidadlatina.com/tradiciones/welcome.asp* **Tradiciones** provides information about the entire Spanish-speaking world outside the United States, organized by countries.

*http://star.ucc.nau.edu/ES/navidad.html* **Elementary Spanish** is a good place to begin and has helpful resources and links. Aimed at youth.

## COMMUNICATIONS

*http://www.loritapia.com/andrestapia/HTML/latinos/othello_pns.htm* **Andrés T. Tapia's** homepage. Includes his many articles on Latino/as and religion and his links.

*http://rozi.com/tu/companero.html* **Tu Compañero Católico** is a new Redemptorist radio ministry that already is broadcast on thirty stations.

*http://www.latinoradio.org/radioframe.htm* **Family Theatre Productions** provides religious radio broadcasting and this site tells all about its activities since 1947.

*http://www.paxcc.org/* **Pax Catholic Communication** is a bilingual media ministry with an especially good radio outreach.

*http://www.vida-nueva.com/* **Vida Nueva** is under construction, but included since it represents the country's most successful Spanish Catholic newspaper.

195

## CURANDERISMO

*http://web2.kpix.com/xtra/remedios/* **Traditional Home Remedies from Mexico** is an electronic bulletin board of cures users cite.

*http://www.globalite.com/shrine/dpjshrine.html* **Don Pedrito Jaramillo is** considered a folk saint; this is the site of his shrine.

*http://unix.utb.edu/~ypea/database.html* **El Niño Fidencio Research Project Database** is limited but interesting. It is under construction, but has technical assistance.

## DAY OF THE DEAD

*http://www.azcentral.com/ent/dead/food.shtml* **Día de los Muertos** provides a very general introduction.

*http://www.indetroit.com/allmedia/dead/default.htm* **Celebration on Sacred Soil** makes assertions without references but has a wealth of related resources and websites.

## EDUCATION

*http://www.jhlt.org/achtus/* **Academy of Catholic Hispanic Theologians of the United States** gives its mission and membership, but also links to the *Journal of Hispanic/Latino Theology*.

*http://www.aeth.org/* **La Asociación para la Educación Teológica Hispana** manages the sites of both the Hispanic Summer Program and the Hispanic Theological Initiative. This is essential information for those who participate in the theological education of Latinos/as.

*http://www.history.swt.edu/Catholic_Southwest.htm* **Catholic Southwest: A Journal of History and Culture** is not dedicated exclusively to Latino/as. However, they play an important part in this periodical and its user-friendly website.

*http://religiousstudies.cua.edu/theo/HISPANIC.htm* **Catholic University of America** offers a Master of Divinity concentration in Hispanic studies. See also their **Programa de Liderato Hispano Pastoral** *http://summer-.cua.edu/special/HPL.htm*.

*http://www.acusd.edu/theo/latino-cath.html* **Center for the Study of Latino/a Catholicism** not only keeps one abreast of their ongoing programs, but has a lot of great links.

*http://www.religionsociety.org/paral/index.htm* **The Program for the Analysis of Religion Among Latinos (PARAL)** has only a rudimentary website at the moment. But their work has been so well received that it is worth bookmarking as it is sure to expand.

## GUADALUPE, OUR LADY OF

*http://spin.com.mx./~msalazar/lupe-e.html* **Interlupe** provides some of the oldest sources for this devotion as well as commentary. The image of Our Lady can also be downloaded.

*http://ng.netgate.net/~norberto/morenita.html* **Nuestra Señora de Guadalupe** is similar to the above, but in Spanish.

## IMMIGRATION AND MIGRATION

*http://www.cmfn.org/index.html* **Catholic Migrant Farmworker Network** provides stories of migrants, comments on current issues, and good links.

*http://www.nccbuscc.org/mrs/index.htm* **Migration and Refugee Services** of the United States Catholic Conference is well maintained and provides excellent links.

*http://clnet.ucr.edu/research/chavez/* **Sal Si Puedes: César E Chávez and His Legacy** has much to offer. Unfortunately, it downplays the role of faith in this lay Catholic's life.

## MARRIAGE

*http://www.bodamagazine.com.ar/notas.htm* **La Boda Magazine** offers history, Christian thoughts, and even a diet for the bride! The history is the best part.

## MISCELLANEOUS

*http://oeop.larc.nasa.gov/hep/hep-links.html* **Hispanic-Related Links** lists hundreds of links arranged by category. Not all the links are active, but there are enough to keep anyone busy.

*http://www.mariachi-publishing.com/MER/* **Mariachi Education Resources** does not deal with religion, but given the importance of mariachi music to liturgy, this is a worthwhile site.

## MISSIONS

*http://www.escusd.k12.ca.us/pages/mission_trail/MissionTrail.html* **California Missions Internet Trail** richly deserved its mention by the *Los Angeles Times*. An excellent site, easily navigated, highly recommended.

*http://www.missiontrail.com/index.html* **El Paso's Historic Mission Trail** is limited and the graphics take an eternity to download, but they offer information on missions the other sites do not.

*http://www.texasmonthly.com/ranch/mission/mission5.html* **Mission Accomplished** is oriented to tourists and is written by *Texas Monthly* magazine.

*http://dizzy.library.arizona.edu/images/swf/mission.html* **Mission Churches of the Sonora Desert** is a fine place to begin virtual visits to the early missions of Arizona, including San Xavier del Bac.

*http://www.sanantoniocvb.com/things/missions.htm* **Mission Trails** is poorly organized but has some interesting links.

*http://www.saconservation.org/mission5.html* the **San Antonio Conservation Society** has links only to missions near it. Includes brief, illustrated descriptions.

## PASTORAL CARE

*http://www.ansh.org/* The **Asociación Nacional de Sacerdotes Hispanos** is limited even in its information for Hispanic priests, but has a lot of good links.

*http://www.nehcc.org/met.htm* **Centro Católico del Nordeste** is a Spanish-only site that keeps one abreast of the center's activities.

*http://socrates.barry.edu/lib-poneill/sepi.htm* **Instituto Pastoral del Sureste (SEPI)** emphasizes its association with Barry University, but also has a very fine page called "Parroquias Católicas en los Estados Unidos" con Paginas del Internet que Tienen Comunidades que Hablan Español .

*http://www.maccsa.org/macc/index.htm* The **Mexican American Cultural Center (MACC)** continues to be a pioneer with this page. While still in development, it gives a good introduction to what MACC has to offer.

*http://www.nccbuscc.org/hispanicaffairs/index.htm* **The Secretariat for Hispanic Affairs** of the National Catholic Conference of Bishops is bilingual and not only offers demographic information but also all pertinent NCCB/USCC publications.

## POLITICS / PUBLIC LIFE

*http://www.hcapl.org/* **Hispanic Churches in American Public Life** "seeks to examine the impact of Catholic, Pentecostal, mainline Protestant, and new religious communities on civic engagement in politics, education, business, social programs, and community activism in the Latino community."

## QUINCEAÑERA

*http://www.youthwired.sat.lib.tx.us/Quinceanera/Quinceanera.htm* **Quinceañera Central** is very commercial, but promises in the future to offer more on traditions and history.

*http://clnet.ucr.edu/research/folklore/quinceaneras/aqlitrep.htm* **the Quinceañera webpage of Orange County** offers a history, interviews, traditional songs, and bibliography.

## SANTERIA AND SPIRITISM

*http://www.nando.net/prof/caribe/caribbean.religions.html* **the Carribean Religion Center** offers information on Santeria in Cuba, New York, and Puerto Rico. Includes a bibliography on this topic, and voodoo as well as information on spiritism. Much is outdated.

*http://www.seanet.com/Users/efunmoyiwa/welcome.html* **OrishaNet** claims it is "Dedicated to being an accurate source of information on La Regla Lucumí for those learning the religion and other interested parties." It is bilingual and includes a soundtrack.

*http://www.religioustolerance.org/santeri.htm* **Religious Tolerance** attempts a balanced review of these practices, but mentions "unintentional murder during Christian exorcisms." This oxymoron is typical. Check out links instead.

*http://santeria.home.mindspring.com/books.htm* **Main Santeria Page** seems somewhat commercial. Nonetheless, it offers much valuable information.

*http://www.religioustolerance.org/santeri.htm* **I Am a Sorcerer** offers a video, stories, and email connections on various controversial topics associated with Santeria as well as many good links.

*http://www.anet.net/~ifa/* **Ijo Orunmila** "a gathering place for students and seekers of wisdom" is very well organized. Probably the best place for a scholar to begin.

## SANTOS / SAINTS

*http://www.atajos.com/cgiin/regresawindow.cgi?palabrota=Santos+Bultos+ Retablos&buscar=B%FAscalo* **Cuando Hablan Los Santos** is somewhat difficult to navigate, but rewarding. Lots of information on the history, sociology, and economy behind the art.

*http://www.si.edu/scmre/santos_e.html* **Santos from Puerto Rico** is very impressive, complete site with wonderful graphics.

## SPANISH LANGUAGE RESOURCES

*http://www.multi-medios.org/* **Biblioteca Electrónica Cristiana** from Lima is a user-friendly place to look for books, Church documents and more.

*http://hmrc.claretianpubs.org/* **Claretian Press' Hispanic Ministry Resources Center** advertises their many fine products.

*http://www.wlp.jspaluch.com/spanish.asp?seasonid=spanish* **J.S. Paluch** makes it easy to locate their Spanish-language wares.

*http://www.liguori.org/libros/libros.htm* **Libros Liguori** may be the most successful marketer of Spanish language Catholic literature in the United States.

*http://www.ltp.org/* **Liturgy Training Publications**' web site is still under construction, but will soon deserve a visit.

*http://www.ocp.org/index.html* **Oregon Catholic Press** offers music and liturgical resources in Spanish—but you would not know it from this site!

*http://www.riial.org/* **Red Informática de la Iglesia en América Latina** is a portal of many links organized by country and by theme.

*http://socrates.barry.edu/lib-poneill/cathspan.htm* **Sitios Católicos en el Internet** arranges entries by country of origin and is especially useful for Marian devotions. It is part of the Catholic Hispanic Ministry site of the Archdiocese of Cincinnati.

# Appendix III: Pastoral Care Resources

♦

The amount of Hispanic pastoral care resources out there has, in no way, kept up with the need experienced by those of us who minister in Hispanic communities. Most of us continue to search for materials that are more than simply adequate in quality. Happily, there is a lot more movement happening in this area. In this appendix you will find information about some of the resources that are available. We do not claim that this information is 100 percent complete but we do hope you find it helpful.

In this appendix you will find the list of members of the National Catholic Council of Hispanic Ministry (NCCHM), the list of addresses for diocesan offices of Hispanic ministry as well as some information on the national Bishops' Secretariat for Hispanic Ministry, and a short list of organizations and publishers that are producing resources for Hispanic ministry. In some cases, in order to avoid repetition, if an institution is already mentioned (i.e., MACC is listed as one of the regional Hispanic leadership institutes), I have not repeated listing them under publishers or bookstores.

We would like to express our gratitude to Armando Contreras of NCCHM and Ron Cruz of the Hispanic Secretariat for the USCCB for their cooperation in helping us gather this information.

# National Catholic Council for Hispanic Ministry, Inc. Directory
# NCCHM Board of Directors

**Msgr. Jaime Soto**
President
2811 E. Villareal Drive
Orange, CA  92667
Phone:      (714) 282-3050
Fax:          (714) 282-3029

**Rev. Kenneth B. Davis, O.F.M.Conv.**
Vice President
The Conventual Franciscans Prov.
of Our Lady of Consolation
St. Meinrad School of Theology,
Hill Drive
St. Meinrad, IN 47577-1021  Phone:
Phone:      (812) 357-6542
Fax:          (812) 357-6792
E-Mail:     Kdavis@saintmeinrad.edu

**Rev. Jose H. Gomez**
Treasurer
Asociación Nacional de Sacerdotes
Hispanos (ANSH)
5505 Chaucer Dr.
Houston, TX 77005
Phone:      (713) 528-6517
Fax:          (713) 528-6379
E-mail:     JoseGomez1@CompuServe.com

**Ms. Carmen Aguinaco**
Secretary
Hispanic Ministry Resource Center
Claretian Publications
205 West Monroe
Chicago, IL 60606
Phone:      (312) 236-7782 ext 439
Fax:          (312) 236-8207
E-mail:     Aquinaco@claretianpubs.org

**Sister Stella Herrera, R.J.M.**
Member at Large
3029 Godwin Terrace
Bronx, NY 10463-5348
Phone:      (718) 543-2454
Fax:          (718) 884-7775
E-mail:     Stellah2@aol.com

**Msgr. Aniceto Villamide**
Member at Large
Northeast Hispanic Pastoral Center
695 Colorado Ave.
Phone:      (203) 372-4301
Fax:          (203) 335-1924

**Sister Joaquina Carrion, M.S.B.T.**
Member at Large
Missionary Servants of the Most
Blessed Trinity
3501 Solly Avenue
Philadelphia, PA 19146
Phone:      (215) 335-7550 ext. 7558
Fax:          (215) 335-7559
E-mail:     JCarrionmsbt@Juno.com

*Editor's Note: As of November, 2001, the members at large are: Sr. María Elizabeth Borobia, F.S.P., Dr. Alicia Marill, and Rev. William Lego.*

# EPISCOPAL MODERATOR

**Most Reverend Ricardo Ramire, C.S.B.**
Bishop of Las Cruces
1280 Med Park Drive
Las Cruces, NM 88005
Phone:     (505) 532-7577
Fax:        (505) 524-3874
E-mail:    diocese@zianet.com

# EX-OFFICIO MEMBER

**Mr. Ron Cruz**
Executive Director – USCCB Secretariat for Hispanic Affairs
3211 4th Street, NE
Washington, DC 20017-1194
Phone:     (202) 541-3150
Fax:        (202) 541-3322
E-mail:    rcruz@nccbuscc.org

# NCCHM MEMBERSHIP LIST

**Amor en Accion**
*Ms. Josefina R.*
*Ms. Alicia C. Marill*
6367 S.W. 15th Street
Miami, FL 33144
Phone:     (305) 266-9533
Fax:        (305) 265-9911
E-mail:    N\A

**Asociación de Diáconos Hispanos**
*Deacon Enrique D. Alonso*
2512 N. Hamlin
Chicago, IL 60647
Bus Phone:  (708) 383-7947
Bus Fax:    (708) 383-4509
E-mail:    N\A

**Asociación Nacional de Sacerdotes Hispanos (ANSH)**
Rev. Enrique Sera
6633 Portwest Dr., Suite #100
Houston, TX 77024
Phone:     (713) 863-1337
Fax:        (713) 426-6916
E-mail:    info@ansh.org

**Augustinians - Province Mother of Good Counsel**
*Fr. William E. Lego, O.S.A.*
6243 S. Fairfield Avenue

Chicago, IL 60629-2309
Bus. Phone:    (773) 434-9600 Ext. 11
Bus. Fax:      (773) 434-2688
E-mail:        Welosa@aol.com

**Augustinians - Province Mother of Good Counsel**
*Rev. Anthony B. Pizzo, O.S.A.*
St. Clare of Montefalco Parish
5443 S. Washtenaw Ave
Chicago, IL 60632-2216
Bus. Phone:    (773) 436-4423
Bus Fax:       (773) 476-1888
E-mail:        ABPIZ@aolcom

**California Catholic Conference**
*Rev. Alejandro Castillo, S.V.D.*
1010 - 11th Street, Suite 200
Sacramento, CA 95814
Bus. Phone:    (916) 443-4851
Bus. Fax:      (916) 443-5629
E-mail:        Acastillo@cacatholic.org

**Catholic Migrant Farmworker Network**
*Celine Caufield*
1915 University Drive
Boise, ID 83706
Bus. Phone:    (208) 384-1778
Bus Fax:       (208) 384-1879
E-mail:        CMFNCC@aol.com
*Sister Charlet Hobelman*
E-mail:        chobelman@nccbuscc.org

**Center for Pastoral Life**
*Sister Judith Vallimont, S.Sp.S*
7900 Loyola Blvd.
Los Angeles, Ca 90045-8364
Bus. Phone:    (310) 338-2799
Bus Fax:       (310) 338-2706
E-mail:        jvallimo@lmumail.lmu.edu

**Charisma in Missions Inc**
*Esther J. Garzon*
1059 S. Gage Avenue
Los Angeles, CA 90023
Mailing Address: P.O. Box 947
Montebello, CA 90640
Bus. Phone:    (323) 260-7031
Bus. Fax:      (323) 260-7221
E-mail:        charisMISN@aol.com

**Christian Foundation for Children and Aging**
*Louis Finocchario*
One Elmwood Avenue
Kansas City, KS 66103
Bus. Phone:  (913) 384-6500
Bus. Fax:  (913) 384-2211
E-mail:  Louf@CFCAUSA.org or
Mail@CFCAUSA.org

**Christian Renewal Center**
*Mr. Joe H. Castro*
P.O. Box 635
Dickinson, TX 77539-0635
Bus. Phone:  (281) 337-1312 Ext. 17
Pager #:  832-722-6160
Bus. Fax:  (281) 337-2615
E-mail:  Center: CRC1515@wt.net
Personal: socks@swbell.net

**Columban Fathers**
*Armida A. Deck, M.A.*
2910–I South Greenville Street
Santa Ana, CA 92704
Bus. Phone:  (714) 549-9594
Bus. Fax:  (714) 997-9588
E-mail:  Armida@Pacbell.net

**The Conv. Franciscans Prov.**
**of Our Lady of Consolation**
*Rev. Kenneth G. Davis, O.F.M., Conv.*
St. Meinrad School of Theology, Hill Drive
St. Meinrad, IN 47577-1021
Bus Phone:  (812) 357-6542
Bus Fax:  (812) 357-6792
E-mail:  kdavis@saintmeinrad.edu

**Daughters of St. Paul/Apostolado Hispano**
*Sister Maria Elizabeth Borobia, F.S.P.*
145 S. W. 107th Ave.
Miami, FL 33174
Bus. Phone:  (305) 225-2513
Bus. Fax:  (305) 225-4189
E-mail:  paulinas@pauline.org
*Sister Maria R. Reyes, F.S.P.*
50 St. Paul's Avenue
Boston, MA 02130-3491
Bus. Phone:  (617) 522-8911
Bus. Fax:  (617) 541-9805
E-mail:  mariaelise@juno.com

**Encuentro Matrimonial Mundial**
*Mr. & Mrs. Jorge Fernández*
424 ½ Exchange Place
Long Branch, NJ 07740

**Family Theater Productions**
*Bro. Joseph Esparza, C.S.C.*
7201 Sunset Blvd.
Hollywood, CA 90046-3488
Bus. Phone:  (323) 874-6633
Bus Fax:  (323) 874-1168
E-mail:  Brojoe@familytheater.org

**Federación Instituto Pastorales (FIP)**
*P. Nelson Perez*
4404 N. 5th Street
Philadelphia, PA 19140
Bus. Phone:  (215) 324-8291
Bus. Fax:  (215) 324-8791
E-mail:  Nperez5797@aol.com

**Harcourt/Brown-Roa**
*Matthew J. Thibeau*
1665 Embassy West Drive
Dubuque, IA 52002
Bus. Phone:  (319) 557-3750
Bus. Fax:  (319) 557-3773
E-mail:  mthibeau@harcourt.com

**Hispanic Ministries of the Congregations
of Holy Cross**
*Bro. Roberto Jiménez, C.S.C.*
4950 Dauphine Street
New Orleáns, LA 70117
Bus. Phone:  (504) 942-3100
Bus. Fax:  (504) 943-7676
E-mail:  HCBRO@aol.com

**Hispanic Ministry Formaiton Mundelein Seminary**
*Fr. Victor Alvarez*
1000 E. Maple Avenue
Mundelein, IL 60060-1174
Bus. Phone:  (847) 970-4842
Bus. Fax:  (874) 566-2583
E-mail:  Valvarez@usml.edu

**Hispanic Ministry Resource Center Claretian Publications**
*Ms. Carmen Aguinaco*
205 West Monroe
Chicago, IL 60606

Bus. Phone:   (312) 236-7782 ext 439
Bus. Fax:     (312) 236-8207
E-mail:       Aguinaco@claretianpubs.org

## Hispanic Telecommunications Network
*Mr. Carlos Amescua*
7711 Madonna Drive
San Antonio, TX 78216
Bus. Phone:   (210) 227-5959
Bus. Fax:     (210) 979-7880
E-mail:       CAAMCA@hotmail.com
*Mr. Roberto Gutierrez*
E-mail:       HTNJRG@aol.com

## International Office of Renew
*Sister Maria Iglesias*
1232 George Street
Gerwood, NJ 07062
Bus. Phone:   (908) 769-5400
Bus. Fax:     (908) 769-5660
E-mail:       Mariai@renewintl.org

## Instituto de Formación Pastoral
*Ms. Margarita Roque*
P.O. Box 4471
Washington, DC 20017
Bus. Phone:   (202) 529-2200
Bus. Fax:     (202) 832-9794
E-mail:       nordeste@gcol.com

## Instituto de Liturgia Hispana
*Rev. Heliodoro Lucatero*
P.O. Box 668
Notre Dame, IN 46556
*Ms. Sylvia Sánchez*
9018 W. Flora Street
Tampa, FL 33615
Bus. Phone:   (813) 885-7861
Bus. Fax:     (813) 884-3624
E-mail:       corproduct@aol.com

## Instituto Fe y Vida
*Carmen Maria Cervantes, Ed.D*
*Joe Matty*
1737 West Benjamín Holt
Stockton, CA 95207
Bus. Phone:   (209) 951-3483
Bus. Fax:     (209) 478-5357
E-mail:       Feyvida@altavista.net

**Jesuit Hispanic Ministry Conference (J.H.M.C.)**
*Rev. Anastasio S. Rivera, S.J.*
480 S. Batavia Street
Orange, CA 92868-3907
Bus. Phone:    (714) 997-9587
Bus. Fax:    (714) 997-9588
E-mail:    Tachor@Juno.com
*Rev. Luis H. Quihuis, S.J.*
21 East Sola Street
Santa Barbara, CA 93101
Bus. Phone:    (617) 522-8911
Bus. Fax:    (617) 541-9805

**The Jesuit School of Theology at Berkeley**
*Dr. Alex R. Garcia*
1735 Leroy Avenue
Berkeley, CA 94709-1193
Bus. Phone:    (510) 841-8804
Bus. Fax:    (510) 841-8536
E-mail:    Agarcia@JSTB.edu
*Sister Gloria Loya*
1735 Leroy Avenue
Berkeley, CA 94709-1193
Phone:    (510) 548-6217
Bus. Fax:    (510) 841-8536
E-mail:    Gloya@JSTB.edu

**La Renovación Carismática Católica Hispana**
*Diacono Rafael De Los Reyes*
500 N.W. 22nd Avenue
Miami, FL 33114-5117
Bus. Phone:    (305) 638-9729
E-mail:    Delosreyes@paxcc.org

**Las Hermanas**
*Sister Linda Chavez*
52nd 3rd Avenue
Gorwood, NJ 07027
Bus. Phone:    (505) 830-0369
Bus. Fax:    (505) 727-7293

**Liguori Publications**
*Ms. Alicia Constamwicc*
One Liguori Drive
Liguori, MO 63057-9999
Bus. Phone:    (314) 464-2500
Bus. Fax:    (314) 464-8449
E-mail:    Avonstamwitz@liguori.org

**Loyola Institute for Spirituality**
*Rev. Allan F. Deck, S.J.*
480 South Batavia Street
Orange, CA 92868
Bus. Phone:   (714) 997-9587
Bus. Fax:       (714) 997-9588
E-mail:          loyinst@pacbell.net

**Institute of Pastoral Studies/Hispanic Institute**
**Loyola University/IPS**
*Rev. William J. Spine, S.J.*
6525 N. Sheridan Road
Chicago, IL 60626
Bus. Phone:   (773) 508-6017
Bus. Fax:       (773) 508-2319
E-mail:          Bspine@luc.edu
*Carmen G. Navarrete*
E-mail:          cnavarr@luc.edu

**Mexican American Cultural Center**
*Sister Maria Elena Gonzalez*
*Rev. Rudy Vella, S.M.*
3019 W. French Place
San Antonio, TX 78228
Bus. Phone:   (210) 732-2156 ext. 137
Bus. Fax:       (210) 732-9072
E-mail:          MACC@maccsa.org

**Missionary Cathechists of Divine Providence**
*Sister Guadalupe Ramirez, M.C.D.P.*
2318 Castroville Rd.
San Antonio, TX 78237-3520
Bus. Phone:   (210) 432-0113
Bus. Fax:       (210) 432-1709
E-mail:          MICADIPR@aol.com

**Mission Serv. of the Most Blessed Trinity (Women)**
*Sister Lourdes Toro, M.S.B.T.*
3501 Solly Avenue
Philadelphia, PA 19136
Bus. Phone:   (215) 335-7550
Bus. Fax:       (215) 335-7559
E-Mail:          LOURDMSBT@HOTMAIL.COM
*Sister Joaquina Carrion, M.S.B.T.*
Bus. Phone:   (215) 335-7550
Bus. Fax:       (215) 335-7559
Home Phone: (215) 335-7562
E-Mail:          Jcarrionmsbt@juno.COM

**Missionary Servants Most Holy Trinity (Men)**
*Rev. Domingo Rodriguez, S.T.*
2717 Curry Drive
Adelphi, MD 20783-1725
Bus. Phone:  (310) 422-6197
*Rev. Jesus Rivera, S.T.*
1215 North Scott Street
Arlington, VA 22209
Bus. Phone:  (703) 276-8646
Bus. Fax:      (703) 522-2656
E-mail:        jriverast@aol.com

**Mount St. Mary's College**
*Mr. Victor Staforelli*
10 Chester Place
Los Angeles, CA 90007-2598
Bus. Phone:  (213) 477-2642
Bus. Fax:      (213) 477-2119
E-mail:        Staforelli@aol.com

**NACFLM**
*Graciela Villalobos*
3424 Wilshire Blvd.
Los Angeles, CA 90010-22481
Bus. Phone:  (213) 637-7227
Bus. Fax:      (213) 637-6681
E-mail:        Gvillalobos@la-archdiocese.org

**NACFLM**
*Sister Janice Mengenhauser, P.B.V.M.*
3214 North 60th Street
Omaha, NE 68104
Bus. Phone:  (402) 551-9003
Bus. Fax:      (402) 551-3050
E-Mail:        Jmengenhauser@omahaflo.creighton.edu

**National Catholic Network de Pastoral Juvenil Hispana/La Red**
*Rey Malave*
6818 Compass Ct.
Orlando, FL 32818
Bus. Phone:  (407) 649-5120 ext.3145
Bus. Fax:      (407) 649-8664
Home Phone: (407) 293-2269
E-Mail:        Reymabel@hotmail.com

**National Organization of Cathechists for Hispanics NOCH**
*Fanny C. Pedraza, President*
3107 Point Clear Dr.
Missouri City, TX 77459
Bus. Phone:  (713) 741-8730 Ext. 714

Bus. Fax:       (713) 741-8775
E-mail:         Robfan2@hotmail.com
*Mr. Rogelio Manrique*
2403 E Holcombe Blvd.
Houston, TX 77021
Bus. Phone:  (407) 246-4914
Bus. Fax:       (407) 246-4940
E-mail:         Romabba@aol.com

### National Pastoral Life Center
*Rev. Phillip J. Murnion*
18 Bleecker Street
New York, NY 10012-2404
Bus. Phone:  (212) 431-7825
Bus. Fax:       (212) 274-9786
E-mail:         Pmurnion@NPLC.org

### Northeast Hispanic Catholic Center
*Mr. Mario J. Paredes*
1011 First Avenue, Suite 1233
New York, NY 10022
Bus. Phone:  (212) 751-7045
Bus. Fax:       (212) 753-5321
E-mail:         NHCC1011@aol.com

### Northeast Hispanic Pastoral Center
*Msgr. Aniceto Villamide*
695 Colorado Avenue
Bridgeport, CT 06605
Bus. Phone:  (203) 372-4301
Bus. Fax:       (203) 335-1924
E-mail:         Villamid@aol.com

### Northwest Regional Office
*Mr. Tadeo Saenz*
2838 E. Burnside Street
Portland, OR 97214-1895
Bus. Phone:  (503) 233-8338
Bus. Fax:       (503) 234-2545
E-mail:         Tsaenz@archdpdx.org

### Oblate School of Theology
*Rev. Robert G. Wright, O.M.I.*
285 Oblate Drive
San Antonio, TX 78216
Bus. Phone:  (210) 341-1366
Bus. Fax:       (210) 341-4519
E-mail:         Wright@Ost.edu

**Oregon Catholic Press**
*Toni Amodeo*
5536 N.E. Hassalo
Portland, OR 97213
Bus. Phone:   (503) 460-5379
Bus. Fax:     (503) 659-5379
E-mail:       Tonia@ocp.org

**Our Lady of Victory Missionary Sisters**
*Sister Lucy Regalado*
P.O. Box 109
Huntington, IN 46750
Bus. Phone:   (219) 356-0628
Bus. Fax:     (219) 358-1504
E-mail:       Victorynoll@olvm.org

**Pastoral Juvenil Hispana Saint Mary's Press**
*Kenneth M. Johnson*
8057 Mariner Drive Dept. #4903
Stockton, CA 95219
Bus. Phone:   (209) 476-0771
Bus. Fax:     (209) 476-7514
E-mail:       K.J.feyvida@altavista.net

**Region XI/RECOSS**
*Luis Velasquez*
Director of Hispanic Ministry
Archdiocese of Los Angeles
3424 Wilshire Blvd.
Los Angeles, CA 90010-2241
Bus. Phone:   (213) 637-7287
Bus. Fax:     (213) 637-6280
E-mail:       ldvelasquez@la-archdiocese.org

**The Religious of Jesus and Mary Provincialate**
*Sister Stella Herrera, R.J.M.*
3029 Godwin Terrace
Bronx, NY 10463-5348
Bus. Phone:   (718) 543-2454
Bus. Fax:     (718) 884-7775
E-mail:       Stellah2@aol.com
*Sister Janet Stollva, RJM*
3706 Rhode Island Avenue
Mt. Rainier, MD 20712
Bus. Phone:   (301) 227-3594
Bus. Fax:     (301) 277-8656
E-mail:       janetstolba@Juno.com

### Sisters of O.L. of Christian Doctrine
*Sister Verónica Mendez*
240 E. 93 Street, #3E
New York, NY 10128
Phone:      (212) 427-9278
E-mail:      VEROICON@aol.com

### Sisters of St. Joseph of Orange
*Sister Carmen Sarati*
480 S. Batavia
Orange, CA 92868
Bus. Phone:  (714) 633-8121
Bus. Fax:     (714) 774-3165

### Society of Helpers Hispanic Ministry
*Sister Dominga Zapata*
1930 N. Kenmore
Chicago, IL 60614-4918
Bus. Phone:  (773) 871-1062
Bus. Fax:     (773) 871-1062 Call First
E-mail:      Dominga_Zapata@claret.org

### Society of St. Sulpice
4835 Mac Arthur Blvd., NW
Washington, DC 20007
Bus. Phone:  (202) 337-4835
Bus. Phone:  (202) 338-4759

### Southeast Regional Office for Hispanic Ministry (SEPI)
*Rev. Mario Vizcaíno, Sch. P.*
*Lydia Menocal*
7700 SW 56th Street
Miami, FL 33155
Bus. Phone:  (305) 279-2333
Bus. Fax:     (305) 279-0925
E-mail:      Lydiamenoc@aol.com Sepimiami@aol.com

### Southern Dominican Province
*Rev. Jorge Presmanes, O.P.*
5909 NW 7th Street
Miami, FL 33126
Bus. Phone:  (305) 264-0181 Press 5
Bus. Fax:     (305) 264-4685
E-mail:      Jorgeop@aol.com

### St. Vincent Seminary
*Rev. Richard B. Michel, O.S.B.*
*Sister Cecilia Murphy, R.S.M.*
300 Fraser Purchase Road
Latrobe, PA 15650-2690

Bus. Phone:    (724) 539-9761
Bus. Fax:      (724) 532-5052
E-mail:        Michel@stvincent.edu
               Scmurphy@stvincent.edu

**Talleres de Oración y Vida/Prayer & Life Workshops**
*Ms. Gloria Ardilla*
15444 SW 113th Street
Miami, FL 33196
Bus. Phone:    (305) 382-4844
Bus. Fax:      (305) 382-8797
E-mail:        Arvacorp@aol.com

**Teresian Association**
*Ms. Araceli Cantero*
2530 SW 3rd Avenue #302
Miami, FL 33129
Bus. Phone:    (305) 757-6241
Bus. Fax:      (305) 762-1130
Phone/Fax:     (305) 285-7159
E-mail:        voxcat#2@miamiarch.org
E-mail:        aracant@aol.com

**Most Reverend Jaime Soto**
President
Auxiliary Bishop/Diocese of Orange
2811 E. Villareal Drive
Orange, CA 92667
Bus. Phone:    (714) 282-3050
Bus. Fax:      (714) 282-3029
E-mail:        bishopjsoto@rcbo.org

**Rev. Kenneth G. Davis, O.F.M.Conv.**
Vice President
The Conventual Franciscans Prov. Of Our Lady of Consolation
St. Meinrad School of Theology, Hill Drive
St. Meinrad, IN 47577-1021
Bus Phone:     (812) 357-6542
Bus Fax:       (812) 357-6792
E-mail:        kdavis@saintmeinrad.edu

**Rev. Jose H. Gomez**
Treasurer
Asociación Nacional de Sacerdotes Hispanos (ANSH)
5505 Chaucer Drive
Houston, TX 77005
Bus Phone:     (713) 528-6517
Bus Fax:       (713) 528-6379
E-mail:        JoseGomez1@CompuServe.com

**Ms. Carmen Aguinaco**
Secretary
Hispanic Ministry Resource Center Claretian Publications
205 West Monroe
Chicago, IL 60606
Bus. Phone:   (312) 236-7782 Ext. 439
Bus. Fax:       (312) 236-8207
E-mail:          Aguinaco@claretianpubs.org

**Sister Stella Herrera, R.J.M.**
Member at Large
The Religious of Jesus and Mary Provincialate
3029 Godwin Terrace
Bronx, NY 10463-5348
Bus. Phone:   (718) 543-2454
Bus. Fax:       (718) 884-7775
E-mail:          Stellah2@aol.com

**Msgr. Aniceto Villamide**
Member at Large
Northeast Hispanic Pastoral Center
695 Colorado Avenue
Bridgeport, CT 06605
Bus. Phone:   (203) 372-4301
Bus. Fax:       (203) 335-1924
E-mail:          villamid@aol.com

**Sister Joaquina Carrion, M.S.B.T.**
Member at Large
Missionary Servants of the Most Blessed Trinity
3501 Solly Avenue
Philadelphia, PA 19146
Bus. Phone:   (215) 335-7550 ext. 7558
Bus. Fax:       (215) 335-7559
E-mail:          JCarrionmsbt@Juno.com
Home Phone: (215) 335-7562

# ADMINISTRATION

**Armando A. Contreras**
Executive Director
2929 N. Central Avenue, #Suite 1500
Phoenix, AZ 85012
Phone:      (602) 266-8623
Fax:         (602) 266-8670
E-mail:     NCCHM1@aol.com

**Adela F. Gallegos**
Director, Leadership Initiative Project
623 Fox Street

Denver, CO 80204
Phone:      (303) 623-9415
Fax:        (303) 623-9419
E-mail:     NCCHMAdela@juno.com

**Secretariat for Hispanic Affairs**
3211 4th Street, NE
Washington, DC 20017
(202) 541-3150

## BISHOPS' COMMITTEE ON HISPANIC AFFAIRS
### 1999-2002
### Most Rev. Arthur Tafoya, D.D., Chairman
Bishop of Pueblo
1001 Grand Avenue
Pueblo, CO 81003
(719) 544-9861
Fax: (719) 544-1220
Email: diocesepueblo @usa.net

**Most Rev. Gilberto Fernández,
D.D., V.G.**
Auxiliary Bishop of Miami
9401 Biscayne Blvd.
Miami, FL 33138
Phone:      (305) 762-1091
Fax:        (305) 758-2027
Email:      miaarch@miamiarch.org

**Most Rev. Theodore E. McCarrick,
Ph.D., D.D.**
Archbishop of Newark
171 Clifton Avenue
Newark, NJ 07104-9500
Phone:      (973) 497-4005
Fax:        (973) 497-4018
Email:      webmaster@rcan.org

**Most Rev. Joseph N. Perry**
Auxiliary Bishop of Chicago
16061 Seton Road / P.O. Box 755
South Holland, IL 60473-0733
Phone:      (708) 339-2474
Fax:        (708) 339-2477

**Most Rev. Plácido Rodríguez, C.M.F.**
Bishop of Lubbock
4620 4th Street P.O. Box 98700
Lubbock, TX 79416

**Most Rev. Michael J. Sheehand,
S.T.L., J.C.D.**
Archbishop of Santa Fe
4000 St. Joseph Pl., NW
Albuquerque, NM 87120
Phone:      (505) 831-8100
Fax:        (505) 831-8345

**Most Rev. James Tamayo,
D.D.**
Auxiliary Bishop of Galveston-Houston
1700 San Jacinto
Houston, TX 77002
Phone:      (713) 659-5461
Fax:        (713) 759-9151

**Most Rev. John G. Vlazny, D.D.**
Archbishop of Portland, Oregon
2838 E. Burnside Street
Portland, OR 97214-1895
Phone:      (503) 234-5334
Fax:        (503) 234-2545
Email:      @archdpdx.org

**Most Rev. Gabino Zavala,
D.D., J.C.L., V.G.**
Auxiliary Bishop of Los Angeles
San Gabriel Pastoral Region

Phone: (806) 792-3943
Fax: (806) 792-2953
Email: ooc@catholiclubbock.org

16009 East Cypress Avenue
Irwindale, CA 91706-2122
Phone: (629) 960-9344
Fax: (629) 962-0455
Email: gabzavala@aol.com

## NON-BISHOP CONSULTANTS:

**Sister María Elena González, President**
Mexican American Cultural Center
3019 W. French Place
San Antonio, TX 78228
Phone: (210) 732-2156 Ext. 101
Fax: (210) 732-9072

**Sister Ana María Pineda, R.S.M.**
Academy of Catholic Hispanic
 Theologians in the United States
Santa Clara University
Religious Studies Department
500 El Camino Real
Santa Clara, CA 95053
Phone: (408) 554-6958
Fax: (408) 554-2387
Email: ampineda@mailer.scu.edu

## LIST OF HISPANIC BISHOPS IN THE UNITED STATES

**Most Rev. Emilio S. Allué**
Auxiliary Bishop of Boston
248 School Street
Watertown, MA 02472-1495
Phone: (617) 926-2117
Fax: (617) 926-2160

**Most Rev. David Arias**
Auxiliary Bishop of Newark
6401 Palisade Avenue
West New York, NJ 07093
Phone: (201) 861-6644
Fax: (201) 861-7799

**Most Rev. Gerald Barnes**
Bishop of San Bernardino
1201 East Highland Avenue
San Bernardino, CA 02404
Phone: (909) 475-5113
Fax: (909) 475-5109

**Most Rev. Gilbert E. Chávez**
Aux. Bishop of San Diego
1535 Third Avenue
San Diego, CA 92101
Phone: (619) 239-0229

**Most Rev. Gilberto Fernández**
Auxiliary Bishop of Miami
9401 Biscayne Blvd.
Miami, FL 33138
Phone: (305) 762-1091
Fax: (305) 758-2027
Email: miaarch@miamiarch.org

**Most Rev. Patrick Flores**
Archbishop of San Antonio
2718 West Woodlawn Avenue
San Antonio, TX 78228
Phone: (210) 734-2620
Fax: (210) 734-2774

**Most Rev. Richard J. García**
Auxiliary Bishop of Sacramento
Diocesan Pastoral Center
2110 Broadway Street
Sacramento, CA 95818-2541
Phone: (916) 733-0200
Fax: (916) 733-0215

**Most Rev. Francisco Garmendia**
Auxiliary Bishop of New York
St. Thomas Aquinas
1900 Crotona Parkway
Bronx, NY 10460

Fax: (619) 239-3788

Phone:    (718) 589-5235
Fax:        (718) 893-0498

**Most Rev. Alvaro Corrada**
Auxiliary Bishop of Washington, DC /
Apostolic Administrator of Caguas, PR
P.O. Box 8698
Caguas, PR 00726
Phone:        (787) 747-5885
Phone:        (787) 747-5787
Fax:            (787) 747-5616

**Most Rev. Rene Gracida**
Former Bishop of Corpus Christi
P.O. Box 2620
Corpus Christi, TX 78403
Phone:        (512) 882-6191
Fax:            (512) 882-1018

**Most Rev. José Madera**
Auxiliary Bishop, Archdiocese
of the Military Services
P.O. Box 4469
415 Michigan Avenue, # 300
Washington, DC 20017-0469
Phone:        (202) 269-9100 Ext. 17
Fax:            (202) 269-9022

**Most Rev. Manuel Moreno**
Bishop of Tucson
192 South Stone Avenue / P.O. Box 31
Tucson, AZ 85702
Phone:        (520) 792-3410
Fax:            (520) 792-0291

**Most Rev. Armand Ochoa**
Bishop of El Paso
499 St. Matthews
El Paso, TX 79907
Phone:        (915) 595-5000
Fax:            (915) 595-5009

**Most Rev. Raymond J. Peña**
Bishop of Brownsville
1910 E. Elizabeth Street
P.O. Box 2279
Brownsville, TX 78522
Phone:        (956) 542-2501
Fax:            (956) 542-6751

**Most Rev. Roberto González**
Archbishop of San Juan
620 Lipan Street / P.O. Box 2620
Corpus Cristi, TX 78403
Phone:        (512) 882-6191
Fax:            (512) 882-1018

**Most Rev. Ricardo Ramirez**
Bishop of Las Cruces
1280 Med Park
Las Cruces, NM 88005
Phone:        (505) 523-7577
Fax:            (505) 524-3874

**Most Rev. Plácido Rodriguez**
Bishop of Lubbock
4620 4th Street / P.O. Box 98700
Lubbock, TX 79416
Phone:        (806) 792-3943
Fax:            (806) 792- 2953

**Most Rev. Agustín Román**
Auxiliary Bishop of Miami
9401 Biscayne Blvd.
Miami, FL
Phone:        (305) 762-1197
Fax:            (305) 762-1138

**Most Rev. Carlos Sevilla**
Bishop of Yakima
5301-A Tieton Drive
Yakima, WA 98908
Phone:        (509) 965- 7117
Fax:            (509) 966-8334

**Most Rev. Arthur Tafoya**
Bishop of Pueblo
1001 Grand Avenue
Pueblo, CO 81003
Phone:        (719) 544-9861
Fax:            (719) 544-1220

**Most Rev. René Valero**
Auxiliary Bishop of Brooklyn
34–43 93rd Street
Jackson Heights, NY 11372
Phone:          (718) 229-8001 Ext. 741
Fax:          (718) 229-2658

**Most Rev. James Tamayo**
Auxiliary Bishop of Galveston-Houston
1700 San Jacinto
Houston, TX 77002
Phone:          (713) 659-5461
Fax:          (713) 759-9151

**Most Rev. Gabino Zavala**
Auxiliary Bishop of Los Angeles
San Gabriel Pastoral Region
16009 East Cypress Avenue
Irwindale, CA 91706-2122
Phone:          (629) 960-9344
Fax:          (629) 962-0455

# REGIONAL OFFICES FOR HISPANIC AFFAIRS

## NORTHWEST

North West Regional Office
2838 E. Burnside Street
Portland, OR 97214-1895
Phone:          (503) 233-8338
Fax:          (503) 234-2545

## MIDWEST

Mid West Hispanic Catholic Community
405 Hayes Street
Saginaw, MI 48602
Phone:          (517) 755-4478
Fax:          (517) 755-5223

## FAR WEST

California Catholic Conference
Division for Hispanic Affairs
1010 11th Street, # 200
Sacramento, CA 95814-3807
Phone:          (916) 443-4851
Fax:          (916) 443-5629

## SOUTHWEST

Sister María Elena González, President
Mexican American Cultural Center
San Antonio, TX 78228
Phone:          (210) 732-2156 Ext. 101
Fax:          (210) 732-9072

## NORTHEAST

North East Pastoral Center
1011 First Avenue
New York, NY 10022
Phone:          (212) 751-7045
Fax:          (212) 753-5321

## SOUTHEAST

Southeast Pastoral Institute
7700 SW 56 Street
Miami, FL 33155
Phone:          (305) 279-2333
Fax:          (305) 279- 0925

## MOUNTAIN STATES

Regina Cleri Center
8800 E 22nd Street
Tucson, AZ 85710-7399
Phone:          (520) 886-5202
Fax:          (520) 886-6481

## NORTH CENTRAL STATES

Diocese of New Ulm
Director for Hispanic Ministry
1400 N 6th Street
New Ulm, MN 56073
Phone:          (507) 359-2966
Fax:(507) 354-3667

**NORTH CENTRAL STATES**
Diocese of St. Louis
Director for Hispanic Ministry
5418 Louisiana Street
St. Louis, MO 63111
Phone:         (314) 351-7009
Fax:            (314) 351- 3372

# DIOCESAN OFFICES FOR HISPANIC MINISTRY

## 1 - DIOCESE OF ALBANY

Coordinator of the Hispanic Apostolate
40 Main Avenue
Albany, NY 12202
Phone:         (518) 452-6655
Fax:            (518) 393-9296

## 2 - DIOCESE OF ALEXANDRIA

Director for Hispanic Ministry
2618 Vanderburg Drive
Alexandria, LA 71303
Phone:         (318) 445-2401
Fax:            (318) 448-6121

## 3. DIOCESE OF ALLENTOWN

Director for Hispanic Ministry
132 South Fifth Street
Easton, PA 18042
Phone:         (610) 866-1121

## 4 - DIOCESE OF ALTOONA-JOHNSTOWN

Hispanic Ministry Coordinator
P.O. Box 126
Hollidaysburg, PA 16648

## 5 - DIOCESE OF AMARILLO

Vicar for Hispanic Ministry
2300 N Spring Street
Amarillo, TX 79107-7258
Phone:         (806) 383-2243

## 6 - ARCHDIOCESE OF ANCHORAGE

Director for Hispanic Ministry
3900 Wisconsin Street
Anchorage, AK 99517
Phone:         (907) 248-2000

## 7. DIOCESE OF ARLINGTON

Director for Hispanic Apostolate
80 N Glebe Road
Arlington, VA 22203
Phone:         (703) 524-2122
Fax:            (703) 524-4261

## 8. ARCHDIOCESE OF ATLANTA

Director for Hispanic Apostolate
680 W Peachtree Street, NW
Atlanta, GA 30308-1984
Phone:         (404) 888-7839
Fax:            (404) 885-7494

## 9. DIOCESE OF AUSTIN

Office of Hispanic Ministry
Pastoral Center
1625 Rutherford Lane
Austin, TX 78754-5105
Phone:         (512) 873-7771

## 10. DIOCESE OF BAKER

Hispanic Ministry Office
St. Patrick "J" & Madison
P.O. Box 823
Madras, OR 97741
Phone:         (541) 475-2564

## 11. ARCHDIOCESE OF BALTIMORE

Director for Hispanic Apostolate
410 S Broadway Street
Baltimore, MD 21231
Phone:          (410) 522-2668
Fax:             (410) 675-1451

## 12. DIOCESE OF BATON ROUGE

Director for Hispanic Ministry
2585 Brightside Drive
Baton Rouge, LA 70820
Phone:     (504) 766-8456
Fax:        (504)766-8973

## 13. DIOCESE OF BEAUMONT

Director of Hispanic Ministry
P.O. Box 3948
Beaumont, TX 77704-3948
Phone:          (409) 838-0451

## 14. DIOCESE OF BELLEVILLE

Director for Hispanic Ministry
P.O. Box 237
Cobden, IL 62920
Phone:     (618) 893-2276

## 15. DIOCESE OF BILOXI

Director for Hispanic Ministry
St. Thomas the Apostle
720 East Beach Blvd.
Long Beach, MS 39560
Phone:          (601) 863-1610

## 16. DIOCESE OF BIRMINGHAM

Director for Hispanic Ministry
P.O. Box 12047
Birmingham, AL 35202-2047
Phone:     (205) 838-8308
Fax:        (205) 836-1910

## 17. DIOCESE OF BISMARCK

Hispanic Ministry Office
P.O. Box 1575
Bismarck, IN 58502-1575

## 18. DIOCESE OF BOISE

Multicultural Office
303 Federal Way
Boise, ID 83705-5925

## 19. ARCHDIOCESE OF BOSTON

Hispanic Apostolate Office
2121 Commonwealth Avenue
Brighton, MA 02135
Phone:          (617) 746- 5816
Fax:             (617) 783-5642

## 20. DIOCESE OF BRIDGEPORT

Vicar for Hispanic Ministry
St. Peter Rectory
695 Colorado Avenue
Bridgeport, CT 06605
Phone:     (203) 366-5611
Fax:        (203) 335-1924

## 21. DIOCESE OF BROOKLYN

Director for Hispanic Ministry
7200 Douglaston Pkwy
Douglaston, NY 11362
Phone:          (718) 229-8001 Ext. 741
Fax:             (718) 229-2658

## 22. DIOCESE OF BROWNSVILLE

Hispanic Ministry Office
P.O. Box 547
Alamo, TX 78516
Phone:     (956) 201-8571

## 23. DIOCESE OF BUFFALO

Director for Hispanic Apostolate
795 Main Street
Buffalo, NY 14203
Phone:      (716) 847- 2217
Fax:        (716) 847- 2206

## 24. DIOCESE OF BURLINGTON

Director for Hispanic Ministry
351 North Avenue
Burlington, VT 05401

## 25. DIOCESE OF CAMDEN

Director for Hispanic Apostolate
410 S 8th Street
Vineland, NJ 08360
Phone:      (609) 692-8992
Fax:        (609) 338-0793

## 26. DIOCESE OF CHARLESTON

Director for Hispanic Ministry
P.O. Box 487
Hardeville, SC 29927
Phone:      (843) 784-6500
Fax:        (843) 784-5338

## 27. DIOCESE OF CHARLOTTE

Director for Hispanic Ministry
2117 Shenandoah Avenue
Charlotte, NC 28205-6021
Phone:      (704) 335-1281

## 28. DIOCESE OF CHEYENNE

Hispanic Ministry Coordinator
1009 9th Street
Wheatland, WY 82001
Phone:      (307) 638-1530

## 29. ARCHDIOCESE OF CHICAGO

Director for Hispanic Ministry
155 East Superior
Chicago, IL 60611
Phone:      (312) 751-8301/8308
Fax:        (312) 751-5313

## 30. ARCHDIOCESE OF CINCINNATI

Hispanic Ministries Office
St. Charles
115 West Seymour Avenue
Phone:      (513) 761-1588
Fax:        (513) 761-9538

## 31. DIOCESE OF CLEVELAND

Director for Hispanic Ministry
1031 Superior Avenue
Cleveland, OH 44114-2519
Phone:      (216) 696-6525 Ext. 2530
Fax:        (216) 696-6243

## 32. DIOCESE OF COLORADO SPRINGS

Catholic Community Services
29 W Kiowa Street
Colorado Springs, CO 80903
Phone:      (719) 636-2345 Ext. 168
Fax:        (719) 636-1216

## 33.DIOCESE OF COLUMBUS

Hispanic Ministry Office
256 E Rich Street
Columbus, OH 43215-5223
Phone:      (614) 469-9178

## 34. DIOCESE OF CORPUS CHRISTI

Director for Hispanic Affairs
1200 Lantana Street
Corpus Christi, TX 78407
Phone:      (512) 589-6501

## 35. DIOCESE OF COVINGTON

Director for Hispanic Ministry
947 Donalson Road / P.O. Box 18548
Erlanger, KY 41018-0548
Phone:     (606) 283- 6337
Fax:       (606) 283- 6334

## 37. DIOCESE OF DALLAS

Pastoral Planning & Diocesan Networks
P.O. Box 190507
Dallas, TX 75219-0507
Phone:     (214) 528-7495

## 39. ARCHDIOCESE OF DENVER

Director for Hispanic Ministry
1300 S Steele Street
Denver, CO 80210
Phone:     (303) 715-3235

## 41. ARCHDIOCESE OF DETROIT

Director for Hispanic Ministry
305 Michigan Avenue
Detroit, MI 48226-2605
Phone:     (313) 237-5761
Fax:       (313) 237-5869

## 43. ARCHDIOCESE OF DUBUQUE

Hispanic Ministry Office
St. Bridget Church
P.O. Box 369
Postville, IA 52162-0369
Phone:     (319)864-3138

## 45. DIOCESE OF EL PASO

Hispanic Ministry Office
499 St. Matthews
El Paso, TX 79907
Phone:     (915) 595-5063

## 36. DIOCESE OF CROOKSTON

Director of Hispanic Ministry
1200 Memorial Drive / P.O. Box 610
Crookston, MN 56716
Phone:     (218) 233-3934
Fax:       (218) 281-3328

## 38. DIOCESE OF DAVENPORT

Vicar for Hispanic Ministry
2706 N Gaines Street
Davenport, IA 52804
Phone:     (319) 324-1911

## 40. DIOCESE OF DES MOINES

Director of Hispanic Affairs
1271 E 9th Street
Des Moines, IA 50316
Phone:     (515) 266-6695
Fax:       (515) 266- 9803

## 42. DIOCESE OF DODGE CITY

Hispanic Ministry Office
P.O. Box 137
Dodge City, KS 67801-0137
Phone:     (316) 223-3442

## 44. DIOCESE OF DULUTH

Hispanic Ministry Coordinator
2830 E 4th Street
Duluth, MN 55812

## 46. DIOCESE OF ERIE

Director for Hispanic Ministry
1237 West 21 Street
Erie, PA 16502
Phone:     (814) 459-0543

## 47. DIOCESE OF EVANSVILLE

Hispanic Ministry Coordinator
P.O. Box 308
Dale, IN 47523-9741
Phone:        (812) 937-2200

## 48. DIOCESE OF FAIRBANKS

Hispanic Ministry Coordinator
2890 N Kobuk
Fairbanks, AK 99709
Phone:        (907) 474-0753
Fax:           (907) 474-8009

## 49. DIOCESE OF FALL RIVER

Director for Hispanic Ministry
P.O. Box 40605
New Bedford, MA 02744-0006
Phone:        (508) 994-2521
Fax:           (508) 997-1462

## 50. DIOCESE OF FARGO

Coordinator for Hispanic Ministry
P.O. Box 1750
Fargo, ND 58107
Phone:        (701) 256-4636

## 51. DIOCESE OF FORT WAYNE-SOUTH BEND

Coordinator for Hispanic Ministry
1108 S. Main Street
Elkhart, IN 46516-3919
Phone:        (219) 293-8231
Fax:           (219)293-1105

## 52. DIOCESE OF FORT WORTH

Hispanic Pastoral Services
800 West Loop, 820 South
Fort Worth, TX 76108-2919
Phone:        (817) 560-3300 Ext. 258
Fax:           (817 244-8839

## 53. DIOCESE OF FRESNO

Coordinator for Hispanic Ministry
1550 N Fresno Street
Fresno, CA 93703-3788
Phone:        (209) 488-7455
Fax:           (209) 488-7444

## 54. DIOCESE OF GALLUP

Hispanic Ministry Coordinator
217 East Wilson Avenue
Gallup, NM 87301
Phone:        (505) 722-5511
Fax:           (505) 863-0075

## 55. DIOCESE OF GALVESTON-HOUSTON

Director for Hispanic Ministry
2403 E Holcombe Blvd.
Houston, TX 77021
Phone:        (713) 741-8727
Fax:           (713) 747-9206

## 56. DIOCESE OF GARY

Director for Hispanic Ministry
1709 East 138 Street
P.O. Box 3027
East Chicago, IN 46312
Phone:        (219) 397-2125
Fax:           (219) 397-2168

## 57. DIOCESE OF GAYLORD

Director for Hispanic Ministry
Immaculate Conception Parish
720 Second Street
Traverse City, MI 49684
Phone:        (616) 946-4211

**58. DIOCESE OF GRAND ISLAND**

Director for Hispanic Ministry
P.O. Box 651
North Plate, NE 69103
Phone:       (308) 532-2707
Fax:         (308) 532-3574

**60. DIOCESE OF GREAT FALLS -
BILLINGS**

Hispanic Affairs Office
121 23rd Street South
Great Falls, MT 59403

**62. DIOCESE OF GREENSBURG**

Hispanic Ministry Office
723 East Pittsburgh Street
Greensburg, PA 15601

**64. ARCHDIOCESE OF HARTFORD**

Director for Hispanic Ministry
467 Bloomfield Avenue
Bloomfield, CT 06002
Phone:       (203) 243-0940

**66. DIOCESE OF HONOLULU**

Hispanic Ministry Coordinator
1184 Bishop Street
Honolulu, HI 96813

**68. ARCHDIOCESE OF INDIANAP-
OLIS**

Multicultural Ministry Office
317 N New Jersey Street / P.O. Box 1410
Indianapolis, IN 46204
Phone:       (317) 637-3938

**59. DIOCESE OF GRAND RAPIDS**

Director for Hispanic Ministry
600 Burton Street, SE
Grand Rapids, MI 49507
Phone:     (616) 243-0491
Fax:       (616) 243-4910

**61. DIOCESE OF GREEN BAY**

Director for Hispanic Services
1825 Riverside Drive
Green Bay, WI 54305
Phone:     (920) 437-7531 Ext. 8247
Fax:       (920) 437-0694

**63. DIOCESE OF HARRISBURG**

Vicar for Hispanic Apostolate
119 South Prince Street
Lancaster, PA 17603
Phone:     (717) 392-2578

**65. DIOCESE OF HELENA**

Hispanic Ministry Coordinator
515 North Ewing Street
Helena, MT 59624

**67. DIOCESE OF HOUMA-
THIBODAUX**

Hispanic Ministry Coordinator
St. Joseph Co-Cathedral
P.O. Box 966 - 721 Canal Blvd.
Thibodaux, LA 70301
Phone:     (504) 446-1387

**69. DIOCESE OF JACKSON**

Director for Hispanic Ministry
237 E Amite Street / P.O. Box 2248
Jackson, MS 39205-2248
Phone:     (601) 969-1880
Fax:       (601) 960-8485

**70. DIOCESE OF JEFFERSON CITY**
Hispanic Ministry Office
P.O. Box 220
373 W Jackson
Marshall, MO 65340
Phone:        (660) 886-3112
Fax:          (660) 886-6601

**71. DIOCESE OF JOLIET**
Director for Hispanic Ministry
402 S Independence Blvd.
Romeoville, IL 60446
Phone:        (815) 838-8100

**72. DIOCESE OF JUNEAU**

Hispanic Ministry Office
5921 Sunset Street
Juneau, AK 99801
Phone:        (907) 780-4918

**73. DIOCESE OF KALAMAZOO**

Director for Hispanic Ministry
215 North Westnedge Avenue
Kalamazoo, MI 49007-3760
Phone:        (616) 349-7769
Fax:          (616)349-6440

**74. ARCHDIOCESE OF KANSAS
CITY IN KANSAS**

Director for Hispanic Ministry
Casa Juan Diego
229 South 8th Street
Kansas City, KS 66101
Phone:        (913) 342-1276
Fax:          (913) 281-1256

**75. DIOCESE OF KANSAS CITY-
ST. JOSEPH**

Coordinator for Hispanic Ministry
P.O. Box 419037
Kansas City, MO 64141-6037
Phone:     (816) 756-1850
Fax:       (816) 756-0878

**76. DIOCESE OF KNOXVILLE**

Director for Hispanic Ministry
119 Dameron Avenue
Knoxville, TN 37917
Phone:        (423) 637-4769
Fax:          (423) 971-3575

**77. DIOCESE OF LA CROSSE**

Office of Justice and Peace
P.O. Box 4004 / 3710 East Avenue S
La Crosse, WI 54601-4004
Phone:     (608) 788-7700
Fax:       (608) 788-8413

**78. DIOCESE OF LAS CRUCES**

Director for Hispanic Ministry
1280 Medpark
Las Cruces, NM 88005
     (505) 523-7577
Fax: (505) 524-3874

**79. DIOCESE OF LAS VEGAS**

Hispanic Ministry Office
P.O. Box 18316
Las Vegas, NV 89114

**80. DIOCESE OF LAFAYETTE
IN INDIANA**

Coordinator for Hispanic Ministry
401 West Buckingham Drive
Marion, IN 46952
Phone:        (765) 662-6078

**81. DIOCESE OF LAFAYETTE IN
LOUISIANA**

Director for Hispanic Ministry
1408 Carmel Avenue
Lafayette, LA 70501
Phone:     (318) 261-5542
Fax:       (318) 261-5635

## 82. DIOCESE OF LAKE CHARLES

Director for Hispanic Ministry
P.O. Box 849
Iowa, LA 70647-0849
Phone:       (318) 582-3503
Fax:          (318) 582-6326

## 84. DIOCESE OF LEXINGTON

Director for Hispanic Ministry
1310 West Main Street
Lexington, KY 40508-2040

## 86. DIOCESE OF LITTLE ROCK

Hispanic Ministry Office
P.O. Box 7565
Little Rock, AR 72217
Phone:       (501) 664-0340
Fax:          (501) 664-9075

## 88. ARCHDIOCESE OF LOUISVILLE

Office for Hispanic Ministry
1200 South Shelby Street
Louisville, KY 40203
Phone:       (502) 636-0296

## 90. DIOCESE OF MADISON

Director for Hispanic Ministry
3577 High Point Road
Madison, WI 53711
Phone:       (608) 821-3092
Fax:          (608) 821-3139

## 92. DIOCESE OF MARQUETTE

Hispanic Ministry Office
P.O. Box 550
Marquette, MI 49855

## 83. DIOCESE OF LANSING

Director for Hispanic Ministry
300 W Ottawa Street
Lansing, MI 48933
Phone:       (517) 342-2498
Fax:          (517) 342-2468

## 85. DIOCESE OF LINCOLN

Director for Hispanic Ministry
3128 "S" Street
Lincoln, NE 68503-3237
Phone:       (402) 435-3559

## 87. ARCHDIOCESE OF LOS ANGELES

Hispanic Ministry Office
3424 Wilshire Blvd.
Los Angeles, CA 90010
Phone:       (213) 637-7280
Fax:          (213) 637-6280

## 89. DIOCESE OF LUBBOCK

Director for Hispanic Ministry
P.O. Box 98700
Lubbock, TX 79499
Phone:       (806) 828-5108

## 91. DIOCESE OF MANCHESTER

Hispanic Ministry Office
41 Chamder Street
Nashua, NH 03060
Phone:       (603) 625-4603

## 93. DIOCESE OF MEMPHIS

Director for Multicultural Ministry
5825 Shelby Oaks Drive
Memphis, TN 38184-1669
Phone:       (901) 373-1200
Fax:          (901) 373-1269

## 94. DIOCESE OF METUCHEN

Director for Hispanic Ministry
Most Holy Rosary Church
625 Florida Grove Road
Perth Amboy, NJ 08861
Phone:          (732) 826-2771

## 95. ARCHDIOCESE OF MIAMI

Director for Hispanic Ministry
9401 Biscayne Blvd.
Miami, FL 33138
Phone:          (305) 762-1091
Fax:             (305) 762-1138

## 96. ARCHDIOCESE FOR THE MILITARY SERVICES, U.S.A.

Hispanic Ministry Office
415 Michigan Ave. Suite 300
P.O. Box 4469
Washington, DC 20017-0469
Phone:          (202) 269-9100 Ext. 17
Fax:             (202) 269-0022

## 97. ARCHDIOCESE OF MILWAUKEE

Director for Hispanic Ministry
3501 S. Lake Dr. - P.O. Box 07912
Milwaukee, WI 53207
Phone:          (414) 769-3393

## 98. ARCHDIOCESE OF MOBILE

Vicar for Hispanic Ministry
4000 Dauphin Street
Mobile, AL 36608
Phone:          (334) 380-4662
Fax:             (334) 460-2194

## 99. DIOCESE OF MONTERREY

Director for Hispanic Ministry
P.O. Box 1684
Salinas, CA 93902-1684
Phone:          (831) 424-4076 Ext. 25

## 100. DIOCESE OF NASHVILLE

Director for Hispanic Ministry
10682 Old Nashville Pike
Smyrna, TN 37167
Phone:          (615) 459-3046
Fax:             (831) 424-5221

## 101. ARCHDIOCESE OF NEWARK

Director for Hispanic Ministry
171 Clifton Avenue / P.O. Box 9500
Newark, NJ 07104
Phone:          (973) 497-4337
Fax:             (973) 497-4317

## 102. ARCHDIOCESE OF NEW ORLEANS

Director for Hispanic Ministry
P.O. Box 19104
New Orleans, LA 70179-0104
Phone:          (504) 486-1983
Fax:             (504 861-9521

## 103. DIOCESE OF NEW ULM

Director for Hispanic Ministry
1400 N. 6th Street
New Ulm, MN 56073
Phone:          (507) 359-2966
Fax:             (507) 354-3667

## 104. ARCHDIOCESE OF NEW YORK

Hispanic Affairs
1011 First Avenue
New York, NY 10022

## 105. DIOCESE OF NORWICH

Director for Hispanic Ministry
61 Club Road
Windham, CT 06280

Phone:     (212) 371-1000 Ext. 2982
Fax:       (212) 319-8265

## 106. DIOCESE OF OAKLAND

Director for Hispanic Ministry
3014 Lakeshore Avenue
Oakland, CA 94610
Phone:     (510) 763-0301
Fax:       (510) 987-8230

## 108. ARCHDIOCESE OF
## OKLAHOMA CITY

Director for Hispanic Ministry
P.O. Box 32180
Oklahoma City, OK 73123
Phone:     (405) 728-3561
Fax:       (405) 721-5210

## 110. DIOCESE OF ORANGE

Vicar for Hispanic Ministry
2811 E Villa Real Drive
Orange, CA 92667-1999

## 112. DIOCESE OF OWENSBORO

Director for Hispanic Ministry
600 Locust Street
Owensboro, KY 42301-2130
Phone:     (270) 764-1983
Fax:       (270) 683-6883

## 114. DIOCESE OF PATERSON

Director for Hispanic Ministry
777 Valley Road
Clifton, NJ 07013
Phone:     (973) 777-8818 Ext. 239
Fax:       (973) 777-8976

Phone:     (860) 456-3349
Fax:       (860) 423-4157

## 107. DIOCESE OF OGDENSBURG

Hispanic Ministry Office
P.O. Box 369
Ogdensburg, NY 13669
Phone:     (315) 393-2920

## 109. ARCHDIOCESE OF OMAHA

Director for Hispanic Ministry
3216 North 60th Street
Omaha, NE 68104

## 111. DIOCESE OF ORLANDO
Director for Hispanic Ministry
421 E. Robinson / P.O. Box 1800
Orlando, FL 32801
Phone:     (407) 246-4930
Fax:       (407) 246-4932

## 113. DIOCESE OF PALM BEACH

Director for Hispanic Ministry
9995 N Military Trail
P.O. Box 109650
Palm Beach Gardens, FL 33410-9650
Phone:     (561) 775-9544
Fax:       (561) 775-9556

## 115. DIOCESE OF PENSACOLA-
## TALLAHASSEE

Director for Hispanic Ministry
11 North B Street / P.O. Box 17329
Pensacola, FL 32522-7329

## 116. DIOCESE OF PEORIA

Hispanic Ministry Office
Sacre Coeur Church
601 Rusche Lane
Creve Coeur, IL 61610
Phone:        (904) 627-2350

## 117. ARCHDIOCESE OF PHILADELPHIA

Director for Hispanic Ministry
222 N 17 Street 8th floor
Philadelphia, PA 19103-1299

## 118. DIOCESE OF PHOENIX

Vicar for Hispanic Ministry
400 E Monroe Street
Phoenix, AZ 85004-2376

## 119. DIOCESE OF PITTSBURGH

Secretariat for Social Concerns
Hispanic Ministry Office
111 Blvd. of the Allies
Pittsburgh, PA 15222

## 120. DIOCESE OF PORTLAND IN MAINE

Hispanic Ministry Coordinator
Cathedral 307 Congress Street
Portland, ME 04101

## 121. ARCHDIOCESE OF PORTLAND IN OREGON

Hispanic Ministry Coordinator
2838 E Burnside Street
Portland, OR 97214
Phone:      (503) 234-5334
Fax:        (503) 234-2545

## 122. DIOCESE OF PROVIDENCE

Director for Hispanic Ministry
One Cathedral Square
Providence, RI 02903
Phone:        (401) 278-4526

## 123. DIOCESE OF PUEBLO

Director of Pastoral Outreach
1001 Grand Avenue
Pueblo, CO 81003
Phone:      (719) 544-9861
Fax:        (719) 544-5202

## 124. DIOCESE OF RALEIGH

Vicar/Director for Hispanic Ministry
715 Nazareth
Raleigh, NC 27606-2187
Phone:        (919) 821-9738
Fax:          (919) 821-9705

## 125. DIOCESE OF RAPID CITY

Coordinator for Hispanic Ministry
P.O. Box 678
Rapid City, SD 57709
Phone:      (605) 343-3541
Fax:        (605) 348-7985

## 126. DIOCESE OF RENO

Hispanic Ministry Office
Pastoral Center
290 South Arlington Avenue
Phone:        (775) 329-9274 Ext. 426

## 127. DIOCESE OF RICHMOND

Office of the Hispanic Apostolate
811 Cathedral Place
Richmond, VA 23220
Phone:      (804) 359-5661

## 128. DIOCESE OF ROCHESTER

Director for Hispanic Ministry
1150 Buffalo Road
Rochester, NY 14624
Phone:      (716) 328-3210 Ext. 329
Fax:         (716) 328-8640

## 129. DIOCESE OF ROCKFORD

Office of the Hispanic Apostolate
Vicar for Hispanic Ministry
921 W State Street
Rockford, IL 61102-2808
Phone:      (815) 962-8042
Fax:         (815) 968-2808

## 130. DIOCESE OF ROCKVILLE

Director for Hispanic Ministry
50 N Park Avenue
Rockville Centre, NY 11570
Phone:      (516) 678-5800 Ext. 618
Fax:         (516) 678-1786

## 131. DIOCESE OF SACRAMENTO

Director for Hispanic Apostolate
2110 Broadway
Sacramento, CA 95818-2541
Phone:      (916) 733-0177
Fax:         (916) 733-0195

## 132. DIOCESE OF SAGINAW

Vicar for Hispanic Ministry
405 Hayes Street
Saginaw, MI 48602
Phone:      (517) 755-4478
Fax:         (517) 755-5223

## 133. DIOCESE OF ST. AUGUSTINE

Director for Hispanic Ministry
134 East Church Street
Jacksonville, FL 32202-3130
Fax:         (904) 632-2135

## 134. DIOCESE OF ST. CLOUD

Coordinator for Multicultural Ministry
115 8th Avenue, SE
Little Falls, MN 56345
Phone:      (218) 863-5161

## 135. ARCHDIOCESE OF ST. LOUIS

Coordinator for Hispanic Ministry
5418 Louisiana Street
St. Louis, MO 63111
Phone:      (314) 351-7009
Fax:         (314) 5351-3372

## 136. ARCHDIOCESE OF ST. PAUL AND MINNEAPOLIS

Director for Hispanic Ministry
840 E 6th Street
St. Paul, MN 55106
Phone:      (651) 793-9791
Fax:         (651) 776-2759

## 137. DIOCESE OF ST. PETERSBURG

Director for Hispanic Ministry
9715 56th Street
Temple Terrace, FL 33617
Phone:      (813) 988-1593
Fax:         (813) 985- 3583

## 138. DIOCESE OF SALINA

Hispanic Ministry Coordinator
P.O. Box 980
Salina, KS 67402

## 139. DIOCESE OF SALT LAKE CITY

Director for Hispanic Ministry
27 "C" Street
Salt Lake City, UT 84103
Phone:      (801) 328-8641 Ext. 331
Fax:         (801) 328-9680

**140. DIOCESE OF SAN ANGELO**

Hispanic Ministry Office
P.O. Box 1829
San Angelo, TX 76902

**141. ARCHDIOCESE OF SAN ANTONIO**

Director for Hispanic Ministry
2718 W Woodlawn
San Antonio, TX 78228
Phone:    (210) 734-2620

**142. DIOCESE OF SAN BERNARDINO**

Director for Hispanic Ministry
1201 East Highland Avenue
San Bernardino, CA 92404
Phone:        (909) 475-5451
Fax:           (909) 475-5360

**143. DIOCESE OF SAN DIEGO**

Director for Hispanic Ministry
3888 Paducah Drive
San Diego, CA 92117
P.O. Box 85728 - ZC 92186
Phone:      (619) 490-8249
Fax:          (619) 490-8272

**144. ARCHDIOCESE OF SAN FRANCISCO**

Hispanic Ministry Office
445 Church Street
San Francisco, CA 94114
Phone:      (415) 565-3668
Fax:          (415) 565-3649

**145. DIOCESE OF SAN JOSE**

Office of Hispanic Ministry
900 Lafayette Street, Suite 301
Santa Clara, CA 95050
Phone:      (408) 983-0141
Fax:          (408) 983-0203

**146. ARCHDIOCESE OF SANTA FE**

Director for Hispanic Ministry
4000 Street Joseph Pl., NW
Albuquerque, NM 87120
Phone:      (505) 831-8152
Fax:          (505) 831-8345

**147. DIOCESE OF SANTA ROSA**

Formador for Hispanic Ministry
286 B Douglas Street
Petaluma, CA 94952
Phone:      (707) 773-4512
Fax:          (707) 763-8188

**148. DIOCESE OF SAVANNAH**

The Catholic Pastoral Center
601 East Liberty Street
Savannah, GA 31401-5196

**149. DIOCESE OF SCRANTON**

Director for Hispanic Ministry
300 Wyoming Avenue
Scranton, PA 18503
Phone:      (570) 346-8969
Fax:          (570) 341-1291

**150. ARCHDIOCESE OF SEATTLE**

Director for Hispanic Affairs
910 Marion Street
Seattle, WA 98104-1299
Phone:      (206) 382-4825
Fax:          (206) 382-2069

**151. DIOCESE OF SHREVEPORT**

Coordinator for Hispanic Ministry
2500 Lane Avenue
Shreveport, LA 71104
Phone:      (318) 222-2006
Fax:          (318) 222-2080

## 152. DIOCESE OF SIOUX CITY

Office of Minorities and Human
    Development
P.O. Box 3379
Sioux City, IA 51102
Phone:          (712) 255-1637

## 153. DIOCESE OF SIOUX FALLS

Hispanic Ministry Coordinator
1220 East 8th Street
Sioux Falls, SD 57103
Phone:          (605) 333-8126
Fax:            (605) 338-0419

## 154. DIOCESE OF SPOKANE

Consultant for Hispanic Ministry
P.O. Box 1453 - ZC 99210
1023 W Riverside Avenue
Spokane, WA 99201
Phone:          (509) 358-7315
Fax:            (509) 456-7108

## 155. DIOCESE OF SPRINGFIELD-CAPE GIRARDEAU

Hispanic Ministry Director
601 South Jefferson Street
Springfield, MO 65806

## 156. DIOCESE OF SPRINGFIELD IN ILLINOIS

Office of Social Concerns
P.O. Box 3187
Springfield, IL 62708-3187
Phone:          (217) 698-8500
Fax:            (217) 698-8650

## 157. DIOCESE OF SPRINGFIELD IN MASSACHUSETTS

Director for Hispanic Ministry
1777 Dwight Street
Springfield, MA 01107
Phone:          (413) 736-8208
Fax:            (413) 731-0962

## 158. DIOCESE OF STEUBENVILLE

Hispanic Ministry Office
P.O. Box 969
Steubenville, OH 43952

## 159. DIOCESE OF STOCKTON

Hispanic Ministry
1125 N Lincoln Street
Stockton, CA 95203
Phone:          (209) 466-5811
Fax:            (209) 941-9722

## 160. DIOCESE OF SUPERIOR

Director of Pastoral Services
P.O. Box 969
Superior, WI 54880

## 161. DIOCESE OF SYRACUSE

Director of Spanish Apostolate
1515 Midland Avenue
Syracuse, NY 13205
Phone:          (315) 422-9390
Fax:            (315) 422-9390

## 162. DIOCESE OF TOLEDO

Director of Hispanic Ministry
P.O. Box 985
Toledo, OH 43697-0985
Phone:          (419) 244-6711
Fax:            (419) 244-4791

## 163. DIOCESE OF TRENTON

Vicar for Hispanic Ministry
St. Mary's Cathedral
151 N Warren Street
Trenton, NJ 08608
Phone:          (609) 396-8447

## 164. DIOCESE OF TUCSON

Regina Cleric Center
8800 E 22nd Street
Tucson, AZ 85710-7399
Phone:        (520) 886-5202
Fax:          (520) 886-6481

## 166. DIOCESE OF TYLER

Hispanic Ministry Office
1015 ESE Loop 323
Tyler, TX 75701-9663
Phone:        (903) 534-1077 Ext. 44
Fax:          (903) 534-1370

## 168. DIOCESE OF VICTORIA

Director for Hispanic Ministry
P.O. Box 4070
Victoria, TX 77903
Phone:        (512) 552-3664

## 170. DIOCESE OF WHEELING - CHARLESTON

Director for Hispanic Ministry
317 Main Street
Bridgeport, WV 26330
Phone:        (304) 842-2283

## 172. DIOCESE OF WILMINGTON

Director for Hispanic Ministry
St. Catherine of Siena
2503 Centerville Road
Wilmington, DE 19808
Phone:        (302) 999-7930
Fax:          (302) 655-7684

## 174. DIOCESE OF WORCESTER

Hispanic Ministry Office
Saint Peter's Church
929 Main Street
Worcester
Phone:        (508) 752-4674

## 165. DIOCESE OF TULSA

Director of Hispanic Ministry
1541 East Newton Place
Tulsa, OK 74106
Phone:        (918) 584-2424
Fax:          (918) 584-2421

## 167. DIOCESE OF VENICE

Spanish Speaking Apostolate
P.O. Box 2006
Venice, FL 34284
Phone:        (941) 484-9543
Fax:          (941) 484-1121

## 169. ARCHDIOCESE OF WASHINGTON

Hispanic Ministry Coordinator
P.O. Box 29260
Washington, DC 20017
Phone:        (301) 853-4567

## 171. DIOCESE OF WICHITA

Hispanic Ministry Office
424 N. Broadway
Wichita, KS 67202
Phone:        (316) 263-6574
Fax: (316) 269-3902

## 173. DIOCESE OF WINONA

Coordinator for Hispanic Ministry
1051 Linn Avenue
Owatonna, MN 55060
Phone:        (507) 451-0516
Fax:          Same

## 175. DIOCESE OF YAKIMA

Director for Hispanic Ministry
213 North Beech
Topenish, WA 98948
Phone:        (509) 864-4040
Fax:          (509) 966-8334

**176. DIOCESE OF YOUNGSTOWN**

Hispanic Ministry Office
50 Struthers-Coitsville Road
Youngstown, OH 44505
Phone:      (216) 755-3633

**177. DIOCESE OF ST. THOMAS
IN THE VIRGIN ISLANDS**

Hispanic Ministry Office
P.O. box 301825
St. Thomas, VI 00803
Phone:      (809) 774-3166

## PASTORAL CARE RESOURCES

## MUSIC

**J.S. Paluch Co.**
3825 N Willow Road
Schiller Park, IL 60176-0703

**OCP Publication**
5536 NE Hassalo
Portland, Oregon 97213

**Rosa Marta Zarate**
1034 Christobal Lane
Colton, CA 92324
Phone:      (909) 875-1779
Email:       rosamartha@genesisnetwork.net

## BOOKS AND PUBLISHING

**ACHTUS (Academy of Catholic Hispanic Theologians in the US)**
Journal of Hispanic/Latino Theology
The Liturgical Press
Collegeville, MN 56321Franciscan Press

**Jaime Vidal, Ph.D.**
Quincy University
Quincy, IL 62301-2699

**Hispanic Ministry Resource Center**
Claretian Publications
205 West Monroe
Chicago, IL 60606
Phone:      (312) 236-7782 Ext. 439
Fax:         (312) 236-8207
E-mail:     Aquinaco@claretianpubs.org

**Liturgical Training Publications**
1800 North Hermitage Avenue
Chicago, IL 60622-1101
Phone:      (800)-933-4213

**Office for Publishing and Promotion Services**
United States Catholic Conference
Washington, DC 20017

**PARAL (Program for the Analysis of Religion among Latinos/as)**
Bildner Center for Western Hemisphere Studies
The Graduate School and University Center
The City University of New York
33 West 42 Street
New York, New York 10036-8099
Phone:        (212)-642-2950
Fax:          ( 212)-642-2789

**Spanish Speaking Bookstore**
4441 N Broadway
Chicago, IL 60640-5659
Phone:        (800)-883-2126 (Outside of Chicago)
Phone:        (773)-878-2117 (Chicago area)
Fax:          (773)-878-0647

**The Redemptorist Fathers**
Theological Book Service
P.O. Box 509
Barnhart, MO 63012

# YOUTH MINISTRY

**Saint Mary's Press**
Carmen Maria Cervantes, Ed.D.
1737 West Benjamin Holt Drive
Stockton, CA 95207-3422

# THEOLOGICAL PREPARATION

**Hispanic Summer Program**
AETH
100 E. 27th Street
Austin, TX 78705-5711

# Name Index

# SUBJECT INDEX